gilbert
LAW SUMMARIES

SECURED TRANSACTIONS

Tenth Edition

Douglas J. Whaley
James W. Shocknessy
Professor of Law
Ohio State University

HARCOURT BRACE LEGAL AND PROFESSIONAL PUBLICATIONS, INC.

EDITORIAL OFFICES: 176 W. Adams, Suite 2100, Chicago, IL 60603

REGIONAL OFFICES: New York, Chicago, Los Angeles, Washington, D.C.

Distributed by: **Harcourt Brace & Company** 6277 Sea Harbor Drive, Orlando, FL 32887 (800)787-8717

PROJECT EDITOR
Steven J. Levin, B.A., J.D.
Attorney At Law

QUALITY CONTROL EDITOR
Blythe C. Smith, B.A.

Titles Available

Administrative Law
Agency & Partnership
Antitrust
Bankruptcy
Basic Accounting for Lawyers
Business Law
California Bar Performance
  Test Skills
Civil Procedure
Commercial Paper &
  Payment Law
Community Property
Conflict of Laws
Constitutional Law
Contracts
Corporations
Criminal Law
Criminal Procedure
Dictionary of Legal Terms
Estate & Gift Tax
Evidence

Family Law
Federal Courts
First Year Questions & Answers
Future Interests
Income Tax I (Individual)
Income Tax II (Corporate)
Labor Law
Legal Ethics (Prof. Responsibility)
Legal Research, Writing,
  & Analysis
Multistate Bar Exam
Personal Property
Property
Remedies
Sales & Lease of Goods
Securities Regulation
Secured Transactions
Torts
Trusts
Wills

Also Available:

First Year Program
Pocket Size Law Dictionary
The Eight Secrets Of Top Exam Performance In Law School

There are two things BAR/BRI will do for you:

1 Get you through **LAW SCHOOL**

2 Get you through the **BAR EXAM**

O.K. we'll throw in a highlighter*

*Available at your local BAR/BRI office.

SUMMARY OF CONTENTS

gilbert

capsule summary

secured transactions

I. INTRODUCTION

A. GOALS OF DEBTOR AND CREDITOR

1. **Debtor's Goal:** To get as much credit as needed *without* giving any more security (collateral or a surety) than necessary . . . . [1]
2. **Creditor's Goal:** To get *repayment plus a profit.* Creditor also wants *priority* over other creditors as against debtor's collateral or surety . . . . [2]
3. **Goal of Security Interest Legislation:** To regulate a *balance* between goals of creditor and debtor . . . . [3]

B. PRE-CODE SECURITY DEVICES

1. **Seller's Retention of Goods After Sale**
   a. **Statute of Elizabeth:** Seller's possession of goods after sale was void and fraudulent as against seller's creditors . . . . [4]
   b. **Early U.S. laws:** U.S. law generally retains the policy against "sham" sales, presuming fraud if the seller retains possession . . . . [5]
   c. **U.C.C.:** The Code incorporates existing law *except* that the seller's retention "in good faith for a commercially reasonable time" is *not* deemed fraudulent . . . . [6]
2. **Pledge:** A pledge (sometimes called a "hypothecation") occurs when the creditor takes *possession* of the debtor's property (collateral) during the debt period. Note that the pledge is still a widely used security device . . . . [8]
3. **Chattel Mortgage:** This was a mortgage on the debtor's personal property filed in the appropriate place to give notice of the creditor's interest . . . . [11]
4. **Conditional Sale:** This occurred when the seller of property retained *title* (but not *possession*) until the buyer completely paid for the goods . . . . [14]
5. **Trust Receipt:** This was a form of *inventory financing* in which a bank purchased goods from a manufacturer and then released them "in trust" to the retailer, after filing a notice that it was engaged in such financing . . . . [19]
6. **Field Warehousing:** This was and is a means of pledging collateral of great bulk. The warehouse is created around the goods and the *warehouse receipt* is issued to the creditor, who then lends the debtor money . . . . [22]
7. **Factor's Acts:** These were state statutes allowing financers to perfect their interests in inventory goods which their extensions of credit had helped to produce . [23]
8. **Assignment of Accounts Receivable:** This method of financing was accomplished in most states by filing notice of the creditor's interest in the outstanding accounts of the debtor-business. The debtor's customers (the obligors) may or may not have been notified that their obligations were assigned to the creditor . [26]

C. THE UNIFORM COMMERCIAL CODE

1. **In General:** Adoption of U.C.C. Article 9 (Secured Transactions) eliminated most of the above pre-Code security devices . . . . [33]
2. **Revised Article 9:** The original (1962) version of Article 9 was substantially rewritten in 1972, and it has been adopted in a great many states . . . . [34]

D. LIENS

1. **In General:** Liens are creditor interests in the debtor's property . . . . [35]

III. **CREATION OF A SECURITY INTEREST**

A. **INTRODUCTION**
   1. **Basic Policies:** The Code guarantees protection to lenders complying with

       (5) ***The secured party can repledge the collateral*** if this action does not impair the debtor's ability to redeem . . . . [179]

       (6) ***The secured party cannot use the collateral*** unless use is necessary to preserve the collateral . . . . [180]

  4. **Perfection with Neither Possession Nor Filing—"Automatic Perfection":** The third method of perfection is "automatic"; *i.e.,* perfection occurs in some situations without filing once attachment of the security interest has happened. Automatic perfection is present in the following situations . . . . [181]

    a. **Purchase money security interest in consumer goods:** A purchase money security interest in consumer goods other than vehicles required to be registered, or fixtures, is automatically perfected on attachment of the security interest . . . . [182]

       (1) **Purchase money transactions:** A purchase money security interest arises when the secured party sells the goods to the purchaser on credit or advances the purchaser the money used to purchase the goods . . . . [183]

         (a) **Extent of security interest:** The purchase money security interest applies only to the extent of ***value advanced*** by the secured party . . . . [185]

       (2) **"Consumer goods":** In determining whether the goods are truly to be used for consumer purposes (and hence qualify for automatic perfection), the creditor may believe what the debtor says . . . . [188]

    b. **Beneficial interests:** Perfection is also automatic in the assignment of a beneficial interest in a trust or decedent's estate . . . . [195]

    c. **Certain accounts:** Automatic perfection occurs in the assignment of an ***insignificant portion*** of the debtor's outstanding accounts . . . . [196]

    d. **Temporary perfection:** Temporary "automatic" perfection is allowed as to certain proceeds of collateral and as to documents and instruments . . . . . . [200]

       (1) **Proceeds**

         (a) **Collateral of same type:** A security interest is automatically perfected in proceeds received on the sale or disposition of collateral. Generally, this security interest ***remains perfected*** if perfection of a security interest in the type of collateral that constitutes the proceeds could be accomplished by filing in the same place as for the original collateral . . . . [202]

         (b) **Proceeds of different type:** If a security interest in the proceeds could not be perfected by filing in the same place as for the original collateral, perfection continues in the proceeds for ***only 10 days*** following disposition of the collateral (after which new filing or possession is required) . . . . [203]

       (2) **Documents and instruments:** Documents of title (*e.g.,* warehouse receipts) and instruments (*e.g.,* promissory notes) in the possession of the creditor may be surrendered to the debtor for a legitimate commercial purpose (such as to reclaim the goods represented by a warehouse receipt or to present a promissory note for payment) for ***21 days*** without a loss of perfection. Similarly, a creditor as to documents or instruments who advances new value enjoys a 21-day grace period of automatic perfection . . . . [204]

B. TIME OF PERFECTION

  1. **Completion of Necessary Requirements:** Perfection occurs when (i) the interest has ***attached*** and (ii) ***all required steps for*** the particular method of ***perfection*** (*e.g.,* filing, possession) have been taken. If the steps for perfection are taken before attachment (*e.g.,* the financing statement is filed before the security agreement is signed), perfection occurs when attachment finally occurs—*i.e.,* when ***both requirements are met*** . . . . [216]

C. **MECHANICS OF FILING**

D. **REQUEST FOR STATEMENT OF ACCOUNT OR LIST OF COLLATERAL**

VII. BANKRUPTCY PROCEEDINGS AND ARTICLE 9

IX. BULK TRANSFERS

A. INTRODUCTION
Bulk sales law aims to protect creditors of an inventoried business that is sold for a

low price to an innocent third party by the debtor, who then departs, leaving the creditors without recourse against the innocent purchaser. U.C.C. Article 6 requires the buyer of an inventoried business to give seller's creditors notice prior to the sale, informing them of the sale and giving them an opportunity to object. Note that repeal of the original Article 6 has been proposed, and a revised, more simplified version of Article 6 has been proposed for states not wanting to eliminate Article 6 altogether . . . .   [638]

B. **SCOPE OF ARTICLE 6**
1. **In General:** Article 6 applies to bulk transfers *not in the ordinary course of the transferor's business* of a *major part* of the materials, supplies, or other inventory. Revised Article 6 defines a bulk sale as one of *more than half* of the seller's inventory where the buyer knows that the seller will not continue to operate a similar business after the sale . . . .   [642]
2. **Sale of Inventory Required:** A bulk transfer involves the sale of an inventoried business, one whose principal activity is the sale of merchandise from stock . . .   [643]
    a. **Sale of equipment:** This is not a bulk transfer unless sold along with the inventory . . . .   [644]
    b. **Restaurants and bars:** States are split on whether sales of restaurants or bars are of an inventoried business, although Official Comments to Article 8 exclude such sales . . . .   [645]
3. **Excluded Transfers**
    a. **Transfer of security interest:** This is not a sale of inventory and so is excluded from Article 6 coverage . . . .   [646]
    b. **Transfers to creditors:** Transfers to creditors to create or realize upon a lien are excluded . . . .   [647]
    c. **Transfers to transferee who assumes all debts:** Such transfers are excluded if the transferee maintains a place of business in the state and gives notice of the assumption . . . .   [649]
    d. **Transfers to new business:** If a business changes form of ownership, the transfer is excluded from Article 6 if the new business assumes the debts of the old business, gives notice, and obtains no rights superior to the old business's creditors . . . .   [650]
    e. **Transfer exempt from execution:** The sale of assets exempt from execution is excluded from Article 6 . . . .   [651]
    f. **Price range:** Revised Article 6 applies only if the sale transfers assets valued between $10,000 and $25 million . . . .   [652]

C. **COMPLIANCE PROCEDURE—ORIGINAL VERSION OF ARTICLE 6**
1. **Schedules:** *Transferor* must prepare a list of existing creditors, and *both parties* must prepare a schedule of the property being transferred . . . .   [653]
2. **List of Creditors:** Must be signed and sworn to, and include names and business addresses of creditors and amounts owed them, and names of those holding what transferor resists as disputed claims . . . .   [654]
    a. **Errors on list of creditors:** Transferee may rely on accuracy of list *unless transferee knows of an error or omission* . . . .   [655]
3. **Preservation of the List and Schedule:** Transferee must preserve both for six months after sale, and permit creditors to examine and copy . . . .   [657]
4. **Notice:** A short form is used where debts of transferor are to be paid in full; otherwise, a long form is used. If in doubt, the long form should be used . . . . .   [658]
    a. **Short form:** This states that a bulk transfer is about to be made, gives the names and addresses of the parties, and states whether the transferor's debts are to be paid in full, and if so, the address to which creditors should send their bills . . . .   [659]
    b. **Long form:** This includes the short form information *plus* the location and description of the property to be transferred, an estimated total of the

transferor's debts, the address where the list and schedule can be examined, what debts will be paid, and the consideration for the transfer . . . . . [660]

c. **Delivery of notice:** Notice may be hand delivered or sent registered or certified mail to all creditors on the list plus any others known by the transferee to be creditors . . . . [661]

d. **Auctions:** If transfer is by auction, auctioneer has the transferee's duties . . . . [662]

e. **Timing of the notice:** Notice must be given at least **10 days** before the transferee takes possession of the goods or pays for them . . . . [663]

5. **Paying the Creditors:** A number of states require the transferee to ensure that the consideration for the transfer is paid **pro rata** to all creditors on the list of creditors who file their claims in writing within 30 days after the mailing of the notice . . . . [664]

D. COMPLIANCE PROCEDURE—REVISED ARTICLE 6

1. **Notice of Filing:** The usual method of compliance under revised Article 6 is for the buyer to send the seller's creditors a notice 45 days in advance of the sale, but where the seller has 200 or more creditors, the buyer may give notice by filing with the secretary of state not less than 45 days before the sale . . . . [665]

2. **Distribution Schedule:** The notice must state how the proceeds will be distributed and comply with the Code's rules for distribution . . . . [666]

E. RIGHTS OF CREDITORS

1. **Omitted Creditors:** If the transferee gave proper notice, an omitted creditor of whom the transferee was unaware has no rights against the transferee or property (absent a valid security interest therein) and must look to the transferor for relief . . . . [667]

2. **Noncompliance with Original Article 6:** Original Article 6 does not specify a remedy for noncompliance, and the courts varied: All courts allowed the transferor's creditors to seize the property transferred, and some also permitted the creditors to reach proceeds of the property transferred. Many courts allowed the transferor's creditors to bring a personal action against the transferee . . . . [668]

3. **Liability Under Revised Article 6:** Revised Article 6 provides for damages to be paid for by the noncomplying buyer. There is a good faith defense and a cap limiting the buyer's liability to twice the value of the contract . . . . [671]

4. **Rights of Secured Creditors:** Creditors with security interests **perfected** at the time of the bulk transfer may seize the transferred property or proceeds thereof regardless of the transferee's compliance with Article 6. However, if the security interest is **unperfected** at the time of the bulk transfer and the transferee had no knowledge of the security interest and gave value for and received the property before perfection, the interest will be cut off . . . . [672]

5. **Statute of Limitations:** Under original Article 6, an action to attack a bulk transfer must be brought within **six months** after the transferee takes possession. Where transfer was **concealed,** period starts to run after transfer is discovered. Under the revision, the statute of limitations is one year from the date of sale. If the sale has been concealed, the period runs from when the person bringing the action should have discovered the sale (in no event more than two years after the sale). Under the revision, note that complete noncompliance with the Act does not of itself constitute concealment . . . . [673]

6. **Subsequent Transfers by Transferee:** If a transfer is defective because of noncompliance with Article 6, a subsequent purchaser of the property from the transferee takes free of the rights of the original transferor's creditors if the purchaser gives value and buys without knowledge of the defect . . . . [674]

TEXT CORRELATION CHART

Gilbert Law Summary Secured Transactions	Farnsworth, Honnold, Harris, Mooney, Jr., Reitz Commercial Law Cases and Materials 1993 (5th ed.)	Jordan, Warren Commercial Law 1992 (3rd ed.)	Schwartz, Scott Commercial Transactions Principles and Policies 1991 (2nd ed.)	Speidel, Summers, White Sales and Secured Transactions Teaching Materials 1993 (5th ed.)	Whaley Problems and Materials on Commercial Law 1995 (4th ed.)
I. INTRODUCTION					
A. Goals of the Debtor and the Creditor	728-732	1-3	545-548	1-4	687-689
B. Pre-Code Security Devices	2-6, 732, 832-845, 934-936	1-3	554-565, 566, 791-814	4-6, 48-55	691-701
C. The Uniform Commercial Code	6-18, 759-760	1-6	1-20	6-7, 9-14	687-689, 692, 701
D. Liens	729-732, 739-743, 745, 1060-1064, 1067-1072	4-6	558, 566	56, 72-73, 291, 304-305	688
II. COVERAGE OF ARTICLE 9					
A. Terminology	741-742, 745-746, 750-754, 759-763, 825-826	3	566-567	10, 39-41, 57	687-689, 703-704, 744-745
B. Scope of Article 9 Coverage	748-763, 822, 890-922, 926-950, 1037	3, 75-76, 129-131, 152-154, 197-198, 215-217, 1068-1078	566, 585, 612-616, 701-713, 736-737	9-10, 55-57, 62-63, 218, 305, 359-423	703-723, 725, 735-743
C. Transactions Excluded from Article 9	107-108, 950-952, 989, 1029, 1134-1135, 1154-1155	197-214, 218-240	566, 666-668, 728-729, 744, 760, 872-874	14-16, 56, 291-295, 359-381	723-733
III. CREATION OF A SECURITY INTEREST					
A. Introduction	759-766, 809-811	4-6	567-568, 598-607	1-6, 9-10, 62-63, 83	743-744
B. Attachment of a Security Interest—In General	762-763, 809-811	4-6	567-569	84-94	769-780
C. Security Agreement	760-763, 769-778, 790-793, 810, 825-830, 863-864, 869-873, 989, 1060-1064	6-21, 22-23	553-554, 567-568, 582, 633, 659, 662, 685-686, 736-737	84-134	735-769, 855, 961
D. Value	810	6-21	567	102	769
E. Debtor's Rights in the Collateral	762-763, 810-811, 827, 871-872, 946, 984, 988-989, 1018-1020, 1046, 1060-1072	55-65	567	83-94	769
IV. PERFECTION					
A. Introduction	764, 811	4-6	568-569	62-63, 135-137	689, 769
B. Methods of Perfection					
1. In General	764, 811-813	4-6, 24-25	568-569	135-137	781
2. Filing of a Financing Statement	764, 813-830, 950-952	24-25	569	62-69, 135-137, 178-192, 214-225	799-806
3. Perfection by Possession	831-851	25, 65-75	569, 774-779		781-788

TEXT CORRELATION CHART—continued

Gilbert Law Summary Secured Transactions	Farnsworth, Honnold, Harris, Mooney, Jr., Reitz Commercial Law Cases and Materials 1993 (5th ed.)	Jordan, Warren Commercial Law 1992 (3rd ed.)	Schwartz, Scott Commercial Transactions Principles and Policies 1991 (2nd ed.)	Speidel, Summers, White Sales and Secured Transactions Teaching Materials 1993 (5th ed.)	Whaley Problems and Materials on Commercial Law 1995 (4th ed.)
4. Perfection with Neither Possession Nor Filing—"Automatic Perfection"	750-753, 850, 869-870, 940-945, 980-983, 985-987, 1001-1002, 1024-1026	75-76, 110-120	568, 586, 653-654, 669, 676-677, 701, 737	136, 192-196	788-799
C. Time of Perfection	770, 811-812, 956-957, 1055-1057	5, 146-148	569, 677	135-136	781
D. Place of Perfection—Multistate Transactions	851-863, 971-972	77-97	591-598	196-214	807-825
V. FILING					
A. The Financing Statement	770-771, 803-804, 808-809, 813-824, 922-924, 940-944, 1002	21-43, 49-55	569-591, 633-634, 665, 701-713, 737	141-178	743, 745-759, 805
B. Where to File	851-863	43-44	569, 724	141-145, 174, 266	799-805, 806
C. Mechanics of Filing	780, 808, 959	44-49	569-591	165-173, 279-286	799-806
D. Request for Statement of Account or List of Collateral		21-24, 108	580-584	144	
VI. PRIORITIES					
A. Competing Interests in Collateral—The Claimants	728-732, 740-748, 760-762, 811-813, 994	98	608-612	226-227, 279	687-689, 827-844
B. Priority—Unperfected Creditors	811-813, 960-974, 1026-1037, 1067-1077	6, 98-110	570-582, 585-586, 616-628, 643	41-48, 226-227	827-828
C. Priority Among Perfected Creditors—General Rule	954-974	98-108, 256-258	608-612, 660-665	228-230	689, 781
D. Priority Among Perfected Creditors—Special Rules for Purchase Money Security Interests	908, 921-926, 976-989	110-137	655-660, 665, 669-685	230-240	844-854
E. Priority Among Perfected Creditors—Special Rules for Certain Types of Collateral					
1. Crop Production Loans	757	152-154		116-122	918-919
2. Fixtures		186-197	713-735	286-291	919-931
3. Accessions		180-181		291-295	931
4. Commingled and Processed Goods	926-929, 991-994	181-185		112-115, 291-295	931
5. Proceeds	991-994, 1064-1067, 1079-1080	155-178	685-699	112-115, 221-225, 267-296	961-982
F. Priority Among Perfected Creditors—As Affected by Terms of Security Agreement	828-830, 958-959, 981	98-129	628-639, 654-655, 659-660, 665-666	110-111, 228-230	829-844, 871-880, 940-942

TEXT CORRELATION CHART—continued

Gilbert Law Summary Secured Transactions	Farnsworth, Honnold, Harris, Mooney, Jr., Reitz Commercial Law Cases and Materials 1993 (5th ed.)	Jordan, Warren Commercial Law 1992 (3rd ed.)	Schwartz, Scott Commercial Transactions Principles and Policies 1991 (2nd ed.)	Speidel, Summers, White Sales and Secured Transactions Teaching Materials 1993 (5th ed.)	Whaley Problems and Materials on Commercial Law 1995 (4th ed.)
G. Priority Among Article 9 Perfected Creditors and Other Claimants					
1. Buyers of the Collateral	994-1026	137-154	639-659	247-279	852-887
2. Statutory Lien Holders	731-732, 811, 950-951, 1060-1063, 1165-1169, 1182, 1191-1192	4-5	585-586, 621-622	291-295, 426-433	917-918
3. Federal Tax Lien	731-732, 741-742, 1165-1169, 1191-1192	241-256	762-772	416-423	932-942
4. Judicial "Lien Creditors"	737-743, 1009-1020,	4-6	585-586, 616-627	304-305	688, 960
5. Article 2 Claimants to the Collateral—Buyers and Sellers	1080-1095, 1183-1187	129-137	261, 655	371-388	889-917
VII. BANKRUPTCY PROCEEDINGS AND ARTICLE 9					
A. Introduction	1038	332-336	827-829	424	689
B. Bankruptcy Code Provisions	1038-1067, 1079-1108	336-444	829-928	424-450	689-691, 943-960, 994
C. After-Acquired Property in Bankruptcy	1067-1078	345-352	882-886	438-446	951-959
VIII. DEFAULT PROCEEDINGS					
A. Introduction	1109-1111	259-260, 262-263	929-930	297-298	984-985
B. Occurrence of Default	1163-1165, 1175-1182	171-178, 259-272	930-950	297-303	985-991
C. Remedies in General	1109-1111	285, 259-260	745, 755, 950-983	297, 303-304	
D. Right of Possession Upon Default	1112-1135, 1154	272-285	950-962	307-319	991-1009, 1020-1026
E. Realizing Upon the Collateral	1135-1173, 1183-1193	285-331	952-962, 971-983	319-357	1009-1020
F. Debtor's Right of Redemption	1173-1183			299	995, 1009-1010
G. Effect of Failure to Comply With Default Provisions	1152-1156, 1132-1144	262-272	962-971	307-319, 325, 326-357	992, 995-1009, 1010-1019
H. Nonwaivable Rights Under the Security Agreement	1150-1152, 1190-1193	279		299, 326, 340-342	1001, 1009
I. Special Default Rules for Intangibles and Fixtures	1183-1187	323-331		305-307	
J. Relation of Default Provisions to Other State Legislation	1129-1135, 1154-1155	272-284	616-621		
IX. BULK TRANSFERS					
A. Introduction	1020-1022		541-544	1032-1033	1027-1029
B. Scope of Article 6	1020, 1023-1026, 1037		541-544	1033-1040	1029-1031

TEXT CORRELATION CHART—continued

Gilbert Law Summary Secured Transactions	Farnsworth, Honnold, Harris, Mooney, Jr., Reitz Commercial Law Cases and Materials 1993 (5th ed.)	Jordan, Warren Commercial Law 1992 (3rd ed.)	Schwartz, Scott Commercial Transactions Principles and Policies 1991 (2nd ed.)	Speidel, Summers, White Sales and Secured Transactions Teaching Materials 1993 (5th ed.)	Whaley Problems and Materials on Commercial Law 1995 (4th ed.)
C. Compliance Procedure— Original Version of Article 6	1020-1023		543-544	1040-1044	1032-1048
D. Compliance Procedure— Revised Article 6				1044	1042, 1048-1049
E. Rights of Creditors	1022-1024, 1027-1037		544	1034-1040	1031-1050

approach to exams

Common to all transactions under Article 9 of the U.C.C. is the fact that there is an advance of value—whether by loan or by outright sale of accounts or other rights—made against some future performance that is guaranteed or *secured by collateral*. In analyzing a secured transactions problem, ask yourself the following questions. (For a more detailed approach to a topic, refer to the chapter approach at the beginning of the appropriate chapter.)

1. ***Does the Transaction Fall Within Article 9?*** Look for an intent to create a security interest, whether the type of collateral or transaction is covered by Article 9, and whether any exclusions apply.

2. ***Has a Valid Security Interest Arisen (Attached to the Collateral)?*** Without attachment, there is no security interest.

3. ***Is the Security Interest Perfected?*** Check for one of the three types of perfection: filing a financing statement, the secured party's taking possession of the collateral, or automatic perfection (*e.g.,* purchase money security interest in consumer goods).

4. ***Against Whom Will the Secured Party Prevail?*** Perfected security interests entitle the holder to priority over unperfected creditors and perfected creditors under the "first-to-file-or-perfect" rule, but not over bona fide purchasers and certain others.

5. ***Is the Secured Party's Interest Valid in Bankruptcy?*** Be sure there was perfection, but also note that the trustee may attack the interest as a fraudulent conveyance or preference.

6. ***What Are the Rights of the Secured Party Upon Default?*** Consider the rights ***and duties*** of ***each party*** upon default. For these, look to the terms of the security agreement and the provisions of the U.C.C.

7. ***Was There a Bulk Transfer of Inventory?*** If so, check that all Article 6 rules have been met.

I. INTRODUCTION

___chapter approach___

In this chapter you are introduced to the basic concepts underlying the law of secured transactions. The rules of Article 9 of the Uniform Commercial Code do not float in a vacuum, and are best understood against a background of the commercial pressures that led to the adoption of legislation and an explanation of the historical solutions that preceded the Code.

Also important to an appreciation of the law of secured lending is mastery of the strange language used in Article 9; some of the key words are introduced in this chapter.

A. GOALS OF THE DEBTOR AND THE CREDITOR

1. **Debtor's Goals:** [§1]   A person wishing to borrow money or obtain goods or services on credit (the debtor) may be able to persuade the person extending credit (the creditor) to trust the debtor to discharge the debt without giving the creditor any kind of security other than the debtor's promise to repay. Such a trusting creditor is said to be "unsecured"; *i.e.,* in the event of default (nonpayment), the creditor will have to go to court, win a judgment, and send out the sheriff to realize on any of the debtor's property. A creditor may, of course, refuse to extend credit on an "unsecured" basis. In this event, the debtor will be required either to get a *surety* (guarantor) to back up the debtor's promise or to furnish *collateral* (the debtor's own property, or property borrowed from a friend) that can be seized in the event of default. Some creditors want *both* a surety and collateral. The debtor's goal is to get as much credit as is needed without tying up any more property than is absolutely necessary. After all, the debtor plans to repay the debt out of income and not by forfeiting property.

2. **Creditor's Goals:** [§2]   The creditor extends credit and wants repayment plus a profit on the transaction. A surety and collateral are back-up devices to insure collection of at least some of the debt if the debtor fails to repay as promised. If the debtor goes bankrupt, the right to go against the surety or the collateral ahead of other creditors is a must, because in bankruptcy proceedings there are rarely enough assets to satisfy debts owed to the unsecured creditors after the "secured" creditors (creditors with rights in collateral) take their property and the bankruptcy expenses are paid. Nonetheless, a creditor's insistence on a security interest (a right to seize the property on the debtor's default) is only a hedge against the debtor's potential failure to repay. The creditor must prepare for the worst, but cannot tie the debtor's hands to the point where the debtor cannot earn enough income to repay the debt.

3. **Goals of Security Interest Legislation:** [§3]   Laws designed to regulate the balance between the goals of the parties must protect the debtor from creditors who want too much collateral, from creditors seizing the debtor's property at will and doing with it as they like, and from excessive regulation of the debtor's affairs. On the other side, the creditor who has taken proper steps to secure the debt must be protected from debtor misbehavior, from other creditors, and from loss of the collateral in the event of default. Article 9 of the Uniform Commercial Code ("U.C.C.")

A TYPICAL SECURED TRANSACTION SCENARIO

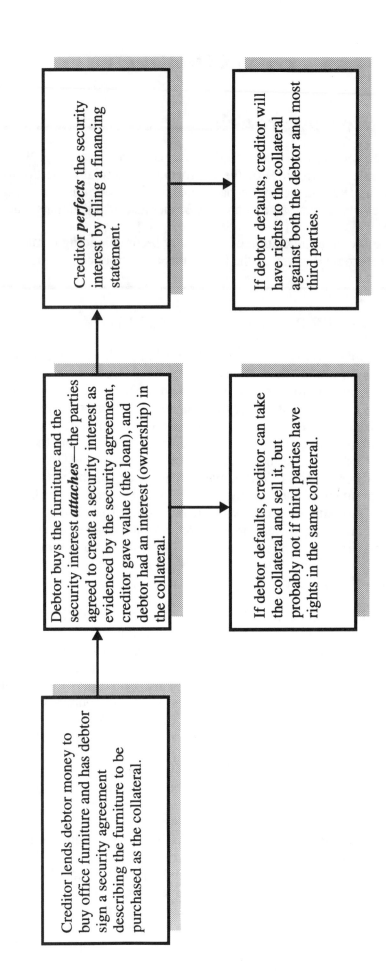

Creditor lends debtor money to buy office furniture and has debtor sign a security agreement describing the furniture to be purchased as the collateral.

Debtor buys the furniture and the security interest *attaches*—the parties agreed to create a security interest as evidenced by the security agreement, creditor gave value (the loan), and debtor had an interest (ownership) in the collateral.

Creditor *perfects* the security interest by filing a financing statement.

If debtor defaults, creditor can take the collateral and sell it, but probably not if third parties have rights in the same collateral.

If debtor defaults, creditor will have rights to the collateral against both the debtor and most third parties.

focuses on the creditor's rights in the collateral. It does not, however, regulate the creditor's recourse against the debtor's surety, which is left to the common law, special statutes [*see, e.g.,* Cal. Civ. Code §§2787 *et seq.*], and other parts of the U.C.C. [U.C.C. §§3-116, 3-419, 3-605].

B. PRE-CODE SECURITY DEVICES

1. Seller's Retention of Goods After Sale

a. **"Statute of Elizabeth":** [§4]   The English Statute of 13 Elizabeth (1570) was designed to prevent "fraudulent conveyances" (*i.e.,* any transfer of the debtor's property that interfered with the legitimate rights of the debtor's creditors). An early reading of the statute interpreted it to mean that a sale of goods in which the buyer had permitted the seller to retain possession of the goods after the sale was void and fraudulent as against the seller's creditors. The purpose was to prevent such a transaction from being used to cheat creditors. [Twyne's Case, 76 Eng. Rep. 809 (1601)]

   (1) **Example:** A creditor might have loaned money on the appearance of the borrower's equipment or goods, and then, upon trying to collect, the creditor would suddenly learn that the merchant had no money and had secretly "sold" the equipment or goods to an obliging confederate.

   (2) **Effect:** Thus, under the English Act, the buyer had to take *possession* of the merchandise purchased. Otherwise, the sale could be set aside to protect the seller's creditors, and the buyer's interest in the goods cut off.

b. **Early U.S. law:** [§5]   This policy against "sham" sales was carried over to the United States in early decisions and statutes and is generally retained in the law today. In most cases where the seller retains possession of the goods, fraud is presumed.

   (1) **Majority view:** In most states, the seller's retention of possession creates only a *rebuttable presumption* of fraud, allowing the buyer to show that there was a bona fide reason for allowing the seller to retain possession (*e.g.,* goods too bulky to move immediately, etc.). [Robertson v. Andrus, 266 P. 53 (Kan. 1928)]

   (2) **Minority view:** In other states, however, such a transaction is *conclusively presumed* fraudulent against the seller's creditors. [*See* Cal. Civ. Code §3440]

c. **U.C.C.:** [§6]   The U.C.C. basically incorporates existing law. It provides that the seller's retention of the goods following sale is fraudulent against the seller's creditors "if fraudulent under any rule of law of the state where the goods are situated." [U.C.C. §2-402(2)]

   (1) **But note:** The Code carves out one *exception:* A merchant-seller's retention of possession "in good faith and current course of trade" for a "commercially reasonable time" is *not* deemed fraudulent. [U.C.C. §2-402(2)]

d. **Risks where seller retains goods:** [§7]   In any event, retention of the goods by the seller is not a good idea for either party. The seller runs the risk of having the "security interest" in the goods voided as a fraudulent transaction, and the buyer hazards a court holding that the seller's creditors or other buyers are entitled to the goods.

2. **Pledge:** [§8]   In most situations in which the creditor gets a security interest in the debtor's property (the collateral), the property itself remains in the debtor's control. In the case of a "pledge," however, the property is kept in the *creditor's* ("pledgee's") physical control until the loan is repaid by the debtor ("pledgor"). A pledge is sometimes called a "hypothecation."

   a. **Possession as notice:** [§9]   Transfer of the pledged collateral acts as *notice* to the world that the pledgee has rights in the property. However, it does not render the transaction fraudulent, because the property still *belongs* to the pledgor.

   b. **Status today:** [§10]   Because of the notice inherent in such transactions, the pledge is still a widely used security device and is given special recognition throughout Article 9. [*See, e.g.,* U.C.C. §§9-203(1)(a), 9-207, 9-301(1)(a), 9-304, 9-305]

3. **Chattel Mortgage:** [§11]   A chattel mortgage was a mortgage on the debtor's personal property filed in the appropriate place to give notice of the creditor's interest.

   a. **Background:** [§12]   Before the nineteenth century, the only effective security devices were the mortgage of real property and the pledge of chattels. However, the pledge of chattels (which required that the creditor take *possession* of the chattels to avoid invalidity as a fraudulent conveyance) was obviously not suited to the needs of an industrial economy in which the debtor invariably needed the goods to use as equipment or inventory.

   b. **Chattel mortgage acts:** [§13]   To meet these needs, chattel mortgage acts were enacted by state legislatures. Generally, these acts allowed the debtor to *retain* the property, but required the debtor to *record or file* the mortgage in a specified manner. Without the filing, the acts provided that conveyances intended as mortgages of chattels were *void* against creditors.

4. **Conditional Sales:** [§14]   To avoid the filing requirements of the chattel mortgage acts, sellers developed the "conditional sale." The basic idea of the conditional sale was that *possession* of the goods would go to the buyer, but *title* would remain in the seller until the buyer had *paid the entire purchase price* (the "condition").

   a. **Varying views on conditional sales:** [§15]   Some courts held that the seller had avoided the language of the chattel mortgage acts since no lien was created. By retaining title, the seller's rights were protected against subsequent lienors and against purchasers from the buyer, even without filing or recording the sale. *Other courts* were bothered by the "secret lien" interest the seller had in the buyer's goods and refused to recognize the seller's unrecorded interest.

   b. **Conditional sales filing statutes:** [§16]   Eventually, most states enacted conditional sales filing statutes similar to the chattel mortgage filing laws.

Even so, the two doctrines maintained a separate existence—sometimes to the embarrassment of creditors who followed the wrong form.

    c.   **U.C.C.:** [§17]   The U.C.C. rejects the whole concept of "title" as being relevant to a seller's rights in goods sold. [U.C.C. §9-202] Under the Code, a seller's retention of title is converted into an "unperfected" security interest—*i.e.,* one that is not good against other parties claiming the goods—unless the seller takes the further steps called for by Article 9 (*see infra,* §§153 *et seq.*). [U.C.C. §§1-201(37), 2-401(1), second sentence in each]

        (1)   **Seller cannot reclaim goods:** [§18]   Contrary to popular belief, an unpaid seller who has not complied with Article 9 has no right to reclaim the specific goods sold to the buyer unless the buyer received the goods while insolvent and the seller demanded their return within 10 days after delivery. [U.C.C. §2-702; *and see infra,* §466]

5.   **Trust Receipt:** [§19]   The trust receipt was a form of inventory financing that sought to adapt the principles of trust law so as to keep *title* to a dealer's inventory in the financing bank while allowing the debtor/dealer to have *possession.*

    a.   **Background:** [§20]   The trust receipt device was originally developed by banks that financed imported goods. It was later extended to domestic transactions—chiefly the financing of the inventories of retail automobile dealers.

    b.   **Procedure:** [§21]   The Uniform Trust Receipts Act first required the bank (the "entruster") to file a *notice* that it was engaging in trust receipt financing with the dealer. Then, the bank would buy the goods (*e.g.,* vehicles) from the manufacturer and turn them over to the dealer (the "trustee") for resale. The bank would *retain title* until the dealer/trustee returned the proceeds of the resale to the bank.

        (1)   **Note:** One difficulty with this financing system was that it was adapted only to goods that could be *specifically identified,* such as automobiles, and could not be used for a store selling many small items.

        (2)   **And note:** Another difficulty was that the Uniform Trust Receipts Act was very complicated, and failure to comply with all its technicalities often invalidated the bank's security interest.

6.   **Field Warehousing:** [§22]   If the collateral is physically awkward to pledge but the creditor requires possession, the goods (typically inventory, sometimes equipment) are physically segregated at their usual location, and a warehouse receipt for them is issued. This *receipt,* which must be surrendered to retrieve the goods, is then *pledged* to the creditor. [U.C.C. §7-403]

    a.   **Effect:** Since a pledge is accomplished—*i.e.,* the pledged collateral being the warehouse receipt over which the creditor maintains control—the debtor cannot (at least in theory) get to the warehoused goods without going through the creditor. For this reason, field warehousing is still a popular means of financing.

7.   **Factor's Acts:** [§23]   Originally, "factors" were sellers who helped finance the operations of their suppliers. Eventually the selling aspect of factoring dropped off,

and only the financing function remained. Thereafter, "factors" were creditors who loaned money used to produce inventory and who acquired a statutory lien in the inventory that attached to the goods from the time of manufacture to the time of retail sale.

    a. **Statutory requirements:** [§24] Factor's acts were not uniform, but three formalities were generally required: (i) the borrower and lender had to execute a written agreement describing which goods were to be subject to the lien; (ii) a notice of lien had to be filed (designating the names and addresses of the parties and containing a general description of goods covered); and (iii) the borrower had to submit periodic designation statements to the lender listing the inventory subject to the lien.

    b. **Only inventory subject to lien:** [§25] The use of the factor's lien was limited to assets acquired by the borrower for sale in the ordinary course of business. Therefore, only inventory could be covered; equipment and machinery were excluded. The borrower was free to sell the inventory, and a purchaser who bought goods in the ordinary course of business would take free of the factor's lien, whether or not the purchaser knew of it.

8. **Assignment of Accounts Receivable:** [§26] Nonnotification assignment of accounts receivable was also a widely used financing device. The lender took an assignment of the borrower's accounts but did not notify the account-debtors of the assignment. They would continue to pay the account-creditor who had assigned the account, and who would then pay the proceeds to the lender.

    a. **Priorities:** [§27] When a borrower wrongly assigned the same account receivable to two different lenders, a problem of priority between the claimants arose:

        (1) **Majority rule:** The majority view was a *"first in time is first in right"* rule. The first assignee took everything the assignor had to assign, so there was nothing that could be assigned to the second assignee. The first assignee would always prevail. [Salem Trust Co. v. Manufacturer's Financial Co., 264 U.S. 182 (1924)]

        (2) **Minority rule:** The minority (English) rule protected the first assignee *if* that assignee gave *notice* of the assignment to the account-debtor. The second assignee could win only if he or she (i) was a *bona fide purchaser* for value of the account *and* (ii) gave the account-debtor *notice* of the assignment before the first assignee did so. [110 A.L.R. 774; *compare* Restatement of Contracts §173]

    b. **Notice filing statutes:** [§28] The interest in allowing lenders to feel secure in lending on accounts receivable led many states to enact notice filing statutes that provided other creditors of the assignee with the information they needed to protect themselves.

    c. **Bankruptcy proceedings:** [§29] The most serious problem with nonnotification financing as a security device was encountered where the borrower went bankrupt and the trustee in bankruptcy attacked the financing arrangement as a fraudulent conveyance or a *voidable preference* (*see infra*, §§489-499).

(1) **Former law—no valid lien:** [§30]   The early rule was that a nonnotification assignment of accounts receivable did *not* create a valid lien on the accounts.

    (a) **Rationale—borrower retains control:** Because the borrower was allowed to maintain dominion over the security, payments made to the lender in the months before the borrower's filing a petition in bankruptcy could be attacked as either a fraudulent conveyance or as a preference by the trustee. And this was true whether the payments were turned over voluntarily by the borrower or whether the lender had, during the period, notified the account-debtors of the lender's interest and seized collections of the account. [Benedict v. Ratner, 268 U.S. 353 (1925)]

        1)   This was a direct blow at nonnotification financing because the operation of the system requires that the borrower maintain the assigned accounts and collect the proceeds from the account-debtors, who have no notice of the assignment.

        2)   The effect of *Benedict* was to force lenders to exercise more formal dominion over the accounts—by more careful scrutiny of the operations of the borrower and by requiring immediate accounting for all proceeds from the accounts.

    (b) **Problem of notice:** [§31]   An additional difficulty for nonnotification accounts receivable financing under the Bankruptcy Act was created in states following the minority (English) rule (which protects the first assignee to give *notice*; *see* above). In such states, a hypothetical bona fide purchaser for value could acquire a better right to the account than the lender because notice to the account-debtor was the controlling factor. This failure to have a perfected security interest was also held to constitute a voidable preference within the months before bankruptcy. [Corn Exchange National Bank & Trust Co. v. Klauder, 318 U.S. 434 (1943)]

(2) **Present law:** [§32]   Today, the U.C.C. provisions allow the lender to perfect a security interest in accounts or contract rights without notification and without creating a voidable preference. [U.C.C. §§9-205, 9-502]

C. THE UNIFORM COMMERCIAL CODE

1. **In General:** [§33]   The U.C.C. was originally promulgated in 1951 and has been adopted in every state. Article 9 of the U.C.C. sets forth a comprehensive statutory framework covering all types of secured transactions in personal property. Thus, the Code has eliminated most of the pre-Code security devices mentioned above and swept away the unnecessary distinctions in form and effect of those remaining viable.

2. **Revised Article 9:** [§34]   The very fact that the original Article 9 was the first basic statute in this complex field led to some imperfections and uncertainties and an unexpected number of variations from state to state in enacting it. This prompted a restudy in depth of the field of secured transactions, and certain revisions to Article 9 were approved by the Permanent Editorial Board in 1971. (The

Code, as revised, is frequently referred to by the courts as the "1972 version," and the original as the "1962 version.") Currently, yet another version of Article 9 is being drafted.

D. LIENS

1. **In General:** [§35] A "lien" is a property interest given to the creditor in the debtor's property.

2. **Types of Liens**

   a. **Judicial liens:** [§36] Judicial liens are those liens acquired in judicial proceedings. They are typically created when the winning party in a lawsuit has the sheriff "levy" on (seize) the property.

   b. **"Statutory" liens:** [§37] Statutory liens are liens created by statute (or common law) in favor of certain unsecured creditors. Examples of creditors accorded this special legislative protection are landlords, attorneys, artisans (TV repairers, automobile mechanics, etc.), and the I.R.S.

   c. **Consensual liens:** [§38] Unlike the two types of liens above, consensual liens arise by agreement between the debtor and creditor. Article 9 security interests (and those created by real estate mortgages) are examples of consensual liens.

II. COVERAGE OF ARTICLE 9

chapter approach

This chapter describes the scope of Article 9. A lawyer must be sensitive to the possibility that the Uniform Commercial Code may apply to a problem because the possible application of the Code to an excluded transaction, or vice versa, could amount to malpractice.

For exam purposes, you also must determine whether Article 9 applies. Ask yourself whether:

1. The parties _intended to create a security interest_ in personal property or fixtures.

2. The _collateral_ is of a type covered by Article 9; look for:

   a. _"Goods"_—consumer goods, inventory, farm products, or equipment (keep in mind that "equipment" is a catchall for goods not falling in the other three categories);

   b. _"Quasi-intangibles"_—negotiable and nonnegotiable instruments, documents of title, or chattel paper;

   c. _"Intangibles"_—accounts receivable or general intangibles; and

   d. _"Investment property"_—stocks and bonds, commodity contracts, and accounts containing these investments.

3. The _transaction_ is of a type covered by Article 9.

If the facts of your question seem to show that Article 9 applies, be sure to consider whether there are any applicable exclusions. Although the Code's coverage is quite broad, there are some exceptions.

A. TERMINOLOGY

1. **Introduction:** [§39] Under pre-Code law, different types of financing arrangements had their own terminology, procedures, and substantive law, although the essence of the underlying transactions—an advance of credit secured by collateral—was often identical. Code efforts at simplifying the preexisting maze begin with the introduction of a set of standard terms to describe the parties in secured transactions, their agreement, and their rights.

2. **"Security Interest":** [§40] The Code definition of "security interest" expands prior law in two respects:

   a. **Interests in personal property:** [§41] First, the Code lays down a blanket definition that includes _every interest_ "in personal property or fixtures that _secures payment or performance_ of an obligation." Pledges, chattel mortgages, conditional sales, and trust receipts all fall under this broad definition. [U.C.C. §1-201(37)]

b. **Certain sales:** [§42] Second, the Code *expands the definition* to include rights and interests not previously considered security interests (*e.g.,* the interests of a buyer of accounts or chattel paper) and makes them subject to Article 9. [U.C.C. §1-201(37)]

(1) **Example:** The outright *sale* of accounts and chattel paper (both defined below) is covered by Article 9 because it is generally too difficult as a factual matter to distinguish the sale of such interests from their transfer as collateral in a financing transaction.

(2) **Example:** Ed's Roofing Co. does a lot of home repairs under oral agreements, generating promises of repayment (accounts). When the company needs money, it *sells* these outstanding accounts to Octopus National Bank for immediate cash. Even though this is a true sale and not a use of the accounts as collateral for a loan, Article 9 is triggered. The parties are treated legally as if the transaction were a loan, with Ed's being the "debtor" and the bank being the "creditor" (for the same reason as in the example above). Of course, Article 9 would also be triggered by the use of Ed's accounts as collateral for a loan.

3. **"Security Agreement":** [§43] Regardless of the manner in which a transaction is structured, "an agreement which *creates or provides for a security interest*" is called a security agreement. [U.C.C. §9-105(1)(h)]

4. **"Secured Party":** [§44] A lender, seller, or person in whose favor there is a security interest is called a "secured party." In the case of a sale of accounts or chattel paper, the purchaser is the secured party. [A. J. Armstrong Co. v. Janburt Embroidery, 234 A.2d 737 (N.J. 1967)]

a. **Note:** When the holders of an obligation under a trust, such as an equipment trust, are represented by a trustee, the trustee is a secured party. [U.C.C. §9-105(1)(i)]

5. **"Debtor":** [§45] The party *owing payment or other performance* of the obligation embodied in the security agreement, whether or not that party owns the collateral, is the debtor. *Sellers of accounts or chattel paper* also fall under the definition. In provisions of Article 9 referring to *collateral,* "debtor" means the person who actually owns the collateral; in provisions dealing with the *duties of the obligor* under a security agreement, "debtor" refers to the obligor. Of course, there are many cases where the obligor and the actual owner will be the same party—*e.g.,* the purchaser of an automobile on installment credit. [U.C.C. §9-105(1)(d)]

6. **Examples:** If a piano company borrows money from Bank A, giving the bank a security interest in the pianos as collateral, the piano company is the "debtor" and the bank is the "secured party." If the piano company sells a piano on credit to a musician, reserving a security interest in the piano until paid for, the piano company is now the "secured party" and the musician is the "debtor." If the piano company then *sells* the musician's promise to pay the debt (an "account," commonly called an "account receivable") to Bank A, the piano company is again, as to this transaction, the "debtor" and Bank A would be the "secured party."

B. SCOPE OF ARTICLE 9 COVERAGE

1. **In General:** [§46]   Article 9 of the U.C.C. "applies (i) to *any transaction* (regardless of its form) which is *intended to create a security interest in personal property or fixtures* including goods, documents, instruments, general intangibles, chattel paper, or accounts and also (ii) to any *sale of accounts or chattel paper*."

2. **Types of Collateral:** [§47]   Because many of the rules in Article 9 turn on the *type* of collateral involved, it is important to classify the property under its proper Article 9 label. Article 9 types of collateral can be divided into the following manageable groups: (i) tangible collateral (*i.e.,* "goods"); (ii) quasi-tangible collateral (*i.e.,* writings having legal significance, such as promissory notes); and (iii) intangible collateral (*i.e.,* collateral having no physical form, such as accounts receivable).

   a. **Tangible collateral—goods:** [§48]   Collateral having a tangible physical form is called "goods" in the U.C.C. The Article 9 definition of "goods" is virtually identical to the definition under Article 2 (the Sales Article). [U.C.C. §§2-105, 9-105(1)(h); *see* Sales Summary]

      (1) **Definition:** [§49]   Included in the term "goods" are "all things which are movable at the time the security interest attaches or which are fixtures." The term also includes unborn young of animals, growing crops, and timber to be cut under a contract or conveyance. [U.C.C. §9-105(1)(h)]

         (a) **Exclusions from definition:** [§50]   Specifically *excluded* from the definition of "goods" are unextracted minerals (like oil and gas) and the types of quasi-intangible and intangible property that are described below (*see infra,* §§56-66). Money is also not included in "goods." [U.C.C. §9-105(1)(h)]

      (2) **Four types of "goods":** [§51]   "Goods" as a category is further broken down into four subgroups. Categorization here depends not on the nature of the goods, but rather on the *principal use* to which the debtor puts the property. The subcategories are mutually exclusive; *i.e.,* a particular piece of property can fit into only one of the following categories with regard to any particular secured transaction: "consumer goods," "inventory," "farm products," or "equipment." [U.C.C. §9-109, Comment 2]

         (a) **"Consumer goods":** [§52]   Goods are "consumer goods" if they are "bought for use primarily for *personal, family, or household purposes*." [U.C.C. §9-109(1)]

         (b) **"Inventory":** [§53]   Goods are "inventory" if they are held for *sale or lease to others in the ordinary course of business*. This category also includes raw materials and materials used or consumed in a business (like pencils and stationery). [U.C.C. §9-109(4)]

         (c) **"Farm products":** [§54]   Goods are "farm products" if they are used or produced in farming operations and are in the possession of the farmer/debtor. The term includes *crops, livestock* (horses, cattle, chickens, etc.), and the *products* of crops and livestock (*e.g.,* maple syrup, milk, eggs, and manure) as long as such products are still in their **unmanufactured** state. Once the products have gone through a manufacturing process (such as canning), they cease to be farm products, and if the farmer holds them out for sale to others, they become "inventory." [U.C.C. §9-109, Comment 4]

(d) **"Equipment":** [§55] Goods are "equipment" if they are used in *a business or by a nonprofit entity or governmental subdivision, or* if they *do not fit into any of the other three categories* of goods. "Equipment," therefore, is the "catchall" category for goods that are used as collateral but are not classifiable as "consumer goods," "inventory," or "farm products." [U.C.C. §9-109, Comment 5]

(e) **Examples:** Under the above definitions, a piano sitting in a music store and used as collateral by the store is "inventory." However, if the piano is sold to an amateur pianist for home enjoyment and used by the amateur as collateral for a loan, it is "consumer goods." And if the piano is owned by a professional pianist and is so used, it is "equipment." [U.C.C. §9-109, Comments 2, 3]

b. **Quasi-tangible collateral:** [§56] Quasi-tangible assets are *legal rights represented by pieces of paper*. When used as collateral, such assets are classified as follows:

(1) **"Instruments":** [§57] "Instruments" includes Article 3 *negotiable and nonnegotiable instruments* (*i.e.,* checks, promissory notes, drafts, and certificates of deposit). [U.C.C. §3-104(2),(3)]

(a) **Compare—chattel paper:** [§58] If the above instruments are coupled with an agreement creating a security interest in favor of a creditor (regardless of whether the agreement is contained in the same piece of paper), the writings taken together are called "chattel paper" (*see* below). Chattel paper formerly was included within the term "instruments," but this is no longer so.

(b) **Compare—investment property:** [§59] Stocks and bonds, commodity contracts, and accounts containing these sorts of investments formerly were covered by the term "instruments," but are now given special treatment under the new catch-all category called "*investment property*." (*See infra,* §209.)

(2) **"Documents":** [§60] "Documents" refers to *documents of title,* such as bills of lading and warehouse receipts. (A company's business documents—such as research reports or corporate papers—do *not* fall under this definition.) [U.C.C. §§9-105(1)(f), 1-201(15)]

(3) **"Chattel paper":** [§61] "Chattel paper" refers to a writing that evidences both a *monetary obligation and a security interest in or a lease of* specific goods. The Code provides that a group of writings evidencing the same two essentials also constitutes chattel paper. [U.C.C. §9-105(1)(b)]

(a) **Example:** Consumer buys a car from a car dealer and signs a contract promising to pay for the car and granting the car dealer a *"security interest"* in the car (thereby making the car collateral, so that it can be repossessed on default). The car dealer then sells the contract outright to a finance company or uses it as collateral for a loan. In either event, the contract constitutes "chattel paper" within Article 9.

    1) **Compare—instrument:** If the contract did not contain the grant of a *security interest* to the dealer (a rare circumstance), it would be an "instrument" when used as collateral by the dealer.

(b) **Example:** Consumer *leases* a car from a car dealer. The lease is "chattel paper" when used by the car dealer as collateral for a loan, or when the car dealer sells the lease to another entity.

    1) **Compare—real estate leases:** However, since Article 9 does not apply to interests in real property (*see* below), a real estate lease used as collateral would **not** be covered by Article 9 and would not be "chattel paper." [U.C.C. §9-102(3), Comment 4]

(c) **Example:** Consumer buys a car and signs *two* pieces of paper: a promissory note and a separate security agreement in favor of the car dealer. If the promissory note alone is sold to a finance company, it is an "instrument," but if the two papers are sold together, they constitute "chattel paper." [U.C.C. §9-105, Comment 4]

(4) **Compare—"accounts":** [§62] Where a consumer buys goods (*e.g.*, groceries) on credit and signs nothing, the seller may use the consumer's *oral promise* of repayment as collateral for a loan. However, in such a case the collateral is called an "account," not chattel paper (*see* below).

c. **Intangible collateral:** [§63] Some types of collateral have *no physical form*. The 1962 version of Article 9 recognized three types of such collateral, but the 1972 version groups all intangibles into two broad categories: "accounts" and "general intangibles."

(1) **"Accounts":** [§64] The term "accounts," commonly called "accounts receivable," refers to a *right of repayment* for goods or services sold or leased that is not evidenced by an instrument or chattel paper. [U.C.C. §9-106]

(a) **"Contract rights":** [§65] Under the revised Code, the term "account" also covers any right to payment under a contract *"whether or not such right has been earned by performance."* The term therefore includes the category of intangibles known as "contract rights" under the 1962 version of Article 9—*i.e.*, rights to payment not contained in an instrument or chattel paper and for which performance has **not** yet been rendered. [U.C.C. §9-106]

    1) **Reason for change:** Under the 1962 version, once performance *occurred*, the "contract right" became an "account." The

purpose behind elimination of the "contract right" category in the 1972 version was to avoid both this technical and confusing distinction between "contract rights" and "accounts" and the drafting errors that sometimes turned a "contract right" into a "general intangible" following performance.

(2) **"General intangibles":** [§66] "General intangibles" is vaguely defined to include any personal property *other than* goods, accounts, chattel paper, documents, instruments, and money. The purpose of this catchall provision is to allow for commercial usage to make use of new forms of personal property as collateral. Some examples are goodwill, literary rights, and rights of performance. [U.C.C. §9-106]

   (a) **Examples:** Blueprints, bid packages, and research reports have been classified as general intangibles [United States v. Antenna Systems, Inc., 251 F. Supp. 1013 (D.N.H. 1966)], as has the right to payment of a federal tax refund [*In re* Certified Packaging, Inc., 8 U.C.C. Rep. 95 (D. Utah 1970)].

   (b) **And note:** Although a *liquor license* is not "property" in the usual sense because it is not freely transferable (it is often described as a mere "privilege" and not a "right"), it is, nevertheless, very much an asset of a business. And several courts have held that it *is* "collateral," so that a security interest in a liquor license *can* be perfected under Article 9. [Gibson v. Alaska Alcoholic Beverage Control Board, 377 F. Supp. 151 (D. Alaska 1974)]

d. **Investment property collateral:** [§67] Stocks and bonds, whether represented by a physical piece of paper (a *"certificated* security") or merely listed on the records of the issuing corporation (an *"uncertificated* security"), commodity contracts, and accounts in which such investments are held ("securities accounts" or "commodity accounts") are given special treatment in Article 9, and thus are all dealt with under the designation of *"investment property."*

gilbert LAW SUMMARIES	**SUMMARY OF COLLATERAL TYPES**	
Tangible	**Quasi-Tangible**	**Intangible**
Consumer goods Inventory Farm products Equipment	Instruments Documents of title Chattel paper Stocks and Bonds	Accounts General intangibles

3. **Types of Transactions:** [§68] Any *financing* transaction, regardless of its name or form, may be held subject to Article 9. If the purpose of the transaction was to *create a security interest* in collateral, Article 9 applies. [Sierra Financial Corp. v. Brooks-Farrer Co., 15 Cal. App. 3d 698 (1971)—what appeared to be an outright *sale* of goods was held to be intended only as a security device and hence subject to Article 9 ("sale" was far below market price and "seller" had reserved the right to repurchase)]

   a. **Leases:** [§69] A true lease is clearly *not* a security transaction and is not subject to Article 9. However, leases are often structured so that the lessee may be entitled to purchase the "leased" goods at the end of the term. The question then arises whether the transaction is a true lease or, in reality, a financing arrangement designed to protect the seller by maintaining title in the seller as *security* for payments from the "lessee" (buyer). If the latter, the "lease" is subject to the filing requirements of Article 9, and the "lessor" had better take the steps required by Article 9 if it wishes to prevail over other creditors of the "lessee."

      (1) **True lease compared with security interest:** [§70] Whether a transaction is a true lease or a sale on credit (*i.e.,* a secured transaction) disguised as a lease depends on the *facts of each case,* but section 1-201(37), defining "security interest," does have some bright line tests in answering the question.

         (a) **Option to purchase:** [§71] If the lessee has the option to purchase the property for no or only nominal consideration, the transaction creates a security interest and is not a true lease. [U.C.C. §1-201(37)(d)]

         (b) **Termination clause:** [§72] If the lessee has the right to *terminate* the lease and return the goods, a true lease occurs, since this is not usually an option given to someone purchasing goods.

            1) **Example:** Consumer leases a suite of furniture from a Rent-To-Own Store, paying on weekly installments. The lease provides that at any time the consumer wishes, he may return the suite and have no further liability. This is a true lease.

         (c) **No value at end of lease:** [§73] If at the end of the lease term (either as originally set or as extended by renewals), the leased goods will have *no remaining economic value,* a disguised sale on credit has occurred, and this is *not* a true lease. This is sometimes called the "junk pile" test because at the end of the so-called lease, the goods are fit only for being discarded. [U.C.C. §1-201(37)(a)-(c)]

         (d) **Other terms irrelevant:** [§74] Section 1-201(37) lists a number of other terms of the lease that are *irrelevant* to the determination of whether a true lease or a secured transaction is intended, even though prior case law found these things important:

            1) **Lease payments exceed value:** [§75] The fact that the payments made under the lease will exceed the fair market value

of the goods does not in any way determine whether a true lease was intended.

   a)   **Example:** Consumer leases a suite of furniture from a Rent-To-Own Store, paying on weekly installments. The lease provides that the furniture will be owned by the consumer once he has made rental payments that are *double* the amount the consumer would have had to pay if he had paid cash for the furniture. The fact that this is an incredibly expensive way to buy furniture in no way affects whether this is a true lease.

   2)   **Option to renew:** [§76]   The fact that the lease gives the lessee the option to renew is also irrelevant, as long as the goods will still have some useful economic life at the end of the lease period.

   3)   **Risk of loss:** [§77]   A term providing that the lessee has the risk of loss is also irrelevant to the true lease/secured transaction issue.

   4)   **Taxes and other charges:** [§78]   Finally, it is also irrelevant that the lessee must pay taxes, insurance, or other service or maintenance fees.

b.   **Consignments:** [§79]   In a typical consignment, the manufacturer or wholesaler of goods (the "consignor") turns them over to a retailer (the "consignee"), who acts as the selling agent of the goods at the retail level. The consignor *retains title* to the consigned goods, and if they are not sold by the consignee at retail, the consignor expects to get the goods back free from any claims of the consignee's creditors. As with leases, it is sometimes difficult to distinguish a "true" consignment from a disguised inventory financing arrangement. Therefore, special rules for consignments were developed in both Article 2 (Sales) and Article 9.

   (1)   **Protection against existing creditors:** [§80]   First, to obtain protection against *existing* creditors of the consignee, the consignor must take the same perfection and notice steps as are required of purchase money secured creditors selling inventory to retailers (*see infra*, §§336-340). [U.C.C. §9-114]

   (2)   **Protection against future creditors:** [§81]   Second, to protect the interest in the assigned goods from *future* creditors of the consignee, the consignor must [U.C.C. §2-326(3)]:

   (a)   *Comply with any special state "sign law"* requiring a sign to be posted on the consignee's premises informing the world that the consignee deals in consigned goods (most states do *not* have such "sign laws"); *or*

   (b)   *Establish that the consignee is "generally known* by the consignee's creditors to be substantially *engaged in selling the goods of others"* (an almost impossible burden of proof [*see In re* Webb, 13 U.C.C. Rep. 394 (S.D. Tex. 1973)]); *or*

(c) *Comply with Article 9 as if* the consignment were primarily a "financing" rather than a "selling" device. This is the only sound choice for all consignors.

(3) **Protection against existing and future creditors:** [§82]   Since the only certain means of protection against *both* existing and future creditors of the consignee is compliance with the usual Article 9 steps, the consignor is wise to comply with Article 9. Under section 9-408, the consignor may file a financing statement that uses the consignment terms (a fail-safe procedure) without this in any way being an admission that anything other than a true consignment was intended. (*See* below.)

C. TRANSACTIONS EXCLUDED FROM ARTICLE 9

Public policy and conflict with other bodies of law governing certain secured transactions give rise to a limited number of exceptions in the Article's otherwise broad coverage.

1. **Federal Statutes:** [§83]   Security interests governed by any statute of the United States are exempt from the Code, but only to the extent that the statutes control the rights of the parties to the security agreement or the rights of third parties. [U.C.C. §9-104(a)]

   a. **Example:** The Federal Aviation Act [49 U.S.C. §1403] provides a method for recording title to airplanes and accords protection to titles thus recorded. This Act, therefore, *preempts* all state *filing* laws—although Article 9 must still be consulted on matters of priority, validity of title documents, good faith purchaser status, etc., as to which the federal statute is silent. [U.C.C. §9-104, Comment 1; Haynes v. General Electric Credit Corp., 432 F. Supp. 763 (W.D. W. Va. 1977)]

   b. **Example:** The Ship Mortgage Act provides an exclusive method for recordation of interests in maritime vessels [46 U.S.C. §911], and the Assignment of Claims Act governs the assignment of payments due under U.S. government contracts [41 U.S.C. §15].

   c. **Note—application of U.C.C. remedies:** [§84]   In some instances, the federal statute merely determines ownership or priorities in the chattels in question but does not specify any *remedy* for enforcement or protection thereof. In such cases, courts apply the remedies available under the U.C.C.

   d. **And note—federal loans:** [§85]   The Supreme Court has held that federal loans are to be governed by the provisions of the U.C.C., which the Court adopted as a matter of federal common law. [United States v. Kimbell Foods, 440 U.S. 715 (1979)]

2. **Landlord's Liens and Liens on Real Property Interests:** [§86]   This exception simply emphasizes that Article 9 applies *only to personal property*; landlord's liens and other interests in real property are all excluded from the Article. [U.C.C. §9-104(b), (j)]

   a. **Rents:** [§87]   A security interest in rents from real property (*e.g.,* an assignment of rental income to secure an indebtedness) is treated the same as a lien on the property itself, and hence it is exempt from Article 9. [Ingram v. Ingram, 521 P.2d 254 (Kan. 1974)—assignment of oil and gas royalties]

b. **Compare—promissory notes:** [§88] If a mortgagee receives a promissory note from the mortgagor and then uses it as collateral for a loan to the mortgagee, Article 9 *applies*, since instruments are covered thereby. [U.C.C. §9-102(3), Comment 4; *and see infra,* §100]

3. **Mechanic's and Artisan's Liens:** [§89] Drafters of the Code felt that the rights of artisans and servicepeople (holders of "statutory" liens) could adequately be governed by local statute or common law. [U.C.C. §9-104(c)]

4. **Claims Arising Out of Judicial Proceedings:** [§90] Judgments, setoffs, rights, and tort claims generally do not serve as collateral in commercial transactions. Hence, they are excluded from the Code. [U.C.C. §9-104(h), (i), (k)]

5. **Wage or Salary Claims:** [§91] The assignment of *current or future wages* represents a question of social importance rather than a purely commercial problem, and so it is left to local law. [U.C.C. §9-104(d)]

6. **Insurance Policies and Deposit Accounts (Bank, Savings and Loan, etc.):** [§92] Sometimes these are put up as collateral, but they are not part of normal commercial financing and are therefore excluded from Article 9. (Note, however, that these may be subject to Article 9 if received by the debtor as "proceeds" on the sale or disposition of other collateral; *infra,* §374.) [U.C.C. §9-104(g), (1)]

7. **Assignments Not for Financing Purposes (So-Called One Shot Assignments):** [§93] As previously mentioned, sales of accounts and chattel paper are normally subject to Article 9. [U.C.C. §9-102(1)(b); *supra,* §42] However, certain transfers of such intangibles have nothing to do with normal commercial financing and hence are specifically *excluded* from Article 9.

a. **Assignment as part of sale of business:** [§94] The sale of a business, along with its assets and liabilities, is not a normal financing transaction. Hence, if the owner of accounts or chattel paper transfers these assets as part of the sale of the business out of which those rights arose, no compliance with Article 9 is required. [U.C.C. §9-104(f)]

b. **Assignment for collection:** [§95] Likewise, the assignment of an overdue account or note to a collection agency is not a financing transaction and is exempt from Article 9. [U.C.C. §9-104(f)]

c. **Assignment coupled with delegation of performance:** [§96] Similarly, where the assignment of the right to payment under contract obligates the assignee to perform the work required for payment (*e.g.,* subcontracting work), this is not a financing transaction and is excluded from Article 9. [U.C.C. §9-104(f)]

d. **Assignment as payment of prior debts:** [§97] Finally, no compliance with Article 9 is required where the assignment of a single account is made in *whole or partial satisfaction* of a preexisting indebtedness. Again, this is not a financing transaction. [U.C.C. §9-104(f)]

8. **Surety's Subrogation Rights:** [§98] When a contractor fails to perform, so that the contractor's surety must therefore do so, the surety's equitable right of "subrogation"—which entitles the surety to the amounts still due the contractor—is *not*

an Article 9 security interest, and the surety need not comply with Article 9 to prevail over the contractor's other creditors. [United States Fidelity & Guaranty Co. v. First State Bank, 494 P.2d 1149 (Kan. 1972)]

9. **Subordination Agreements:** [§99]   An agreement whereby two creditors, both having security interests in the same collateral, decide to reverse which one is senior and which junior is not an Article 9 security interest and is excluded from Code coverage. [U.C.C. §§1-209, 9-316]

10. **Effect of Underlying Transaction Not Within Code:** [§100]   Even though the basic obligation that secures a security interest may be exempt from the U.C.C., subsequent transactions involving the security interest may fall within the coverage of Article 9. [U.C.C. §9-102(3)]

    a. **Example:** Buyer purchases a ranch from Seller, paying a portion in cash and giving a note and mortgage on the ranch for the remainder. This is a real property transaction and is excluded from the Code. [U.C.C. §9-104(j); *supra,* §86] However, suppose that Seller then takes Buyer's note and mortgage and pledges them to secure Seller's obligation to Third Party. Third Party's security interest in the note and mortgage *is governed by the Code.* [U.C.C. §9-102, Comment 4]

11. **Consumer Protection Statutes:** [§101]   The federal government and most states have enacted special statutes regulating security interests in consumer goods. These statutes provide important *additional* requirements in *consumer financing* arrangements to validate a security interest.

    a. **Example:** Where a consumer credit transaction may result in the creation of a security interest in the debtor's principal residence, these statutes may require that the consumer be given certain notices and a three-day "cooling off" period in which to back out of the deal. [16 U.S.C. §1635]

    b. **Example:** Similarly, consumer laws in most states require certain disclosures to be made in the security agreement, prohibit the creation of security interests in certain kinds of consumer collateral, and regulate the creditor's foreclosure rights on default. [Uniform Consumer Credit Code §§3.203, 3.103, 5.103; Cal. Civ. Code §§1803.2, 1804.3, 1812.2]

III. CREATION OF A SECURITY INTEREST

chapter approach

In this chapter you are introduced to the first substantive area of the law of secured transactions—the basic steps necessary before the creditor's security interest *"attaches"* to the collateral nominated by the debtor.

Attachment is a condition precedent to the success of the creditor's attempt to reach any collateral protecting the credit extended by the creditor. Be careful to determine whether the mandatory rules for creation of a security interest have been met:

1. Is there a *security agreement* that is complete (formalities, signatures, description of collateral)?

2. Did the secured party *give value* sufficient to support the agreement?

3. Does the debtor have *existing rights* in the collateral?

If you cannot answer yes to these three questions, there has been no attachment, and if a creditor makes a mistake here, the whole process thereafter is wasted.

A. INTRODUCTION

1. **Basic Policies**

    a. **Protection of lenders complying with Code:** [§102]   The Code contains a basic guarantee to lenders that if they follow its language and avoid the exceptions created therein, their security interests will be protected. Thus, the U.C.C. states: "Except as otherwise provided *by this Act,* a security agreement is effective according to its terms between creditors." [U.C.C. §9-201]

        (1) **Effect:** This greatly simplifies the problems in secured financing and is quite a departure from earlier systems of secured financing, where statutes or case law sometimes left "implied" or unstated exceptions to trip an unwary lender.

    b. **Prevention of systems outside Code:** [§103]   Lenders are also prevented from attempting to exploit gaps in the Code to create new types of security interests that need not be filed. U.C.C. section 9-302 provides that a "financing statement must be filed to perfect *all* security interests except . . . [certain named types of interests]." Thus, the all-inclusive nature of the Code both protects the lender from unknown pitfalls and prevents the creation of a private system outside the framework of the Code.

        (1) **Example:** Prior to the U.C.C., a creditor who failed to take all the steps required by law to create or protect an interest in the collateral might still prevail under the theory that the creditor had an "equitable" lien (*i.e.,*

one that would be recognized by courts of equity). Under the Code, however, equitable liens are *not* recognized. [U.C.C. §9-203, Comment 5]

2. Creation of a Security Interest—An Overview

a. **Attachment and perfection:** [§104]   The process by which the debtor and creditor create a security interest in the debtor's collateral effective *between these two parties* is called *"attachment"* (*see* detailed discussion, below). The process by which this security interest is then made good against most of the *rest of the world* (*e.g.,* buyers, other creditors, the debtor's trustee in bankruptcy) is called *"perfection"* (*see infra,* §§153 *et seq.* for the steps required for "perfection").

b. **Security agreement and financing statement:** [§105]   The two primary pieces of paper involved in an Article 9 financing transaction are the security agreement and the financing statement (each of which is discussed in detail, *infra*). Basically, the *security agreement is a contract between the debtor and creditor* that spells out the rights and duties of the parties and is required for "attachment" of the security interest. The *financing statement is a document containing certain information* about the creditor's secured interest and is typically (although not always) used to accomplish "perfection"; *i.e.,* the creditor perfects by *filing* the financing statement in the appropriate place. Thus, the function of the financing statement is to give *notice* to others of the creditor's interest in the debtor's property.

B. ATTACHMENT OF A SECURITY INTEREST—IN GENERAL

1. **Definition:** [§106]   As indicated above, "attachment" is the label the U.C.C. uses to describe the *process* by which the security interest is *created* in the property of the debtor in favor of the secured party. The steps required for "perfection" of a security interest (*infra*) may be taken before or after the time when it attaches to the collateral, but the security interest is not perfected until it has attached—*i.e.,* it cannot be good against other parties ("perfection") until it is effective between the debtor and creditor ("attachment").

2. **Requirements:** [§107]   There are three requirements for "attachment" of a security interest:

(i)   The parties must have an *agreement* that the security interest attach;

(ii)   *Value* must be given by the secured party; and

(iii)   The *debtor* must have *rights* in the collateral.

[U.C.C. §9-203] Each of these requirements is discussed in detail in following sections.

a. **Coexistence required:** [§108]   The security interest attaches as soon as these three requirements have been met, unless the parties have explicitly agreed to postpone the time of attachment. The three events may occur in *any order*, but they must *co-exist* before the interest attaches. [U.C.C. §9-203(2)]

(1) **Example:** Borrower borrowed $10,000 from Lender on May 1 and signed a security agreement giving Lender a security interest in Borrower's existing factory equipment. Lender also agreed to lend an additional $20,000 to Borrower against Borrower's inventory and an automobile Borrower was planning to buy. Borrower received the $20,000 loan June 1 and bought the automobile on July 1. The security interest in the factory equipment attached on May 1, when the three steps were completed. The security interest in the inventory did not attach until June 1, when Borrower received value from Lender. The security interest in the car did not attach until July 1, when Borrower acquired the automobile.

(2) **Example:** On April 10, Borrower signed an agreement with Lender giving Lender a security interest in Borrower's stamp collection. On April 15, Lender filed a financing statement in the appropriate place. On April 18, Lender loaned Borrower the money. Attachment did not occur until April 18, when Lender gave *value*. [U.C.C. §9-303, Comment 1]

b. **Agreement as to time of attachment:** [§109] As mentioned above, the parties may specifically agree to postpone the time of attachment. For example, on June 1, the debtor and creditor sign an agreement giving the creditor a security interest in collateral the debtor owned, with the creditor giving current "value" in the form of a binding commitment to make the loan (*see infra,* §143). However, the agreement provides that attachment will not take place until July 10. The agreement will be given effect. The parties may wish to have control over the moment of attachment because it is the legal event that determines matters such as where to file the financing statement.

C. SECURITY AGREEMENT

1. **Necessity of a Writing:** [§110] Whether a written security agreement is required depends on whether the secured party has possession of the collateral.

    a. **Collateral in possession of secured party—oral agreement sufficient:** [§111] If the secured party has *possession* of the collateral to which the security agreement attaches (a "pledge" transaction), a *written* security agreement is *not* required. A security agreement is still necessary for attachment, but it may be *oral* since the collateral is pledged. [U.C.C. §9-203(1)(a)]

        (1) **Example:** Bummer leaves his wristwatch at the pawn shop in exchange for $10 and a pawn ticket. Even though Bummer did not sign a security agreement, the oral agreement is enough to give the pawn shop a security interest.

    b. **Collateral not in secured party's possession—writing required:** [§112] If the secured party is *not* in possession of the collateral, the security interest will be valid only if there is a *written* security agreement *signed by the debtor* and *containing a description* of the collateral. [U.C.C. §9-203(1)(a)]

        (1) **Effect of requirement:** [§113] The formal requisite of a written agreement is not only a condition to the enforceability of a security interest against third parties but it is also in the nature of a *Statute of Frauds* requirement; *i.e.,* a nonpossessory security interest without a written

agreement is *not enforceable* against the debtor and cannot be made so under any common law lien theory. [U.C.C. §9-203, Comment 5]

(2) **Can financing statement satisfy?** [§114]   As mentioned above, to *perfect* a security interest, it is usually necessary to file a *financing statement* in an appropriate state office. Since financing statements must be signed and contain a description of the collateral, the question arises whether the financing statement can be used to satisfy the requirement of a "signed security agreement" where there is no other written agreement between the parties.

   (a) **General rule:** [§115]   By itself, a financing statement is usually *not* enough to satisfy the requirement of a "signed security agreement."

      1) **Rationale:** A "security agreement" is one that *creates* a security interest [U.C.C. §9-105(1)]—by language *granting* the creditor an interest in the collateral—and a financing statement usually *does not purport to create* a security interest. Rather, it merely serves as notice to third parties that a security interest is *claimed.*

         a) **Note:** The requirement that the security agreement contain language actually *granting* the security interest is not found in the U.C.C. but comes from the case of *American Card Co. v. H.M.H. Co.,* 196 A.2d 150 (R.I. 1963)—holding that a financing statement could not serve as a security agreement because it contained no "granting" language.

      2) **Further rationale:** Another reason why the financing statement is not a sufficient security agreement is that it is often filed *before* the financing arrangements are complete (to assure the creditor of priority). Hence, the mere fact that a financing statement is on file is no proof that a security *agreement* was ever reached. [*In re* Shoreline Electric Supply, Inc., 18 U.C.C. Rep. 231 (D. Conn. 1975)]

      3) **Compare:** If there *is* a "signed security agreement," the creditor can use it as the financing statement (*see infra,* §247).

   (b) **Modern trend:** [§116]   There is now a discernible trend to liberalize the above general rule.

      1) **Criticism—technicality:** First of all, the *American Card* case, *supra,* has been much criticized by commentators for adding a technicality to the Code and has not been followed by all courts. [*See, e.g.,* Kreiger v. Hartig, 527 P.2d 483 (Wash. 1974)—holding that parol evidence may be used to show an intention to "grant" a security interest where the writing did not do so]

      2) **Extrinsic evidence allowed:** Furthermore, a number of courts now hold that where a financing statement has been executed

and filed, it is proper to consider *extrinsic evidence* (*e.g.,* correspondence, invoices, promissory notes, etc.) in determining whether a "security agreement" has been *reached*. This, in effect, allows the executed financing statement *plus some other evidence* to satisfy the "signed security agreement" requirement of section 9-203(1), above. [*In re* Numeric, 485 F.2d 1328 (1st Cir. 1973)—financing statement plus corporate resolution of debtor approving proposed financing held sufficient]

    (c) **Addition of granting language to financing statement:** [§117] Note that if "granting" language is added to a financing statement before it is filed, the language will satisfy the requirements of the U.C.C. and *American Card* and will allow the financing statement to serve as the parties' security agreement. This can be a useful backup if for one reason or another the "real" security agreement is held insufficient.

2. **Conveyance of Security Interest:** [§118] As indicated above, an essential ingredient of a security agreement is that it *create or provide for* a security interest in specific collateral. [U.C.C. §9-105(1)]

    a. **Test—evidence of debtor's intent:** [§119] Whether the agreement creates or provides for a security interest turns on the language used. It must appear from the wording that the *debtor intended* to grant the creditor some present lien or interest in the collateral. [Komas v. Future Systems, Inc., 71 Cal. App. 3d 809 (1977)]

    b. **Terminology:** [§120] No particular words are required. Certainly, the term "security interest" is not essential; provisions for "liens" or "mortgages" or "rights" may be held sufficient. [*In re* Mann, 318 F. Supp. 32 (W.D. Va. 1970)]

        (1) *The word "grants" or "conveys"* is normally used to create the interest. But again, neither of these is essential. The intent to create a security interest may be implied from other provisions of the agreement. [*In re* Amex-Protein Development Corp., 504 F.2d 1056 (9th Cir. 1974)]

        (2) *If the agreement calls itself a "conditional sale,"* it still qualifies as a security agreement if it is signed by the debtor-buyer and describes the collateral. [Sommers v. I.B.M., 640 F.2d 686 (5th Cir. 1981)]

        (3) *The security agreement is not limited in what it may contain.* Since it is the basic *contract,* it should include everything that the parties agree upon (repayment terms, grounds for default, etc.).

3. **Description of the Collateral:** [§121] The security agreement must always contain a description of the collateral involved. (Where the collateral is growing crops or timber to be cut, it must also contain a description of the real estate on which the crops or timber are located.) [U.C.C. §9-203(1)]

    a. **Sufficiency of description:** [§122] Following its policy of reducing formal requirements, the U.C.C. provides that the description is sufficient if it *reasonably identifies* what is described. [U.C.C. §9-110]

(1) **Test:** [§123]   The description must be such that it can be determined therefrom *what collateral the parties intended* the security interest to cover. [*In* re Swanson, 104 B.R. 1 (Bankr. C.D. Ill. 1989)—"all personal property" held not descriptive enough]

    (a) **Compare—description in financing statement:** [§124]   Note that this may require a more detailed description than is required in the *financing statement*, where the test is simply whether it is enough to put a reasonable person **on inquiry** as to whether particular collateral is covered by some previously filed security interest (*see infra,* §263).

(2) **Application:** [§125]   Under the foregoing approach, it is sufficient if the security agreement contains a description that *reasonably* covers the collateral in question. The so-called serial number description required by old law is certainly *not* required. Wording such as "all equipment located at . . ." or "all inventory at . . ." may be held sufficient. [James Talcott, Inc. v. Franklin National Bank, 194 N.W.2d 775 (Minn. 1972)]

    (a) **Example—"contents":** Lender had a perfected security interest in all "contents" of Debtor's luncheonette and "all property used" in the business. The seller of a cash register (who had failed to perfect a security interest) sought to reclaim the cash register on the ground that it was not covered by the Lender's security agreement. *Held:* The description "contents . . . and property used" in the luncheonette covered the cash register. [National Cash Register Co. v. Firestone Co., 191 N.E.2d 471 (Mass. 1963)]

    (b) **Incorporation by reference:** [§126]   It is not required that the description be contained in the four corners of the security agreement itself. The agreement may incorporate by reference a description contained in the financing statement or in some **other documents** altogether. [*In re* Amex-Protein Development Corp., *supra,* §120—agreement covered "subject personal property as per invoices" attached]

(3) **Effect of errors in description:** [§127]   An error in description is *not fatal* as long as there is some other proof that the parties intended the collateral in question to be covered by the security agreement.

    (a) **Example:** Thus, an error in copying the *serial or license numbers* of vehicles or equipment may be disregarded where the agreement also contains a correct description of the make, model, and year of manufacture. [Still Associates v. Murphy, 267 N.E.2d 217 (Mass. 1971)]

        1) **But note:** On the other hand, where the debtor had several trucks of the same make, model, and year of manufacture, so that the serial number was the *only means of identifying* the collateral, an error in the serial number may be held fatal to the lender's claim—at least in litigation with an innocent purchaser or the debtor's trustee in bankruptcy. [*In re* Aragon Industries, 14 U.C.C. Rep. 1218 (S.D. Fla. 1973)]

(b) **Compare—errors in location:** [§128]   Errors in describing the *location* of the collateral are more likely to be held material. Still, where the chattels are otherwise identifiable by description contained in the agreement, even a misstatement of their location may be disregarded. [First State Bank v. Waychus, 183 N.W.2d 728 (Iowa 1971)—livestock]

b. **"Proceeds":** [§129]   While permissible, it is *no longer necessary* that the security agreement expressly mention "proceeds." The reason is that, unless otherwise agreed, it is presumed that the parties intended the security agreement to cover proceeds (cash or noncash) obtained upon the sale or exchange of the collateral, and hence such proceeds are covered as a matter of law. [U.C.C. §9-306(2); *see infra,* §376]

c. **"After-acquired property":** [§130]   A security interest may be created in "after-acquired property"—*i.e.,* collateral that the debtor does not now own, but that the debtor may or will acquire in the *future.* [U.C.C. §9-204(1); *see* further discussion *infra,* §335] This means that as the debtor becomes the owner of new property in the future, the creditor's security interest will automatically attach to that property without the need to do anything further. Whether it is wise or not to allow the debtor to encumber future as well as existing property was a much debated issue when the Code was being drafted, but, with the exception mentioned below for consumer goods, the drafters decided to allow this much freedom of contract.

(1) **Exceptions for consumer goods:** [§131]   There are two major exceptions to this rule. Under the U.C.C., no security interest attaches to *consumer goods* (other than accessions; *see infra,* §359) given as additional security under an after-acquired property clause unless the debtor acquires rights in the consumer goods *within 10 days* after the secured party gives value. (This is to prevent overreaching creditors from tying up all the property of consumers.) [U.C.C. §9-204(2)] The second exception is mandated by federal regulation and is called the "Credit Practices Rule." Under the Rule, both the Federal Trade Commission and the Federal Reserve Board prohibit the creation of non-purchase money, nonpossessory security interests in *household goods.* [16 C.F.R. 444; 12 C.F.R. 227; for a discussion of what constitutes a purchase money security interest, *see infra,* §183] The policy here is to prevent overreaching creditors from seizing property having value only to the consumer.

(a) **Example:** Mr. and Mrs. Debtor applied for a loan from Finance Company. They signed a security agreement that claimed as collateral "all Debtors' consumer goods now owned or hereafter acquired until their deaths." The Debtors received a $1,000 loan from Finance Company on October 10. On October 31, they bought a sewing machine. Finance Company's security interest does *not* attach to the sewing machine. Under U.C.C. section 9-204, the sewing machine constitutes consumer goods purchased more than 10 days after value was given, and so no attachment occurs. Under the federal regulations, an after-acquired interest cannot arise because the sewing machine is a household good, and the secured party does not have a purchase money security interest therein, and has not taken possession.

(b) **Compare:** Farmer borrowed $10,000 from the Farmer's Friend Bank on October 10, signing a security agreement giving the bank a security interest in "all livestock now owned or hereinafter acquired." On October 31, Farmer bought 20 new cows. The bank's security interest attaches to the 20 cows since they are "farm products," not "consumer goods."

(2) **Specificity required:** [§132] Where the security agreement is intended to cover "after-acquired property," most courts hold that the agreement itself must *expressly* use that term or otherwise clearly refer to collateral to be acquired in the *future*. [*In re* Atlantic Stud Welding Co., 503 F.2d 1133 (3d Cir. 1974)]

(a) **Less required for inventory:** [§133] However, it is generally held that where the security agreement covers *"inventory,"* this term *implies* that it covers not only present inventory, but also inventory *to be acquired* in the future. *Rationale:* Inventory by its nature changes from day to day; thus, the parties must have intended the security interest to do likewise. [Borg-Warner Acceptance Corp. v. Wolfe City National Bank, 544 S.W.2d 947 (Tex. 1976)]

(b) **Accounts and farm equipment similar:** [§134] Similarly, if the collateral is accounts receivable or farm equipment, most courts hold that there is no need to use the words "now owned or after-acquired" since in the usual case the parties would contemplate that after-acquired collateral of this type would automatically be covered by the security agreement, although the careful attorney will not leave this in doubt and will actually put "now owned or after-acquired" in both the security agreement and the financing statement. [*In re* Nightway Transportation Co., 96 B.R. 854 (N.D. Ill. 1989)—accounts; Kubota Tractor Corp. v. Citizens & Southern National Bank, 403 S.E.2d 218 (Ga. 1991)—farm equipment]

(3) **Interest attaches when property acquired:** [§135] Even though the security agreement clearly is intended to cover "after-acquired property," the security interest itself *attaches* only when the debtor *acquires* the property. However, once the debtor has an interest in the collateral, the security interest attaches *automatically* (no further agreement or formalities are required).

d. **"Floating liens":** [§136] A "floating lien" is one that attaches to a debtor's accounts, stock, inventory of goods, or other aggregation of items of collateral. However, the debtor has the right to transfer and dispose of *individual* items of collateral. Thus, the actual identity of the collateral may always be changing, but the stock or aggregation as a whole continues to be subject to the lien; *i.e.,* the lien "floats" over the collateral, attaching to an item when it comes into the debtor's possession and terminating when the item is sold or the account is paid.

(1) **Code provisions:** [§137] Although the term "floating lien" is not expressly used, it is authorized by the provisions of U.C.C. section 9-204(1), validating after-acquired property clauses (above), and U.C.C.

section 9-205, validating arrangements under which the debtor has the right to transfer or dispose of the collateral.

    (2) **Caution—bankruptcy proceedings:** [§138] However, there is a problem with using a floating lien on inventory or accounts if the debtor goes bankrupt. The trustee in bankruptcy may try to attack the transaction as creating a *voidable preference* (*infra,* §499).

4. **Signature of the Debtor:** [§139] The *debtor* must sign the security agreement. [U.C.C. §9-203(1)] This may be done by any means satisfying the requirements of U.C.C. section 1-201(39). Thus, *any symbol* used by a party to authenticate a writing is sufficient—*e.g.,* a typed signature if affixed with the requisite intent to authenticate the writing. [*In re* Save-On-Carpets of Arizona, Inc., 545 F.2d 1239 (9th Cir. 1976)]

    a. **Compare—signature of secured party:** [§140] It is *not* necessary that the secured party sign the security agreement (although in practice, this is often done).

5. **Other Terms of Agreement:** [§141] In addition to the minimum requirements for validity (*i.e.,* writing, "granting" language, description of the collateral, and debtor's signature) [U.C.C. §9-203(1)], the security agreement (*i.e.,* the loan agreement between the parties) typically contains the details of the entire credit transaction, including the rights and duties of the parties.

    a. **Provisions for default:** [§142] For example, although U.C.C. section 9-503 permits the creditor to repossess the collateral on "default," the term "default" is not defined in the Code. Therefore, a well-drafted security agreement will specify what circumstances constitute "default"—*e.g.,* nonpayment, the debtor's death, etc.—even though this is not required by the U.C.C.

D. VALUE [§143]

The security interest cannot attach until the creditor has given "value." [U.C.C. §9-203(1)(b)] This is usually an advance of money or a delivery of goods, but may be anything satisfying the definition of "value" in U.C.C. section 1-201(44). Under this section, a person gives "value" for rights in collateral by acquiring them:

1. *In return for any consideration sufficient to support a simple contract*;

2. *As security for a preexisting claim* or in partial or total *satisfaction* thereof;

3. *By accepting delivery* under a preexisting contract for purchase; or

4. *In return for a binding commitment to extend credit*—whether or not the credit is ever drawn upon.

E. DEBTOR'S RIGHTS IN THE COLLATERAL

1. **Rights in the Collateral:** [§144] Before a security interest can attach, the debtor must have "rights in the collateral." This makes sense, since a debtor can hardly grant a security interest in property in which the debtor has no interest. [U.C.C. §9-203(1)(c)]

a. **Definition:** [§145]   The term "rights in the collateral" is not defined by the Code, but it would seem to mean that the debtor must have some *ownership interest or right to obtain possession.* The term "rights" is defined to include *remedies.* [U.C.C. §1-201(36)]

b. **Title to collateral irrelevant:** [§146]   Since the provisions of the Code on rights, obligations, and remedies of parties apply whether title to the collateral is in the secured party or the debtor, the concept of *title can be ignored* in considering whether the debtor has "rights in the collateral." [U.C.C. §9-202; Brandywine Lanes, Inc. v. Pittsburgh National Bank, 261 A.2d 330 (Pa. 1970)]

  (1) **Effect:** Even in bankruptcy proceedings, the courts look at the substance of the transaction in light of the U.C.C. provisions, and not at where the formal title may rest. [*In re* Yale Express Systems, Inc., 370 F.2d 433 (2d Cir. 1966)]

c. **When "rights" acquired:** [§147]   The question as to whether and when "rights" have been acquired is left to determination by the courts on a case-by-case basis.

  (1) **"Identification":** [§148]   In a sale of goods transaction, a buyer has rights in the goods as soon as they have been *"identified"* by the seller *as intended for the buyer,* even though the buyer has yet to receive possession. [U.C.C. §2-501; *see* Sales Summary] Thus, if the other steps are met, a creditor's security interest in goods purchased by the debtor will attach upon the seller's "identification" of those goods. [*In re* Pelletier, 5 U.C.C. Rep. 327 (D. Me. 1968)]

    (a) **Example:** Bank loaned Farmer $20,000 to buy a tractor from Tractor Company, and Farmer signed a security agreement in favor of Bank. Farmer ordered the tractor on February 6. On February 10, Tractor Co. picked out a tractor from its warehouse and tagged it for eventual shipment to Farmer. The moment the tractor was picked out, "identification" occurred, Farmer obtained "rights in the collateral," and Bank's security interest "attached" to the tractor. (And this is true even though Farmer had not yet received or paid for the tractor.)

  (2) **Effect on priority:** [§149]   Determining the *exact* moment of attachment may be important in establishing priorities among creditors—*e.g.,* if the debtor were to go bankrupt prior to delivery of identified goods (*see infra,* §497).

2. **Effect of Restriction on Debtor's Right to Transfer the Collateral:** [§150] Any provision in the security agreement that purports to prohibit transfer of the debtor's rights in the collateral is void and unenforceable, and the debtor's interest may be transferred notwithstanding. This includes both voluntary and involuntary transfers (*e.g.,* by execution sale or other judicial process). [U.C.C. §9-311]

a. **Compare—acceleration or insecurity clauses:** [§151]   A provision in the security agreement giving the secured party the right to *accelerate payment* or *demand additional security* in the event of the debtor's transfer of the collateral may be valid and enforceable; *see infra,* §§523-524.

b. **Other rights:** [§152]   The debtor's transfer of the collateral in spite of this restriction does not necessarily preclude the secured party from finding and repossessing the collateral (*see infra,* §429), and, if the security agreement so provides, it may itself be a ground for default.

IV. PERFECTION

chapter approach

"Perfection" is the process that the parties must go through to make sure that the creditor's security interest in the collateral is good _against most of the rest of the world._ Particularly important is the creditor's freedom from the possibility that the debtor will go bankrupt and the debtor's trustee in bankruptcy will be able to find a way to attack and destroy the security interest.

You will learn in this chapter that there are a number of ways that a creditor can perfect the security interest. Be sure to examine the facts of your question to look for perfection by:

1. **Filing a financing statement:** This is the _usual method_—the _filing_ of a public notice (the "financing statement") in the appropriate office. This notice describes the encumbered collateral and names the parties. Since it is indexed under the debtor's name, later creditors who are contemplating a transaction with the same debtor can check the records and discover what property is already subject to the claims of creditors. Be sure that the financing statement has been filed in the proper place.

2. **Possession of collateral:** If the creditor takes _possession_ of the collateral, the security interest is perfected.

3. **Automatic perfection:** Some security interests can be perfected _without_ filing or possession; perfection is accomplished by attachment alone (_e.g.,_ purchase money security interest in consumer goods). Also, if an interest has been perfected, the protection may carry over to _proceeds,_ but the protection may be lost if goods or negotiable documents are released to the debtor to effect a sale or refinancing. Be sure to consider the rules regarding _temporary perfection._

When the facts of your question involve more than one state, consider the rules governing choice of law in secured lending problems. For example, if collateral is purchased in one jurisdiction for immediate use in another, in which jurisdiction should the steps for perfection be taken? Or for highly mobile collateral (_e.g.,_ railroad cars), where should the creditor perfect? If the collateral has no physical form (_i.e.,_ accounts receivable), what jurisdiction controls?

A. INTRODUCTION [§153]

Although the U.C.C. specifies _methods_ of perfection and the _time_ of perfection, it does not include a definition of perfection itself. However, section 9-301 of the Code, in listing the classes of creditors over whom an _unperfected_ security interest will not prevail, obliquely indicates that the process of perfection is a set of actions which, when complied with, give the secured party _priority over certain other classes of the debtor's creditors_ in the exercise of the security interest.

B. METHODS OF PERFECTION

1. **In General:** [§154]   The Code provides three methods of perfecting a security interest: (i) the filing of a financing agreement; (ii) _possession_ of the collateral; and

(iii) the mere *attachment* of the security interest. The applicability of each method depends on the type of collateral; however, as a general rule, *filing is available for all types* of collateral *except "instruments."*

gilbert LAW SUMMARIES	COMPARISON OF ATTACHMENT VS. PERFECTION	
	Attachment	**Perfection**
Purpose	Establishes secured party's rights in the collateral as *against the debtor*.	Establishes secured party's rights in the collateral as *against third parties*.
Requirements	(i) An agreement evidenced by possession or a written security agreement signed by the debtor; (ii) Value given by the secured party; and (iii)Debtor has rights in the collateral	(i) Attachment; and (ii) One of the following: *Filing* (in the proper place) of *a financing statement* describing the collateral, *Taking possession* of the collateral, *Automatic* perfection

2. **Filing of a Financing Statement:** [§155]   A financing statement is a document that (i) notes the secured party's interest and (ii) generally describes the type of collateral included under the security agreement. The document is filed in the public office specified under each state's adoption of the Code. (The method is discussed in detail *infra,* §247.)

   a. **Note—filing sometimes exclusive method:** [§156]   Filing is the most common method of perfecting a security interest. However, as to certain kinds of property—*accounts and intangibles*—it is the *only* method by which an interest can be perfected. [U.C.C. §9-302]

3. **Perfection by Possession:** [§157]   A *pledge* occurs when the creditor takes physical possession of the collateral (*e.g.,* creditor bank takes debtor's stamp collection and places into its vault) and holds onto it during the term of the loan. The Code provides that the creditor's *possession* of the collateral results in perfection as soon as all the requirements for attachment have been met. [U.C.C. §9-305]

   a. **Pros and cons:** [§158]   If there is a single "best way" to perfect a security interest, it is for the creditor to take physical possession of the collateral. With one stroke, this solves any Statute of Frauds problems (*supra,* §§111-113) and assures perfection. [U.C.C. §9-302(1)(a)]

(1) **And note:** Possession of the collateral also reduces the risk of third parties being misled: Since the debtor's assets are in "hock," they cannot be used to deceive potential lenders as to the debtor's solvency, and as a result, the secured party in possession of the collateral is generally entitled to priority in any contest with third parties (*see infra,* §327).

(2) **But note:** On the other hand, of course, physical possession carries with it problems of storage, care, and maintenance (*see infra,* §§169-170).

b. **Types of property covered:** [§159]   Possession of the collateral by the secured party (without filing) perfects the security interest when the collateral consists of *goods, money, documents, instruments,* or *chattel paper.* [U.C.C. §9-305]

(1) **Money and instruments:** [§160]   If the collateral is money or instruments, taking possession is the *only* way in which a security interest can be perfected. [U.C.C. §9-304(1)]

(a) **Filing of financing statement:** [§161]   It follows that the mere filing of a financing statement normally does *not* perfect a security interest in money or instruments. However, the result may be contra where the money or instruments are "proceeds" from the sale of other collateral (*see infra,* §§378, 380).

(2) **Compare—property not covered:** [§162]   Property that does not fall within the above categories is not "pledgeable." This includes intangibles such as a liquor license, country club membership, seat on a stock exchange, debt, etc. A certificate of title or other registration document is also considered too intangible to be pledgeable property. [Lee v. Cox, 18 U.C.C. Rep. 807 (M.D. Tenn. 1976)]

c. **Means of taking "possession":** [§163]   "Possession" is not defined in the Code. At common law, it means unequivocal, absolute *physical control* over the property sufficient to put third parties on *notice* of the possessor's interest. However, the means of acquiring such control vary according to the type or location of the collateral involved. [Transport Equipment Co. v. Guaranty State Bank, 518 F.2d 377 (10th Cir. 1975)]

(1) **Inventory:** [§164]   A common method for obtaining possession of the debtor's inventory is for the creditor to have the inventory placed in a warehouse (sometimes a *field warehouse, supra,* §22) and then take possession of the negotiable warehouse receipt (a document) issued by the warehouseman. Since no one can get the warehoused goods without surrendering the warehouse receipt [U.C.C. §7-403(3)], possession of the document constitutes possession of the goods [U.C.C. §9-304(2)].

(2) **Goods in possession of bailee:** [§165]   Where goods are being held by a bailee, perfection of a security interest by possession is accomplished by having a *receipt* or other document issued in the name of the secured party or by *notifying the bailee* of the secured party's interest. [U.C.C. §9-304(3)]

(a) **Example:** Debtor's pet lion grew too large to keep at home, and so she boarded it at the local zoo. Thereafter, Debtor used the lion as collateral for a loan from Bank. Bank's interest will attach and become perfected as soon as Bank and Debtor sign a security agreement, Bank loans the money, and the zoo is notified of Bank's security interest. [U.C.C. §9-304(3)]

(b) **Alternative method:** [§166]   Of course, perfection could also be accomplished in bailed goods by *fling a financing statement*. This may actually be a safer method since the Code is unclear as to the type of notice to be given a bailee and any possible effect of a debtor's control over the bailee. [*See In re* Miller, 545 F.2d 916 (5th Cir. 1977)]

    1) **Example:** Farmer stored grain in an elevator and received in return a *nonnegotiable* warehouse receipt listing Farmer as the bailor. Farmer then borrowed money from Bank using the grain as collateral. To perfect its security interest in the grain, Bank should: (i) get the document reissued in Bank's name, *or* (ii) notify the grain elevator that Bank now has an interest in the goods, *or* (iii) file a financing statement covering the grain (classified as "farm products").

    2) **Effect of document issued:** [§167]   Note that possession of a *nonnegotiable* document has no legal effect on the filing because its surrender is not required on termination of the bailment. However, when a *negotiable* document of title as to bailed goods has been issued, the filing must cover the *document* (rather than just the goods) to be effective. [U.C.C. §9-304(2)]

d. **Duration of perfection:** [§168]   When a security interest is perfected through possession, it becomes effective from the time *possession is taken* (without relation back) and continues only so long as possession *continues*. [U.C.C. §9-305]

(1) **Effect of requiring transfer:** The U.C.C. thus brings state law into line with the policy of the Federal Bankruptcy Code. Article 9 rejects the concept of the "equitable lien," which under former law allowed a secured party to claim a perfected interest from the date on which the security interest *attached*, despite the fact that the promise of placing the collateral in the hands of the secured party had not been carried out prior to bankruptcy or default by the debtor. Article 9 makes it clear that where perfection is claimed by possession, no perfection occurs until possession *is* transferred.

e. **Rights and duties of secured party in possession:** [§169]   The U.C.C. confers certain rights and imposes certain duties on a secured party in possession of collateral.

(1) **Duty of reasonable care:** [§170]   First, the secured party must use reasonable care in storing and preserving the collateral. In the case of instruments or chattel paper, this requires the secured party to take all steps

necessary to preserve the rights of the debtor in the paper. [U.C.C. §9-207(1); Grace v. Sterling Grace & Co., 30 App. Div. 2d 61 (1968)]

(a) **Example:** Bank took possession of certain debentures of XYZ Corp. as collateral for loan to Debtor. These debentures were convertible into XYZ common stock. Bank received notice from XYZ that it was going to redeem the debentures—the redemption price being significantly lower than the value of the common stock into which the debentures were convertible. Bank failed to convert the debentures and allowed XYZ to redeem them. Bank was held liable to Debtor for the difference between the redemption price and the value of the XYZ common stock. [Reed v. Central National Bank, 421 F.2d 113 (10th Cir. 1970)]

(b) **Notice to debtor:** [§171]   The creditor in possession may satisfy the duty of reasonable care by *notifying the debtor* of any act that must be taken with respect to the collateral and allowing the *debtor* to perform the act.

(c) **No liability for market slump:** [§172]   A pledgee in possession of securities is not liable for a *decline in value* of the pledged instrument—even if timely action could have prevented the decline. [Hutchinson v. Southern California First National Bank, 27 Cal. App. 3d 572 (1972)—stock pledged at $44 per share fell in value to $14]

(d) **Waivers of liability void:** [§173]   An *exculpatory clause* (totally absolving the secured party from any liability) is unenforceable. Section 1-102(3) prohibits disclaimers of the due care obligation. (However, reasonable limitations on what is required by the secured party may be upheld.) [Brodheim v. Chase Manhattan Bank, 75 Misc. 2d 285 (1973)—holding that parties may not disclaim liability, but may set standards by which to measure duties]

(2) **Right to reimburse for expenses:** [§174]   The secured party may charge the debtor for any reasonable expenses incurred during the secured party's custody of the collateral, including insurance costs. In addition, the secured party may hold the collateral as security for these expenses. [U.C.C. §9-207(2)(a)]

(3) **Accounting for rents, issues, and profits:** [§175]   The secured party may keep any increase in profits on the collateral as additional security; however, any *money* received from the collateral must either be returned to the debtor or applied against the secured obligation. [U.C.C. §9-207(2)(c)]

(4) **Risk of loss:** [§176]   The risk of accidental loss or damage to the collateral is borne by the debtor to the extent that the secured party's insurance is insufficient. [U.C.C. §9-207(2)(b)]

(a) **Secured party's duty to insure:** [§177]   However, the Code imposes liability for loss on the secured party for any failure to meet the duty of reasonable care. Note that it is arguably **unreasonable** for a secured party to take possession of collateral **without any insurance** on the collateral. [U.C.C. §9-207(3)]

(b) **Use of insurance proceeds:** [§178]   Where insurance covers loss of the collateral, the insurance is used to pay the debt. The insurance company **cannot** pay the creditor and then (through the doctrine of subrogation) turn around and sue the original debtor. [*See* G. Gilmore, Security Interests in Personal Property §42.7 (1965)]

(5) **Right to repledge:** [§179]   The secured party may **repledge** the collateral if this action does not impair the ability of the debtor to redeem. [U.C.C. §9-207(2)(e)]

(a) **Example:** When consumer borrowed money from Big Bank, the bank made him pledge his valuable stamp collection as collateral, keeping it in the bank vault. If the **bank** needs to borrow money, it may use consumer's stamp collection as collateral, as long as the terms of the deal between the bank and its lender in no way affect the ability of the consumer to pay off the original debt and retrieve the stamp collection.

(6) **Right to use collateral:** [§180]   The secured party may operate or use the collateral **only** if such action is necessary to preserve the collateral or its value. [U.C.C. §9-207(4)]

4. **Perfection with Neither Possession Nor Filing—"Automatic" Perfection:** [§181] The Code carves out a set of transactions that may be perfected simply by the **attachment** of a security interest; *i.e.,* upon attachment, perfection occurs **automatically,** and no further steps are necessary. The logic behind the U.C.C. drafters' decision to allow perfection upon attachment in these cases is based on commercial convenience and the availability of other methods for protecting creditors.

a. **Purchase money security interest in consumer goods:** [§182]   A security interest in **consumer goods** that arises in connection with the purchase of the goods is perfected automatically upon attachment; *i.e.,* no filing is required. [U.C.C. §9-302(1)(d)]

(1) **Rationale:** The financial burden that filing would place on retail merchants, who typically advance credit in the form of retail-installment contracts, would outweigh any interest in protecting other creditors of the consumer who might look to the collateral in payment of their claims. Furthermore, since consumer goods are rarely used twice as collateral, there are usually no later creditors who would benefit from a filing.

(2) **"Purchase money" transactions:** [§183]   A purchase money security interest ("PMSI") arises when the secured party advances money or credit to **enable the debtor to purchase** the collateral. [U.C.C. §9-107]

(a) **Example:** Buyer buys a dishwasher on credit from Seller, who reserves "title" to the dishwasher in himself until Buyer pays for it (a "conditional sale"; *see supra,* §14). Since this extension of credit enables Buyer to buy the goods, Seller's interest qualifies as a purchase money security interest [U.C.C. §9-107(a)], and is perfected automatically on attachment [U.C.C. §9-302(1)(d)].

1) **Compare:** Borrower needs money to finance her child's tonsillectomy and borrows it from Consumer Finance Co. ("CFC"), giving CFC a security interest in her valuable stamp collection. In this case, CFC must file for perfection since its money was not used to *buy the stamp collection* and hence is not of the "purchase money" variety.

(b) **Who gets automatic perfection:** [§184] A purchase money secured party may be either the *seller* who has advanced credit for all or part of the price or *any other person* (*e.g.,* finance company, lender) who gives value or incurs an obligation to enable the debtor to acquire the collateral or rights in it, but *only* if the value is *actually used* in the transaction by the debtor. [U.C.C. §9-107(a), (b)]

1) **Example:** In the first example above, if a *bank,* rather than Seller, had loaned Buyer the money to buy the dishwasher, the bank's lien therein would also qualify as a "purchase money security interest" *if* Buyer actually used the borrowed money to buy the dishwasher. If Buyer told the bank that Buyer planned to use the money to buy the dishwasher (and signed a security agreement giving the bank an interest in the dishwasher), but *actually* used the money to pay a tax bill and bought the dishwasher with money taken from a savings account, the bank's interest would not be of the "purchase money" type, and the bank would have to file a financing statement to perfect its interest. [U.C.C. §9-107(b)]

(c) **Extent of security interest:** [§185] A secured party has a purchase money security interest only *to the extent of the value* that the secured party has advanced in the purchase transaction.

1) **Example:** Where the purchaser already owes the merchant on an earlier deal and the merchant carries forward the earlier debt as part of the purchase price of the new item, the earlier balance is *not* part of the purchase money interest. [*In re* Manuel, 507 F.2d 990 (5th Cir. 1975)]

2) **And note:** Where the secured party consolidates a purchase money security interest with non-PMSI debts, some courts hold that no part of the debt is a purchase money security interest. Other courts require the secured party to demonstrate what portion is so covered. [*In re* Ionosphere Clubs, Inc., 123 B.R. 166 (S.D.N.Y. 1991)]

(d) **Note—security agreement required:** [§186] Even though the creditor is not required to *file* notice of his interest in a purchase money transaction involving consumer goods, the creditor must still have a *signed security agreement* with the debtor to obtain a valid security interest in the first place. [Food Service Equipment Co. v. First National Bank, 174 S.E.2d 216 (Ga. 1970)]

    (e) **Priority:** [§187] Special rules of priority apply in favor of purchase money security interests—in consumer goods or otherwise (*see infra,* §§330-340).

(3) **"Consumer goods":** [§188] As indicated *supra,* §52, the Code defines "consumer goods" as goods "used or bought primarily for personal, family or household purposes." [U.C.C. §9-109(1)]

    (a) **Primary use test:** [§189] Whether a particular purchase falls under the definition depends on the purchaser's *primary* use. Thus, a sofa sold for a dentist's reception room would not constitute consumer goods because of the business use; however, the purchase of the same sofa for the dentist's family room would fall under the definition. [U.C.C. §9-109, Comment 2]

    (b) **Creditor may trust consumer:** [§190] However, actual use of the goods may not be determinative if it differs from what the consumer told the creditor at the time of *attachment*. In other words, if the consumer says the goods are for personal use and is lying (really planning a business use), the creditor is still protected without filing if the creditor believed the debtor. [Balon v. Cadillac Automobile Co., 303 A.2d 194 (N.H. 1973); Commercial Credit Equipment Co. v. Carter, 516 P.2d 767 (Wash. 1973)]

    (c) **Motor vehicles:** [§191] The Code specifically *excludes* from the consumer goods exception "motor vehicles required to be registered." As to such vehicles, a *filing is required* to perfect the security interest—at least as far as section 9-302(1)(d) is concerned.

        1) **Certificate of title systems:** [§192] However, section 9-302(3) exempts from the filing requirement various kinds of personal property that are covered by *certificates of title* or central filing statutes under state law (motor vehicles, boats, mobile homes, etc.).

            a) **Effect:** In all states, certificates of title are issued evidencing the ownership of motor vehicles. Security interests in such vehicles must be perfected by notation of the interest *on the face of the certificate.* [*See, e.g.,* Cal. Veh. Code §6300]

        2) **Other rules:** [§193] Automobile financing presents a number of unique problems that are discussed in detail, *infra,* §§240 *et seq.*

    (d) **Fixtures:** [§194] Consumer goods that are to become fixtures (*e.g.,* a furnace) require special steps for perfection (*see infra,* §§347-349).

b. **Beneficial interests:** [§195] Like purchase money security interests, perfection of a security interest created by an assignment of a beneficial interest in a trust or decedent's estate is automatic; *i.e.,* no filing is required. [U.C.C. §9-302(1)(c)]

(1) **Example:** Debtor borrows $1,000 from Lender, and to secure payment, he assigns to Lender his interest as beneficiary under an existing trust. Lender need not file to perfect his security interest.

(2) **Rationale:** Such assignments are not normally commercial transactions, and hence the Code drafters decided to exclude them from the filing requirements of Article 9.

c. **Certain accounts:** [§196]   Another exemption to the filing requirement (another automatic perfection transaction) covers assignments of accounts that—either alone or combined with other assignments to the same assignee—do ***not*** constitute a ***significant portion*** of the assignor's outstanding accounts. [U.C.C. §9-302(1)(e)]

(1) **What constitutes "significant" portion:** [§197]   For the purposes of determining a "significant portion," the Code focuses on all transfers made to the ***particular assignee,*** including other earlier assignments made in conjunction with the assignment that is supposedly exempt. Thus, an assignor cannot avoid the Code perfection requirements by serial assignment.

(a) **Note:** Some courts measure "significant portion" ***mathematically***— comparing the unfiled assignment amount to the assignor's total accounts receivable—and hold the assignee unsecured if the assignment is a large percentage of the total. [*See, e.g.,* Consolidated Film Industries v. United States, 547 F.2d 533 (10th Cir. 1977)—assignment of assignor's ***only*** account receivable held "significant" so that assignee who did not file was deemed unperfected]

(b) **Compare:** Most courts, however, take the position that whatever the percentage, the true test is whether the assignment is ***"casual or isolated"*** or part of a regular commercial financing pattern. [U.C.C. §9-302, Comment 5]

1) **Rationale:** An assignee who does not regularly engage in assignments may not realize filing is required; furthermore, as a practical matter, it may be difficult for an assignee to discover the total amount of the assignor's accounts. [*See, e.g.,* Architectural Woods, Inc. v. Washington, 562 P.2d 248 (Wash. 1977)—assignee not in the regular business of taking assignments of accounts held perfected and hence not required to file]

(2) **State variations:** [§198]   A few states (notably California) have rejected the above exemption. In its place, California permits automatic perfection in deposit accounts and insurance policies used as collateral (which most states exempt from the scope of Article 9 but which California includes). [U.C.C. §9-104(1)] Perfection in these types of collateral arises as soon as written notice of the security interest is given to the institution with whom the deposit account is maintained, or, for insurance policies, to the insurer. [Cal. Comm. Code §9-302(1)(h)]

(3) **Compare—assignment of perfected security interest:** [§199]   If the creditor perfects by filing a financing statement in the proper place and

then assigns or sells the debtor's obligation to another creditor, the second creditor may wish to change the records to reflect that the name of the creditor has changed. This may be accomplished by the filing of an *assignment statement,* but such a filing is permissive and not mandatory, so that even without it, the second creditor's security interest remains perfected. [U.C.C. §9-405]

(a) **Constitutes sale of an account:** Recall, however, that assignments of accounts are treated as security interests (*see supra,* §42). Thus, even though the second creditor's security interest remains perfected as to the original debtor, the second creditor must file a financing statement to be perfected as to the first creditor's creditors. If the second creditor fails to do this, it risks losing the account to other creditors of the first creditor.

(b) **Example:** Debtor borrowed money from Lender A and gave Lender A a security interest in her accounts receivable, which Lender A perfected by filing a financing statement in the appropriate place. Lender A then assigned this debt to Lender B, so that the debtor would have to make the payments directly to Lender B. There is no legal duty to change the name of the secured parties on the financing statement, and whether or not this is done, Lender B will be protected against those trying to seize the accounts receivable from the original debtor. However, the transaction between Lender A and Lender B is itself a secured transaction (the sale of an account), and for Lender B to have priority over the creditors of Lender A, Lender B will have to file a financing statement showing that Lender A has granted it a security interest in these accounts.

d. **Temporary "automatic" protection:** [§200] The Code provides for *temporary* protection of a security interest (without filing or taking possession) as to certain *proceeds* from collateral or in *documents and instruments.* [U.C.C. §9-302(1)(b)]

(1) **Proceeds:** [§201] This topic is discussed in detail, *infra,* §§368 *et seq.* Suffice it to note at this point, that proceeds covers anything received (cash or noncash) *on the sale or disposition* of the collateral in which the security interest exists.

(a) **Collateral of same type:** [§202] Broadly, as long as the proceeds are collateral as to which a security interest *could* be perfected by *filing in the same place* where the original financing statement was filed, the security interest *continues* in the proceeds; *i.e.,* no new filing is required. [U.C.C. §9-306(2); *see infra,* §378]

1) **Example:** When a debtor trades in an old machine on a new machine, the filed security interest on the old machine continues in the new machine. No new filing is required.

(b) **Proceeds of different type:** [§203] However, where the proceeds are a different kind of collateral—as to which the original filing would not: have been an appropriate means of perfection or the appropriate place for filing—then the secured party must act diligently. The original security interest terminates *10 days* after the sale or disposition of the original collateral, and a *new perfection* must be obtained (by filing or possession, whichever is appropriate) within that 10-day period to protect the secured party. [U.C.C. §9-306(3); *see infra*, §§380-381]

1) **Example:** Creditor perfects a security interest in Debtor's machine by filing a financing statement in the appropriate office. Debtor sells the machine in return for a promissory note. Because a security interest in a promissory note can be perfected by the secured party's taking possession of the note (*supra*, §160), the security interest in the note terminates after 10 days unless the secured party obtains new perfection (*e.g.*, by obtaining possession of the note).

2) **Priority:** If such new perfection is obtained during the 10-day period, it "relates back" to the date of perfection of the security interest in the original collateral so as to give the secured party priority over later creditors.

3) **Effect in bankruptcy:** Both the continuity of the interest and its relation back to the perfection in the original collateral are of vital importance in determining the secured party's rights in a bankruptcy proceeding.

(2) **Documents and instruments:** [§204] A secured party as to documents or instruments who advances *new value* under an existing written agreement obtains a *21-day* perfection period, even though the secured party does not file and the collateral remains with the debtor. [U.C.C. §9-304(4)]

(a) **Rationale:** There are often commercial reasons why the debtor must remain in possession of the documents or instruments, and there would be no point in forcing the secured party, who is willing to extend new value, to first file or take possession of the instruments or else lose protection. The briefness of the period of protection assures that the secured party will be watchful.

(b) **Other twenty-one-day extensions:** [§205] There are two other situations (besides the giving of new value) in which the Code specifies that a security interest already in existence in documents or instruments shall remain perfected (without additional filing) for a 21-day "grace" period:

1) **Delivery of goods or documents:** [§206] If a secured party makes available to the debtor *either the goods* themselves *or documents representing the goods,* for the purpose of ultimate sale or exchange, or for loading, shipping, storing, or like purposes, the Code grants a 21-day extension of perfection. [U.C.C. §9-304(5)(a)]

2) **Delivery of instrument:** [§207] A secured party is granted a similar extension when delivering the instrument to the debtor for the purpose of sale, exchange, collection, renewal, or registration of transfer of the instrument. [U.C.C. §9-304(5)(b)]

(c) **Note—methods of perfection limited:** [§208]   Other than possession, these temporary procedures for perfection of interests in instruments are the only way in which the secured holder of such collateral may perfect. Filing will not do it. [U.C.C. §9-304(1)]

5. **Investment Property:** [§209]   The rules for perfection of a security interest in investment property (defined, *supra*, §67) are contained in section 9-115. Generally there are two methods: *control* or the *filing* of a financing statement.

a. **Priority:** [§210]   It is important to appreciate the following rule: if one creditor perfects by gaining control and another by filing, the creditor with control prevails over the creditor who perfected merely by filing. [U.C.C. §9-115(5)(a)]

b. **Control:** [§211]   A creditor has *control*, and is therefore perfected, by doing one of the following things:

(1) **Certificated securities:** [§212]   If stocks or bonds are represented by a physical certificate (*i.e., certificated securities*), the creditor gains control by taking delivery of it with any necessary indorsements. [U.C.C. §8-106(a), (b)]

(2) **Uncertificated securities:** [§213]   Some corporations issuing stocks or bonds do not issue physical pieces of paper, but instead simply record the names of the owners of these securities at the corporate office or that of its transfer agent. Such securities are said to be *"uncertificated"* [U.C.C. §8-102(a)(18)] In this case, a creditor gains control, and thus is perfected, either by becoming the registered owner in the records of the issuer or by having the issuer agree to comply with instructions by the creditor without further consent by the registered owner (the debtor). [U.C.C. §§8-106(c), 8-301(b)]

(3) **Securities or commodity accounts or rights to particular investments in such accounts:** [§214]   If the stocks or bonds are deposited in an account with a broker or a clearing corporation (both are called *"security intermediaries"*), or commodity contracts are similarly held, security interests can be taken in the entire account or portions thereof (a *"security entitlement"*) by gaining control over the account. This is done in a number of ways: changing the name of the account to that of the creditor, or obtaining the agreement of the broker/clearing corporation that it will act according to the instructions of the creditor without any further consent of the debtor. [U.C.C. §8-108(d)]

(a) **Example:** Investor bought 100 shares of Monopoly Telephone Company stock through her broker and allowed the broker to register the stock in the broker's name so that the stock could be easily sold when Investor so decided. Investor needed to borrow money and use this stock as collateral, so she applied to Bank for a loan. Bank can perfect its security interest in the stock in a number of ways: have the stock moved to an account on which Bank is the record owner, or have the broker transfer the stock to Bank so that Bank becomes the registered owner, or have Investor procure the agreement of the broker that it will act according to the instructions of Bank without having to get the consent of Investor. Any of these methods would establish *control* and lead to perfection. Bank could also file a financing statement covering the stock, but it would then risk losing priority to another creditor who perfected by gaining control.

(4) **Securities intermediary as creditor:** [§215]   If the securities intermediary (*i.e,* the broker or clearing corporation) itself becomes the creditor, perfection is automatic on attachment. Further, since the securities will be in the possession of the securities intermediary, the securities intermediary will have control. In this situation, the securities intermediary gets *superpriority* over all other creditors, even those having prior control. [U.C.C. §9-115(5)(c), (d)]

   (a) **Example:** Suppose in the last example, Bank gained control by having Investor instruct her broker to follow the instructions of Bank, but in the meantime to also follow her instructions (such dual ownership is permitted). If Investor then borrows money from her own broker, granting the broker a security interest in the Monopoly Telephone stock, both the broker and Bank have perfected security interests, but broker has priority over Bank.

   (b) **Compare—two parties with control:** Except for the superpriority given to securities intermediaries, the general rule is that where two creditors both have control, their securities interests *rank equally* and they will have to share the collateral pro rata. [U.C.C. §9-115(5)(b)]

SUMMARY OF METHODS OF PERFECTION

Filing—   Effective for *all types* of collateral except instruments.

Possession— Effective for goods, money, documents, instruments, and chattel paper.

Automatic— Effective for PMSIs in *consumer goods*, assignments of an insignificant portion of the assignor's accounts, and assignments of interests in trusts. There are also a number of temporary periods of automatic perfection: 10 days for proceeds; 21 days when a secured party gives new value under a security agreement where collateral is an instrument; 21 days where a secured party makes available an instrument, negotiable document, or goods in possession of a bailee on a temporary basis (*e.g.*, for the debtor to sell); and four months where collateral is moved from one state to another.

Control—   Effective for investment property.

C. TIME OF PERFECTION

1. **Completion of Filing or Other Requirements:** [§216]   A security interest becomes perfected when (i) it has **attached and** (ii) **all the applicable steps** for the methods of perfection being used by the secured party have taken place. A secured party may take the steps necessary for perfection (such as filing or acquiring possession of the collateral) **in advance** of the attachment of the security interest, but perfection does not take place until the interest has attached. [U.C.C. §9-303(1); **and see** **supra,** §§107-108]

2. **Effect of Secondary Perfections:** [§217]   A security interest may be perfected more than once. If this occurs, the later perfection by another means is deemed to **relate back** to the date of the original perfection, **provided** that there has been no intervening unperfected period. [U.C.C. §9-303(2)]

   a. **Example:** On June 1, Debtor pledges his crop of jelly beans, placing the entire harvest in a silo in Secured Party's name in return for an advance of $1,000. (Secured Party's interest is therefore perfected by possession under section 9-302(1)(a).) On July 1, Debtor needs to regain control of the jelly beans, so Secured Party files a financing statement covering the transaction and then allows Debtor to have possession. The perfection is deemed to have taken place on June 1, since there was no intervening period of nonperfection.

   b. **Example:** Suppose instead that Secured Party released the jelly beans to Debtor on July 1, without filing a financing statement, so that Debtor could sell the jelly beans at a market. Secured Party no longer enjoys perfection by possession, but has a 21-day temporary perfection commencing on July 1, since the secured party has released the collateral to allow Debtor to sell. [U.C.C. §9-304(5)(a); **supra,** §206]

   c. **Compare:** But suppose Secured Party released the jelly beans for a purpose that does not fall within section 9-304(5)(a) or failed to file within the 21-day period. In such a case, Secured Party's perfected interest will no longer date from June 1, the original date of perfection, since there was a lapse in the continuity of perfection, and intervening liens or purchasers could prevail. [U.C.C. §9-303(2)]

D. PLACE OF PERFECTION—MULTISTATE TRANSACTIONS

1. **Introduction:** [§218]   The Code deals with the problems of multistate transactions and removal of the collateral from one state to another by special rules governing the place where a security interest must be perfected. [U.C.C. §9-103]

2. **General Rule—"Last Event Test:"** [§219]   The controlling law as to perfection of a security interest, and the effect of perfection or nonperfection, is the law of the state **where the collateral is located when the last event occurs** upon which is based the assertion that the security interest is perfected or nonperfected. [U.C.C. §9-103(1)(b)]

   a. **Example:** Buyer and Seller sign a security agreement in New York for the sale of a yacht located in California. Buyer lives in Illinois and the yacht is delivered there. Since no filing is required to perfect a purchase money security interest in consumer goods and the "last event" for automatic perfection is the creditor's giving of "value" by delivering the goods, Illinois law would govern perfection (*see supra,* §182).

b. **Filing as last event:** [§220] In most cases, of course, *filing* is the "last event" on which a claim of perfection is based. This being so, the filing must be made in the state where the collateral is located when the filing occurs. Prior filing in another state does not perfect the interest (and is not saved by the four-month rule discussed below, which applies only when the security interest *was perfected* in the jurisdiction from which it has been removed).

3. **Removal of Collateral to Another State—New Perfection Required (Four-Month Rule):** [§221] Even though the security interest was properly perfected in the state where the collateral was originally located, if the debtor thereafter moves the collateral to another state (with or without the secured party's knowledge or consent), a reperfection in the new state is required *within four months* after removal. [U.C.C. §9-103(1)(d)]

a. **New perfection "relates back":** [§222] As long as the secured party reperfects the security interest in the new state within the four-month period (by a new filing or taking possession), the interest is deemed perfected from the date of the original perfection—*i.e.,* there is a "relation back" as against any subsequent interest holder. [U.C.C. §9-303(2)]

b. **Effect of failure to reperfect:** [§223] On the other hand, if the secured party fails to reperfect within four months of removal, the interest becomes unperfected as against *any* "purchaser" of the collateral after removal (and under section 1-201, "purchaser" includes secured parties). In this case, there is *no* "relation back," so that even if the secured party later perfects in the new state, the interest will be subordinate to intervening lien creditors, etc.

   (1) **Example:** Big Bank financed Retailer's inventory in Utah and perfected its security interest by filing a financing statement in Utah. On January 1, Retailer moved its business to Texas. On February 1, another creditor sued Retailer and sent out the sheriff to attach a lien to the inventory. On March 1, Retailer took a new loan from Small Bank of Texas, which loan was also secured by the inventory. Small Bank filed a financing statement in Texas on March 1. On March 2, Big Bank learned of the move and filed a new financing statement in Texas. Big Bank's filing "relates back" to the original perfection in Utah, so that Big Bank's security interest prevails over all other parties.

   (2) **Compare:** If, however, Big Bank did not refile in Texas until August 1, it would still have a perfected security interest in the inventory, but it would be *junior* (paid off last) to the rights of Small Bank of Texas.

   (3) **Note—judicial lien creditor not protected:** The Code's definitions of "purchaser" and "purchase" [U.C.C. §1-201(32), (33)] require a voluntary transaction. The judicial lien created by the suing creditor in the example above does not so qualify. Thus, Big Bank remains perfected as to that creditor even if it takes no steps to reperfect within the four-month period.

c. **Effect of lapsing perfection:** [§224] As discussed *infra,* §287, a filed financing statement is effective only for five years and then it lapses unless renewed.

If the collateral moves across state lines and the financing statement lapses in the first state *before* four months have passed since the move, there is *no four-month "grace" period*; rather, the time for reperfecting in the second state ends when the financing statement lapses in the first state. [U.C.C. §§9-403(2), 9-103(1)(d), (i), *and see* Comment 7]

(1) **Example:** Big Bank filed a financing statement in Utah on March 1, 1996, to perfect a security interest in Retailer's inventory. This financing statement will lapse (cease to be effective) at the end of five years (March 1, 2001). If on February 1, 2001, Retailer moves the business to Texas, Big Bank will have only until March 1, 2001, to refile in Texas, or its security interest will become unperfected.

d. **Exception to four-month rule—automatic perfection:** [§225] If the collateral is of the type requiring no steps other than attachment for automatic perfection (*e.g.*, a purchase money security interest in consumer goods; *supra*, §182), the four-month rule does not apply. Thus, on removal of the collateral to a new state, no steps need be taken to continue the original perfection. [U.C.C. §9-103(1)(d)]

(1) **Example:** Debtor purchased a dog in Arkansas on credit, giving Seller a purchase money security interest. One year later, Debtor and the dog moved to North Carolina. No filing was required in Arkansas since Seller's perfection occurred automatically on attachment. [U.C.C. §9-302(1)(d)] Therefore, perfection continues without filing in North Carolina. [*In re* Marshall, 10 U.C.C. Rep. 1290 (N.D. Ohio 1969)]

e. **Intrastate removal:** [§226] Note that the above rules apply only where collateral is moved from one state to another. No refiling is required where goods are merely moved from one city or county to another within the same state. [U.C.C. §9-401(3)]

4. **Special Rules:** [§227] The general rules above give way when dealing with certain types of collateral, as to which special rules govern the place for perfection of the security interest.

a. **Goods intended for use in another state (thirty-day rule):** [§228] A *purchase money security interest* in goods must be perfected in the state for which the goods are destined if: (i) *both parties understand* at the time of attachment that the goods are to be kept in another state; and (ii) the goods are moved into the new state *within 30 days after the debtor receives possession*. [U.C.C. §9-103(1)(c)]

(1) **Rationale:** It is much more likely that someone searching for filings would look in the state where the parties intended the collateral to be used than in the state where it happened to be purchased.

(2) **Example:** Buyer signed a security agreement in favor of Seller of goods on September 1 in New York, and Seller delivered the goods to Buyer in New York on October 1. Both parties understood that Buyer was going to use the goods as equipment in Buyer's business in Minnesota.

(a) *If Seller files in Minnesota before letting buyer have possession* in New York, Seller's interest will be perfected from the moment of attachment *provided* the goods are in fact removed to Minnesota within 30 days of Buyer's possession.

(b) *If Seller waits to file until later,* perfection will date from the moment of filing in Minnesota.

(c) *If the goods never get to Minnesota,* but stay in New York, Seller's interest will become *unperfected* (even though on file in Minnesota) 30 days after Buyer gets possession, unless Seller refiles in the jurisdiction in which the goods are then located. [U.C.C. §9-103, Comments 2, 3]

(3) **Subsequent removal of goods:** [§229]   Note that the four-month grace period still applies in the event of removal after the original perfection.

b. **Goods covered by a certificate of title:** [§230]   A completely different set of rules governs the place for perfection of interests in goods covered by a state "certificate of title"—*e.g.,* automobiles, airplanes, mobile homes, etc. (*See* detailed discussion, *infra,* §§240-242.)

(1) **Interstate removal of goods:** [§231]   A different rule also applies where property covered by a certificate of title is removed from one state to another (*see infra,* §§243-246).

c. **Accounts, intangibles, certain mobile goods:** [§232]   Certain assets have no readily visible "home base," and for these assets the Code provides that a security interest must be perfected under the laws of the state *where the debtor is located.* [U.C.C. §9-103(3)]

(1) **Assets covered:** [§233]   Included under this rule are the debtor's accounts; general intangibles (copyrights, trademarks, patents, etc.); and any goods that are *normally used in more than one jurisdiction* (*e.g.,* aircraft, road building machinery, etc.) if they are *not* covered by a certificate of title and *are* a part of the debtor's *equipment* or *inventory leased to others* (*e.g.,* machinery leased by an equipment leasing company).

(2) **Rationale for special rule:** [§234]   Since the collateral is not "stationed" anywhere, it makes more sense to search for filings at the debtor's location than anywhere else. [U.C.C. §9-103, Comment 5]

(3) **"Debtor's location":** [§235]   The debtor is deemed to be located at the debtor's place of business if there is but one; if the debtor has several places of business, then at the chief place of business (home office); if no place of business, then at the debtor's residence. Note that the debtor's location is pegged to where *executive control* is centered, rather than to where the debtor merely has plants or property. [U.C.C. §9-103(3)(d)]

(a) **Example:** Rent-A-Tractor Co. rents tractors to farmers all over the country. It has its offices in West Virginia, but none of the tractors are used or located in West Virginia. If Rent-A-Tractor borrows money from Bank using the tractors as collateral, Bank will be perfected if it files a financing statement in West Virginia. It need not file wherever the tractors are located.

(4) **Effect of change of "debtor's location":** [§236]   A *refiling* is required whenever there has been a change of the debtor's "location" (*e.g.,* the head office) from one jurisdiction to another. The secured party must obtain a new perfection in the new jurisdiction within four months or the security interest will become unperfected against any person who became a "purchaser" of the collateral (including secured parties) after the change. [U.C.C. §9-103(3)(e)]

d. **Chattel paper**

(1) **Perfection by possession:** [§237]   Where a security interest in chattel paper is claimed to be perfected by *possession* thereof, the general rule of location of the collateral (paper) applies. [U.C.C. §9-103(4)]

(2) **Perfection by filing:** [§238]   Where, however, the security interest in chattel paper is assertedly perfected by *filing*, the Code reverts to the rule applicable to general intangibles (above)—*i.e.,* the filing must be at the "debtor's location" (head office). [U.C.C. §9-103(4)]

(a) **Rationale:** Chattel paper is readily transportable, and there may even be duplicate copies of the paper; hence, the safest place to search for such filing is at the debtor's head office, rather than checking every state in which the debtor may have assets.

(b) **Example:** In the above example, if Rent-A-Tractor had used the tractor *leases* as collateral, Bank would be perfected by filing in West Virginia *or* by taking possession of the leases ("chattel paper"). Possession constitutes proper perfection even if Bank is located in another state. [U.C.C. §9-103, Comment 6]

e. **Minerals:** [§239]   A security interest that attaches to minerals (coal, oil, gas, etc.) as extracted from the earth is perfected according to the law of the jurisdiction in which the point of extraction (wellhead or minehead) is located. Likewise, perfection of an interest in an *account* created by a sale of minerals at the well or mine is governed by the law of the same jurisdiction. [U.C.C. §9-103(5)]

5. **Motor Vehicles**

a. **Perfection of security interest:** [§240]   As previously indicated (*supra,* §230), the Code expressly *exempts* from the filing requirements of Article 9 any personal property covered by a *certificate of title* under state law—*e.g.,* autos, boats, trailers, mobile homes, etc. [U.C.C. §9-302(3)]

(1) **State methods exclusive:** [§241]   The Code goes on to provide that in states having certificate of title systems, compliance with those laws is the *only* way in which a security interest can be perfected in collateral subject to the laws. Filing in the normal U.C.C. manner is *ineffective*. [U.C.C. §9-302(4)]

(a) **Example:** Under California law, a security interest in a motor vehicle can be perfected only by *notation* of the interest on the certificate of title to the vehicle. [Cal. Veh. Code §6300] (Except that if the vehicle is part of a dealer's inventory, the secured party can perfect by taking ***possession of the certificate*** of title even though his interest is not noted thereon.) [Cal. Veh. Code §5907]

(2) **Certificate of title now uniform:** [§242]   All states now require that security interests in motor vehicles be perfected by notation of the creditor's lien interest on the certificate of title (unless the vehicles are still part of inventory, in which case perfection is obtained by the filing of a financing statement covering the dealer's inventory).

b. **Interstate transfer of motor vehicles**

(1) **Four-month grace period:** [§243]   Where a motor vehicle is covered by a certificate of title and the secured party's interest is properly noted on the certificate, interstate movement of the automobile generally has ***no effect*** on the security interest, even if the vehicle is re-registered in the new jurisdiction within the four-month period. Perfection of the interest generally is governed exclusively by the law of the state that issued the certificate for at least four months after the vehicle leaves the original state, and the secured creditor remains perfected for four months without doing anything. [U.C.C. §9-103(2)(b)]

   (a) **Example:** Debtor purchased a car in Virginia and Finance Company's security interest was noted on the certificate of title. Later, Debtor moved to the District of Columbia. Finance company's security interest will remain perfected for at least four months.

   (b) **Example:** Same facts as above, but Debtor registered the car in the District the week after moving there. No new certificate of title was issued. Finance Company remains perfected for four months after the car arrives in the District despite the registration. Thus, it will have a grace period in which to get its interest perfected in the District of Columbia. Note, however, that if Finance Company had given the certificate of title to Debtor, it would lose the benefit of any four-month grace period (*see infra,* §245).

      1) **Note:** Some jurisdictions allow a car to be registered without surrender of the old certificate of title and without issuing a new certificate (sometimes called a "memo registration"). While such registration will not cut short the four-month grace period, it does set a potential trap for the secured party, who might be unaware that the car has been moved and re-registered and so would be unaware of the impending lapse of the security interest. Where jurisdictions require surrender of the old certificate of title, this trap does not exist (*see infra,* §245).

(2) **Perfection continues absent new registration:** [§244]   Note that perfection continues ***beyond the four-month grace period*** until the car is registered in the new state.

   (a) **Example:** Under the facts in (1)(a), above, Finance Company's security interest will remain perfected beyond the four-month grace period as long as the car is not registered in the District.

(3) Where four-month rule not applicable

    (a) Secured party gives certificate to debtor: [§245]   Registration in the new state usually requires surrender of the certificate of title covering the vehicle. Normally, the secured party holds the certificate of title, and so the secured party would be alerted to any attempt to get a new certificate and could insist that its security interest be noted on the new certificate. However, if the secured party allows the debtor to obtain possession of the certificate of title and the debtor uses the certificate to re-register the vehicle in the new jurisdiction during the four-month grace period, the grace period is cut off. [U.C.C. §9-103(2)(b)]

    (b) Failure to note interest: [§246]   Similarly, if for any reason the vehicle is registered in the new state and the certificate of title does not show the existence of any liens, the prior perfected security interest becomes subordinate to the rights of an innocent purchaser for value of the car (other than a dealer or other professional). However, if the new certificate states that the vehicle might be subject to liens not shown on the certificate, no purchaser within the four-month grace period is protected. [U.C.C. §9-103(2)(d)]

        1) Compare—dealers and other professionals: If the purchaser is a dealer (*i.e.,* in the business of selling cars), or if a bank or finance company makes a loan on the car, the original security interest is *not* automatically subordinated. Rather, the normal four-month grace period (above) applies, during which the original secured party can retain seniority by reperfecting the security interest in the new state. [*See* U.C.C. §9-103, Comment 4—helpful discussion of certificates of title]

V. FILING

chapter approach

This chapter looks into the *formalities* of the financing statement, which is important because failure to create a valid financing statement means that the creditor is unsecured. If the debtor goes bankrupt while the creditor is unsecured, or if other creditors attach the collateral, the unsecured creditor will not be able to reach the collateral if the debtor defaults on the debt.

The chapter also discusses the *mechanics* of filing: where to file, how often to file, and what documents can be filed. It is important for you to analyze the facts of your question to determine whether these technical requirements have been met.

A. THE FINANCING STATEMENT

1. **Notice Filing:** [§247]   The parties may, if they choose, file a copy of their *security agreement* as a financing statement, thus giving complete notice of the debt and collateral to all who read the record. However, the Code also authorizes the filing of a brief *financing statement*—a system favored by most debtors and creditors. The financing statement may give little specific information about the details of the underlying transaction, but it does put other creditors "on notice" that a security agreement of *some* kind is in effect. [U.C.C. §9-402(1)]

   a. **Form of financing statement:** [§248]   A sample form of a financing statement is set forth in U.C.C. section 9-402(3), and blank forms (commonly referred to as "UCC l"s) are available at the office of the secretary of state and at other filing offices.

   b. **Indexed under debtor's name:** [§249]   The financing statement is indexed in the records under the debtor's name. The idea here is that later creditors, contemplating a loan to the debtor, can then search the records under the debtor's name and see what property of the debtor is already encumbered in favor of other creditors.

2. **Required Contents of Financing Statement:** [§250]   The following is the information required to be included in the financing statement under the Code [U.C.C. §9-402(1)]:

   (i) *The names of both the debtor and the secured party*;

   (ii) *The address of the secured party* from which information concerning the secured interest may be obtained;

   (iii) *A mailing address of the debtor;*

   (iv) *A statement indicating the types or describing* the items of *collateral*; and

(v) *The signature of the debtor* (the secured party need not sign under revised Article 9)

a. **State variations:** [§251]   Various states have added other requirements to the financing statement. Check your state's version of section 9-402 for variations from the uniform requirements.

3. **Sufficiency of the Financing Statement**

a. **"Minor errors . . . not seriously misleading" rule:** [§252]   The stated policy of the Code is that a financing statement *substantially complying* with the requirements of section 9-402 is effective even though it contains *minor errors* that are *not seriously misleading*. The courts are bluntly told to avoid the supertechnical reading of statutory requirements sometimes practiced in the past. [U.C.C. §9-402(8), *and see* Comment 5]

(1) **Example:** A financing statement gave the name of the debtor as "Upton, Inc.," but the signature line was signed by two corporate officers as individuals (without designations such as "Pres." or "Sec." following their names). Applying the "minor errors . . . not seriously misleading" rule, the court held this was a sufficient "signature of the debtor" to satisfy the requirement of section 9-402(1). [Sherman v. Upton, Inc., 242 N.W.2d 666 (S.D. 1976)—stressing the court's lack of "intention of going back into the morass of nit picking from which the U.C.C. has refreshingly led us"]

b. **Name and address of secured party:** [§253]   The requirement that the address of the secured party be listed on the financing statement is intended to give anyone interested notice of where to go for more information. Hence, creditors may jeopardize their secured status by providing incomplete or inadequate names and addresses. On the other hand, a complete street address is not always required.

(1) **Example:** Coca-Cola sold a Coke machine to a gas station. The financing statement gave the address of the secured party as "Coca-Cola Bottling Co., East Hartford, Conn." The court held the address sufficient because there was only one Coca-Cola Bottling Co. in the entire Hartford phone book, so a creditor would not have been misled by the incomplete address. [*In re* Bengtson, 3 U.C.C. Rep. 283 (D. Conn. 1965)]

(2) **Compare:** Creditor lived on a rural route outside the small town of Harvard, Illinois. The financing statement gave the creditor's address only as "Harvard." This was held insufficient since another creditor trying to get more information would have a "difficult task" locating the creditor. [Burlington National Bank v. Strauss, 184 N.W.2d 122 (Wis. 1971)]

c. **Name and address of debtor:** [§254]   The name and mailing address of the debtor must be included in the financing statement to give notice of the existing interest to the other creditors of the debtor—especially future creditors considering extending credit. Since the financing statement is indexed under the name of the debtor, it is particularly important that this information be correct.

(1) **Trade names:** [§255]   Individuals doing business under trade names must be identified by their *real names,* not their company names. Trade names are too uncertain (and may be unknown to a person searching the record) to serve as the basis for a filing system. [U.C.C. §9-402(1)]

    (a) **Example:** Lender took a security interest in the inventory of "Carolyn's Fashions," a dress store owned by Mary Carolyn Hill. The financing statement listed "Carolyn's Fashions by Mary Carolyn Hill." When the store went bankrupt, the Lender's security interest was held *invalid* because the financing statement had been filed under the debtor's trade name instead of her real name. [*In re* Hill, 363 F. Supp. 1205 (N.D. Miss. 1973)]

(2) **Partnerships:** [§256]   Where a partnership is the debtor, the financing statement *is* sufficient if it states the partnership name; it need not name the individual partners. [U.C.C. §9-402(7)]

(3) **Change of name, etc.—"seriously misleading" rule:** [§257]   If the debtor so changes his/her name (or a corporation so changes its identity or structure, *e.g.,* by merger) that a filed financial statement is *"seriously misleading,"* the filing ceases to be effective as to any *new* collateral acquired by the debtor after four months, unless a new statement or amendment is filed before then. [U.C.C. §9-402(7)]

(4) **Change of debtor's address or location of collateral**

    (a) **Intrastate moves:** [§258]   The U.C.C. drafters of section 9-401(3) gave the states two alternatives to choose from as to the effect of a change of the debtor's address *within* the state:

        1) **No need to refile:** [§259]   Most states adopted the first alternative, providing that a change in the debtor's address to a new county within the state or a change in the location of the collateral does *not* affect perfection—*i.e.,* the original filing continues to be valid.

        2) **Four-month rule:** [§260]   Some states (Delaware, Oklahoma, Pennsylvania, Texas, West Virginia, Wyoming, and the Virgin Islands) adopted the second alternative and require a refiling within four months after a change of either the debtor's address or the location of the collateral.

        3) **Change in use of collateral immaterial:** [§261]   Under either version of section 9-401(3), a mere change in the *use* of the collateral does *not* require a change in the original filing.

    (b) **Interstate moves:** [§262]   A change of the debtor's address (chief executive office or if none, residence) from *one state to another* may require a new filing in the new state—at least as to the kinds of collateral discussed *supra,* §§232, 236. [U.C.C. §9-103(3)]

d. **Description of collateral:** [§263]   The financing statement must contain a description of the collateral. The description of the property must be sufficient to allow a party to identify it by **_reasonable further inquiry_**. **_Less specificity_** of description is required in the financing statement than in the security agreement because the financing statement's purpose is to provide mere notice to others to check further, whereas the security agreement's description is the more specific contractual understanding of the two parties. For the financing statement, the description need be neither complete, nor completely accurate, as long as the collateral is reasonably identified; a trade description or statement of the **_type_** of collateral will usually suffice. [U.C.C. §9-110]

(1) **Example:** Seller sold a tractor to Buyer under a conditional sales contract. The financing statement described the collateral by model type and serial number, but did not state what type of appliance or object it was. The description was held sufficient, on the basis that the collateral was obviously some type of vehicle sold by Seller, and inquiry of the parties would have definitely determined what it was. [*In re* Richards, 455 F.2d 281 (6th Cir. 1972)]

(2) **Code terminology sufficient:** [§264]   Courts are inclined to find the description sufficient if it uses Code terms—*e.g.,* "inventory," "goods," "accounts receivable"—even though a creditor might not be able to determine the exact items covered. However, equally broad **_non-Code_** terms are more likely to be held to be an **_insufficient_** description. [Mammoth Cave Production Credit Association v. York, 429 S.W.2d 26 (Ky. 1968)—"all farm equipment" too vague]

    (a) **Note:** Because of the broad and general Code terms permitted ("equipment," "inventory," etc.), disputes frequently arise as to whether a particular item is covered by a broad description in the financing statement.

        1) **Example:** Where X purchases a fancy sports car, ostensibly for use in connection with his auto repair business, is it covered by a lender's financing statement that referred only to "equipment"? (Since many cars are used as "equipment," most courts would answer "yes" to this question.)

        2) **Comment:** Normally, classification depends on **_intended use._** Thus, the same automobile could conceivably be classified as "inventory" (in the hands of a dealer), "consumer goods" (in the hands of a consumer buyer) or "equipment" (in the hands of a business buyer). [U.C.C. §9-109, Comment 2]

(3) **After-acquired property:** [§265]   The security agreement may cover not only existing collateral but also collateral to be acquired in the future—*i.e.,* "after-acquired property" (*supra,* §130). This does **_not have to be mentioned in the financing statement,_** as long as the **_types_** of collateral subject to the after-acquired property provision are sufficiently described. [Bank of Utica v. Smith Richfield Springs, Inc., 58 Misc. 2d 113 (1968)—security agreement covered auto dealer's present inventory and after-acquired cars as well: financing statement specified merely "motor vehicles," but this was sufficient description to alert other creditors that secured party's interest might extend to both present and after-acquired stock of cars]

(4) **Fixtures:** [§266]   Where the collateral is goods that are or will be affixed to realty, the financing statement must expressly state this fact, must describe the realty, and further recite that the financing statement is to be recorded in the real estate records. (*See* further discussion of fixture filings, *infra,* §§350 *et seq.*)

e. **Signature of debtor:** [§267]   Finally, the financing statement must include the signature of the debtor. In an appropriate case, a court will uphold a "signature" that is *typed or printed* rather than handwritten if it is clear that it was *intended* as the debtor's signature.

(1) **Example:** In a case involving the validity of a secured party's signature (which was required under the 1962 Code), the court upheld the financing statement where the name was typewritten in the appropriate box on the form. The fact that the party had thereafter filed the form was held evidence of his intent that his typewritten name constitute his "signature" within the meaning of U.C.C. section 1-201(39); hence his handwritten signature was not required. [Benedict v. Lebowitz, 346 F.2d 120 (2d Cir. 1965)]

4. **Effect of Financing Statement Signed by Secured Party Only:** [§268]   Under revised Article 9, the financing statement need be signed only by the *debtor*. While the secured party must be *named* (above), the secured party's signature is not required. It follows that where the financing statement has been signed only by the secured party and *not* by the debtor, it is normally *invalid*.

a. **Exceptions:** [§269]   However, such a financing statement (signed by the secured party instead of the debtor) will be effective to perfect a security interest in the following limited cases:

(1) *Where the collateral was acquired after the debtor had changed name, identity, or corporate structure.* [U.C.C. §9-402(2)(d)]

(2) *Where the secured party had previously perfected a security interest* in the debtor's accounts, intangibles, or mobile goods, and the *debtor* thereafter *changed location* to a new state (*supra,* §236); or, where the secured party had previously perfected a security interest in other collateral that the debtor had *removed* to a new state (*supra,* §221). [U.C.C. §9-402(2)(a)] (The financing statement must recite the fact of such removal or relocation.)

(3) *Where the collateral is "proceeds"* received by the debtor on sale or other disposition of property in which the secured party had the perfected interest, and the "proceeds" are of a kind in which the security interest does not continue automatically (*supra,* §203). [U.C.C. §9-402(2)(b)]

(4) *Where the collateral was acquired after the original filing had lapsed* (*i.e.,* after five years; *see infra,* §290). [U.C.C. §9-402(2)(c)]

b. **Rationale:** The reason for dispensing with the debtor's signature in each of the above cases is that the *necessity for refiling arises from actions of the debtor that may have been unauthorized* or even fraudulent. A secured party might be unable to find the debtor or get the debtor to sign the new statement and therefore is permitted to proceed without the debtor's signature. [U.C.C. §9-402, Comment 4]

5. **Amendments:** [§270]   Amendments to the original financing statements that merely change names, amounts, or descriptions are considered part of the original financing statement and therefore have *no effect* on perfection or priority of the secured interest. However, if an amendment *adds collateral*, it is deemed effective (as to the added collateral) only from the filing date of the amendment. [U.C.C. §9-402(4)]

   a. **Signatures of both parties required:** [§271]   Whereas the original financing statement need be signed by the debtor only, *both parties must sign* an amendment. [U.C.C. §9-402(4)]

   b. **No extension of filing period:** [§272]   As developed below, a filing is normally effective for a period of five years (*infra,* §287). That period is *not extended* by amendments to the original financing statement. [U.C.C. §9-402(4)] (However, *continuation statements* may extend the period; *see infra,* §291.)

   c. **Compare—"floating lien":** [§273]   Note the important distinction between a floating lien (*supra,* §136) and an amendment adding collateral:

   (1) **"Floating lien":** The specific items of inventory covered by a "floating lien" are *covered from the date of filing*, regardless of when they come into the inventory.

   (a) **Example:** Retailer gives Bank a security interest in its "inventory, now existing or after-acquired," and Bank files a financing statement in the proper place. This creates a lien (security interest) in favor of Bank that "floats" over the inventory as it changes components— *i.e.,* Bank does *not* have to file amendments to the financing statement each time the specific items in the inventory change.

   (2) **Amendment adding collateral:** On the other hand, an amendment enlarging the collateral to include a new item covers the *new* item only from the *date of amendment*. (This underscores the advantage of an "after-acquired property" clause in the original security agreement; *supra,* §130.)

   (a) **Example:** Thus, in the above example, if Retailer had given Bank a security interest in its "office furniture," and then later, in return for a new loan, gave Bank a new security interest in its truck, the financing statement would have to be amended to cover the truck, and perfection as to the security interest in the truck would date only from the filing of the amended financing statement.

B.   WHERE TO FILE

1. **General Policy:** [§274]   No general statement about *where* to file can cover all states because the official draft of the U.C.C. provides three different filing systems from which states may choose. [U.C.C. §9-401]

a. **Alternative 1:** [§275]   The first alternative, adopted in only four states, provides that when the collateral is *minerals*, *timber* to be cut, or goods that are or are to become *fixtures*, filing shall be in the same office as that in which a mortgage on the real estate would be filed (*i.e.,* usually a county recorder's office). In all other cases, the filing shall be in the office of the secretary of state. (Most filings under this system therefore are statewide.)

b. **Alternative 2:** [§276]   The second alternative, adopted by a *majority* of jurisdictions, provides for local filing for *consumer goods, farm equipment, and farm products*. (Generally, "local" filing means in the office of some designated *county* official in the county of the debtor's residence or the county where the collateral is located, if owned by a nonresident.) Fixtures, minerals, timber, or growing crops require filing in the office where the land is located (again, county), and all other filings are with the secretary of state. (This system thus *combines* local and state-wide filing.)

c. **Alternative 3:** [§277]   The third alternative, adopted in a substantial minority of the states, follows the requirements of Alternative 2, but adds a requirement: In cases where the filing is with the secretary of state, the financing statement must *also* be filed in the county of the debtor's place of business if only one county is the place of business, or in the county of the debtor's residence if the debtor has no place of business in the state, but resides in the state.

2. **Rationale of Combination State-Local Filing System—Alternatives 2 and 3**

a. **Convenience for local creditors:** [§278]   A creditor dealing with a consumer need look only in the local records to find all security interests the debtor has granted. The same is true for farm goods and products (except that two-county filing is required where the farmer lives in one county and farms in another county). This saves the trouble of looking through a mass of state-wide records for a small consumer transaction and is intended to benefit small local creditors.

b. **Single filing system for state-wide transactions:** [§279]   On the other hand, every non-farm business transaction must be filed in the central office of the state, thus allowing major creditors and credit reporting agencies to rely on a single source to check for large-scale commercial debtors.

3. **Fixture Filings:** [§280]   Note that with respect to fixtures, to assure priority, the financing statement must be filed *locally* (*e.g.,* in county where land located), and this must be done in the *real estate records*. (This is true under all three alternatives.) The purpose is that such filings would be disclosed by any real estate search, just as any encumbrance on land; *see infra,* §350.

4. **Improper Filing:** [§281]   A filing made in good faith in the wrong place (or not in every place required) is still effective as to any collateral for which the filing did comply with the requirements of the Code. It is also effective against any person who had knowledge of the contents of the improperly filed statement. [U.C.C. §9-401(2)]

a. **Example:** Farmer, a resident of state X, takes a loan from Bank, using as collateral her horses and a tractor. State X's version of section 9-401(1) requires financing statements covering farm products collateral to be filed in the county of the debtor's residence, and statements for all other types of collateral to be filed in the office of the secretary of state.

(1) *If Bank files only in the secretary of state's office,* this will not perfect a security interest in the horses ("farm products"), but will perfect a security interest in the tractor ("equipment").

(2) *However if a later creditor* who is planning to lend money to Farmer *actually sees* the financing statement in the secretary of state's office, and then takes a security interest in the *horses* and files a financing statement in the proper county, the later creditor would be *junior in priority* to Bank because of that creditor's "knowledge of the contents" of the misfiled statement. [U.C.C. §9-401, Comment 5]

b. **Limitation:** [§282]   This protection does *not* extend to bankruptcy proceedings or to the filing of a tax lien by the federal government. [*In re* Babcock Box Co., 200 F. Supp. 80 (D. Mass. 1961); Dragstrem v. Obermeyer, 549 F.2d 20 (7th Cir. 1977)]

(1) **Rationale:** Under federal law, both the bankruptcy trustee and the I.R.S. are given the status of "hypothetical ideal lien creditors," and "ideal" is construed as meaning "without notice of an improperly filed financing statement." [Bankruptcy Code §544(a)]

5. **Federal Filing Acts:** [§283]   Local filing is not required for certain types of security interests covered by federal statutes. [U.C.C. §9-302(3)] For example, railroad equipment filing is with the Interstate Commerce Commission, and aircraft, aircraft parts, and engines require filing with the Administrator of Civil Aeronautics. Ship mortgages are required by the Ship Mortgage Act of 1920 to be filed with the office of the collector of customs of the ship's port of documentation. For interstate trucks and buses, Congress has provided that compliance with the filing and perfection laws of any state perfects the security interest in all jurisdictions. [49 U.S.C. §313]

C. MECHANICS OF FILING

1. **When Effective:** [§284]   Filing under the Code is deemed effective on the presentation of a financing statement for filing and tender of the filing fee or acceptance of the statement by the filing officer. What the filing officer does with the statement does not matter, as long as the secured party *presents* a conforming statement and *pays* the filing fee. [U.C.C. §9-403(1)]

a. **Indexing:** [§285]   The filing officer must mark each statement with a consecutive file number and the date and hour of filing, and must allow public inspection of the statement. The officer is required to index the statements according to the name of the *debtor*. The index must include the file number and the address of the debtor. [U.C.C. §9-403(4)]

b. **Errors in filing or indexing:** [§286]   However, the creditor's job is over on delivery of the financing statement and proper filing fee at the proper filing office. The security interest is protected even if the filing officer somehow fails to file the financing statement or files it under the wrong name. [*In re Royal Electrotype Corp.*, 485 F.2d 394 (3d Cir. 1973)—filing clerk negligently filed financing statement under name of secured party instead of under debtor's name]

(1) **Note:** In this situation, a creditor has a perfected security interest even though no other creditor could discover it! It is simply a question of protecting the earlier of two innocent parties.

2. **Duration of Filing:** [§287]   The financing statement is effective for a period of five years from the date of filing. [U.C.C. §9-403(2)]

   a. **Former rule:** [§288]   Under the original Article 9, a filed financing statement was effective only for whatever loan period was specified therein plus 60 days—creating a booby-trap for the creditor when the loan was past due. Revised Article 9 eliminates the problem by making the filing effective for five years regardless of the due date on the loan.

   b. **Extension during insolvency:** [§289]   If insolvency proceedings are instituted against the debtor during the five-year period, and the proceedings are still pending at the expiration thereof, the security interest will remain perfected until 60 days after the termination of the insolvency proceedings. [U.C.C. §9-403(7)]

   c. **Effect of lapse:** [§290]   Unless a continuation statement is filed in the six months before the expiration of the five-year period, the security interest becomes *unperfected*. The effect is that purchasers, junior security interest holders, and even lien creditors whose interests have attached before the lapse *gain priority* over the lapsed security interest. [U.C.C. §9-403(2)]

     (1) **Example:** A and B both make advances against the same collateral. A files on March 1, 1995, and B files on September 1, 1996. Unless A files a continuation statement before March 1, 2000, his filing lapses, his security interest becomes unperfected, and B will have priority until September 1, 2001. Any purchaser or lien creditor whose interest attaches on or after March 1, 2000, and before A refiles will also have priority over A.

3. **Continuation Statements:** [§291]   The secured party can extend the effectiveness of a financing statement about to expire by filing a *continuation statement*. Such a statement may be filed within *six months* before the expiration of the financing statement. The continuation statement must be signed by the secured party, must identify the original statement by file number, and must state that the original statement is still effective. It need *not be signed by the debtor*. This adds another five years to the effectiveness of the financing statement; succeeding continuation statements can be filed to add additional five-year periods. [U.C.C. §9-403]

4. **Termination Statement and Release of Collateral:** [§292]   Whenever there is no outstanding secured obligation and no commitment to make advances, incur obligations, or otherwise give value, the secured party *must, on written demand* by the debtor, send the debtor a statement that the secured party no longer claims a security interest under the financing statement, identified by file number. The debtor can then file this termination statement. If the secured party does not send such a

termination statement within 10 days after a proper demand is made, the debtor may recover for any damages suffered plus a statutory $100 penalty. [U.C.C. §9-404]

a. **Necessity of demand:** [§293]   As to *consumer goods* financing, an affirmative duty is placed on the secured party to file a termination statement within one month following payment *regardless of demand* by the debtor (consumer). In all other cases, however, the secured party is *not* under a duty to file until the debtor makes written demand therefore. [U.C.C. §9-404(1)]

b. **Who can demand:** [§294]   Only the debtor can force the secured party to give such a statement; another potential creditor cannot, although such a creditor can condition a new loan to the debtor on having the old outstanding security interest canceled.

c. **Releases:** [§295]   A secured party can also *release* collateral described in the financing statement from the security interest by a signed release. The release must contain a description of the collateral being released, the name and address of the debtor, the name and address of the secured party, and the file number of the financing statement. [U.C.C. §9-406]

5. **Assignment:** [§296]   A secured party may assign all or part of his/her rights under a financing statement by filing a separate written statement of assignment signed by the secured party of record (*see supra,* §199). The instrument must state the name of the secured party and the debtor, file number and date of filing of the financing statement, name and address of the assignee, and a description of the collateral assigned. A copy of the assignment can be used if it complies with the requirements as to contents. [U.C.C. §9-405]

a. **Procedure permissive:** [§297]   Note that the section 9-405 procedure is only a *permissive* method whereby a secured party can have an assignment noted "of record" (so that inquiries regarding the transaction will be addressed to the assignee). A secured party who assigns ("sells") the security interest of another creditor *need not file* to preserve the perfected status of the assignee. [U.C.C. §9-405]

D. REQUEST FOR STATEMENT OF ACCOUNT OR LIST OF COLLATERAL

1. **Request by Debtor:** [§298]   The debtor has the power to force the secured party to provide information under the Code. [U.C.C. §9-208] The debtor may send the secured party a statement indicating the aggregate amount of the unpaid debt as of a specified date, and may request that the secured party approve or correct the statement and return it to the debtor. If the security agreement or some other record kept by the secured party identifies the collateral, the debtor may also request that the secured party approve or correct a list of the collateral.

a. **Response by secured party:** [§299]   The secured party has two weeks in which to comply by sending a written correction or approval. If the secured party claims a security interest in all of a particular type of collateral owned by the debtor (*e.g.,* all inventory), the secured party may state that in the reply and does not have to approve or correct an *itemized* list of such collateral.

b. **Failure to reply:** [§300]   If the secured party fails to comply without a reasonable excuse, he is liable for any loss caused to the debtor. If the debtor included a good faith statement of the total obligation or a list of collateral, or both, in the statement, and the secured party failed to comply without a reasonable excuse, the secured party is barred from claiming a security interest in anything not shown in the statement against any person who has been misled by the failure to comply. This penalty provides a secured party with a strong incentive to reply in order to avoid losing part of the collateral. [U.C.C. §9-208(2)]

2. **Protection of Secured Party:** [§301]   The secured party is protected against burdensome requests by U.C.C. section 9-208(3), which limits a debtor to *one* such statement every six months without charge. A debtor has a right to statements more often, but the secured party may charge for them.

a. **State variations:** [§302]   Several states (notably California) added a subsection 4 to provide that if the secured party maintains branch offices, the request by the debtor must be sent to the branch at which the security transaction was entered into or the branch at which the debtor is to make payments, and that the secured party's answer relates only to debts owed the branch and to security taken at the branch.

3. **Third Party Problems:** [§303]   A secured party is often unwilling to disclose to third parties detailed information about the secured party's secured interest, either because it is costly or because the interests of the inquirer conflict with those of the secured party. Third parties *cannot* compel the secured party to provide such information; they are limited to the information on file—and usually, only the *types* of collateral are described.

a. **Third party recourse:** [§304]   As a result, a third party (*e.g.,* a prospective lender) must prevail upon the debtor to get a statement of the secured party's claim.

   (1) **Note:** Of course, this is of no help where the third party is a present creditor trying to learn the extent of another creditor's security interest in order to levy upon the goods for a prior debt.

   (2) **And note:** Even for a prospective lender aided by the debtor, the statement relates only to obligations and collateral at the time of the statement and does not protect against future advances or after-acquired property.

b. **Estoppel:** [§305]   Although there is no duty to reply to a third party's inquiry, the secured party may be *estopped* to deny *misstatements* regarding the secured party's relationship with the debtor, if the misstatements cause detriment to a third party who advances credit on this information. [United States v. Gleaners & Farmers Cooperative Elevator Co., 314 F. Supp. 1148 (N.D. Ind. 1970)—where government told prospective buyer it did not have lien on farmer's crops, it was held estopped to claim one later]

VI. PRIORITIES

chapter approach

If more than one person claims the right to certain property, which of them prevails over the others? This is the issue of priority, and the Code contains a wealth of rules on point. The competitors in the fight to claim the property include not only the original lender and debtor, but also people such as other secured parties, judicial lienors, buyers of the collateral, taxing authorities, and the debtor's trustee in bankruptcy.

To establish the priorities, ask:

1. Is the secured party's interest **unperfected**? If so, that party is entitled to little priority (only over certain subsequent parties).

2. Is the secured party's interest **perfected**? If so, then that party is entitled to priority over unperfected creditors and perfected creditors under the *"first-to-file-or-perfect"* rule, **purchase money security interest** rules, and **special rules** applicable to fixtures, accessions, and commingled goods.

Remember that more than one creditor may claim the **proceeds** of the sale or disposition of the collateral. The priority rules regulate this dispute as well.

Finally, recall that there are certain kinds of parties against whom even a perfected interest affords **no protection**—*e.g.,* a bona fide purchaser from a dealer in goods, a holder in due course of a negotiable instrument, certain statutory lien holders, etc.

A. COMPETING INTERESTS IN COLLATERAL—THE CLAIMANTS

1. **Introduction:** [§306] Sometimes there are several competing interests in the same piece of collateral. In such a case, the question arises as to which of these interests is entitled to priority. Of course, the simplest answer would be to rank each according to the time it arose. However, the Code has rejected this approach in favor of protecting certain classes of interest holders over others (*e.g.,* creditors who have gone through the requisite formalities to perfect their interests take priority over unperfected creditors). Therefore, before considering specific rules of priority, it is necessary to keep in mind who the possible claimants to a piece of collateral are.

2. **Debtor:** [§307] The person who owes payment or other performance of the secured obligation is the "debtor." Usually, the debtor will also be the **owner** of the collateral. [U.C.C. §9-105(1)(d); *see supra,* §45]

3. **Unsecured ("General") Creditor:** [§308] A creditor who has no security interest in the collateral but has a **personal** claim against the debtor (*e.g.,* a doctor to whom bills are owed) is called an unsecured creditor. Note that this type of creditor may acquire an interest in the debtor's collateral if the debtor **agrees** to grant the creditor a security interest or if the creditor **sues** the debtor, recovers judgment, and

uses the judicial process to *levy* on the collateral (thereby creating a judicial "lien" on it; below).

4. **Judicial "Lien Creditor":** [§309]   A creditor who was formerly unsecured ("general"), but who has acquired a lien on the debtor's property by judicial process (attachment, levy, etc.) is a judicial "lien creditor." Under the U.C.C., the term "lien creditor" also includes the trustee appointed in the debtor's bankruptcy, the assignee appointed to represent the debtor's creditors in a state liquidation procedure (called an "assignment for the benefit of creditors"), and a receiver appointed by a court of equity to take over and control the debtor's property. [U.C.C. §9-301(3)]

   a. **Time of lien:** [§310]   In most states, a lien creditor's interest arises at the time of "levy," meaning the moment a judicial officer (typically the sheriff) physically *seizes* the property. In a minority of states, the moment of "levy" relates back to the moment the court clerk issued the writ of execution.

      (1) **Insolvency proceedings:** [§311]   For a trustee in bankruptcy, a judicial lien is automatically created on all the bankrupt debtor's nonexempt property at the moment the *bankruptcy petition is filed* (*infra,* §475); in an assignment for the benefit of creditors, the judicial lien on all the debtor's nonexempt property arises on *assignment*; and for a receiver in equity, the lien arises at the time of *appointment* of the receiver. [U.C.C. §9-301(3)]

5. **Secured Creditor:** [§312]   Where the debtor has agreed to give a security interest in specific collateral to a creditor, and that creditor has taken the steps necessary for the security interest to "attach" (become valid between the two parties), the creditor is "secured." [U.C.C. §9-203; *see supra,* §§106-149]

6. **Perfected and Secured Creditor:** [§313]   A secured creditor who has also taken the steps necessary to protect the security interest from other claimants (*see supra,* §153) is both *secured and perfected*.

7. **Statutory Lien Creditor:** [§314]   A creditor whose lien interest arises *automatically* by statute or common law is called a statutory lien creditor. "Statutory" liens are granted to taxing authorities (*e.g.,* the federal tax lien, discussed *infra,* §448), landlords, mechanics, artisans, lawyers, innkeepers, and certain other people who have performed services for the debtor.

   a. **When lien arises:** [§315]   The lien attaches to the debtor's property at the time specified in the statute creating the lien (typically on the lienholder's *possession* of the collateral).

8. **Buyers of the Property:** [§316]   If the debtor (owner) sells the collateral, the buyer may then face the claims of the debtor's various creditors having interests in the property. As a general rule, the law tends to favor a good faith buyer over such creditors—although, as will be seen, the buyer does not always win.

B. PRIORITY—UNPERFECTED CREDITORS [§317]

An unperfected creditor (one whose security interest has "attached" (*see supra,* §106) but is not yet perfected) ranks among competing interest holders as follows:

1. **Other Unperfected Creditors—First-to-Attach Rule:** [§318]   Where there are two conflicting security interests in the same collateral, neither of which has been perfected, the *order of attachment determines* priority in the collateral. [U.C.C. §9-312(5)(b)]

   a. **Note:** As a practical matter, this type of dispute is never litigated because it is simply easier for a creditor to perfect prior to suit and thus prevail as a perfected creditor (*see* below). This means that when the collateral is repossessed and sold, the perfected creditor will first be paid in full, and only then, if there is any surplus money, will the unperfected creditor be paid. Thus, if the sale's proceeds are insufficient to pay the full amount, the debtor owes the unperfected creditor; the latter's only recourse is to sue the debtor personally for the "deficiency" (the amount still owing). [U.C.C. §9-301, Comment 2]

2. **Perfected Creditors Have Priority:** [§319]   An unperfected creditor is *junior* (or "subordinate") to a creditor who has *perfected* a security interest in the collateral first.

   a. **Knowledge and time of attachment irrelevant:** [§320]   The above rule (perfected over unperfected) applies no matter which security interest "attached" first, and regardless of whether the perfected creditor had *knowledge* at all times of the unperfected creditor's interest—even with knowledge of the other interest *before* the perfection.

      (1) **Example:** Debtor gives a security interest in collateral to Creditor A and another security interest in the same collateral to Creditor B. Both creditors know of each other. If *neither* perfects, they have priority in the collateral according to the order in which their interests attach (*supra*, §318). However, if one creditor perfects, that creditor has the senior interest no matter whose security interest attached first.

   b. **Exception—knowledge of misfiled financing statement:** [§321]   The only exception to this rule is when the creditor knows of the *contents* of a misfiled financing statement and obtains this knowledge *before* becoming perfected. In such case, the later-perfected interest is subordinate to the misfiled interest. [U.C.C. §9-401(2); *see supra*, §281]

      (1) **Example:** Creditors A and B are given security interests in the same collateral. Creditor A tries to perfect by filing, but files the financing statement in the wrong place. If Creditor B perfects without *seeing* the misfiled statement (even though Creditor B knows it exists), Creditor B wins. But if, prior to perfection, Creditor B knows the "contents" of the misfiled financing statement, Creditor B is junior to A, even though B is the first to file correctly. [U.C.C. §9-401 (2); *see supra*, §281]

3. **Judicial Lien Creditors:** [§322]   Section 9-301 of the Code provides that an unperfected creditor is also junior to a judicial lien creditor who levies before the unperfected creditor perfects his interest.

4. **Statutory Lien Holders:** [§323]   Holders of statutory liens (auto mechanics, landlords, taxing authorities, etc.) are *senior* to unperfected security interests unless the statutes creating their liens state otherwise (and typically they do not). [U.C.C. §9-310]

5. **Buyers:** [§324]   Those who purchase the collateral from the debtor and pay value take *free* of unperfected security interests in the collateral as long as they have no *knowledge* of the unperfected interest. [U.C.C. §9-301(1)]

    a. **Purchase of inventory:** [§325]   Moreover, if the collateral is *inventory* and the buyer purchases in the *ordinary course of business* (*i.e.,* a "normal" retail sale), the buyer takes free of *all* security interests in the inventory (perfected or not), even if the buyer *knows* of the security interest. [U.C.C. §9-307(1), *and see* Comment 1; *see infra,* §421 for detailed discussion on buyers of inventory]

C. PRIORITY AMONG PERFECTED CREDITORS—GENERAL RULE [§326]

As mentioned above, perfected security interests are senior to unperfected security interests in the same collateral. But when two *perfected* security interests exist in the same collateral, who prevails?

1. **General Rule—First to File or Perfect:** [§327]   Priority goes to whichever secured party is the first either to *file or perfect* the security interest (whichever is earlier), provided there is no period thereafter when there is neither filing nor perfection. [U.C.C. §9-312(5)]

2. **Effect:** [§328]   This gives the party who *files first* top priority—even though a later creditor *perfected* first (*e.g.,* by taking possession after the first creditor's filing). Alternatively, an interest perfected by a method *other than filing* is entitled to priority over a filed interest only if the nonfiling creditor in fact perfected *before* the other creditor's filing.

    a. **Example:** Debtor sought to borrow $10,000 from Bank using her valuable art collection as collateral. The parties signed a security agreement and financing statement as to this, and Bank filed the financing statement in the appropriate place, but did not immediately loan her the money nor make a commitment to do so. Two days later the debtor borrowed $8,000 from Loan Company, also using the art collection as collateral, which Loan Company then took into its possession as it loaned her the money (a perfection by pledge). The day after that, Bank loaned debtor the $10,000. In this situation Bank has filed its financing statement *first* but perfected its security interest *second* (since perfection cannot occur before attachment, and attachment cannot occur until the creditor gives value—*see supra,* §216). Nonetheless, Bank has priority over Loan Company because Bank filed first, and section 9-312(5) gives priority to the *first to file or perfect*, whichever came first between the two. This rule permits reliance on the filing system; Bank got on file first, and its filing should have alerted later creditors, like Loan Company, that it would therefore claim top priority in the collateral.

3. **Knowledge and Time of Attachment Not Determinative:** [§329]   One creditor's knowledge of the other's unperfected security interest is irrelevant. Furthermore, the time when the competing security interest first *attached* is also immaterial.

    a. **Example:** A files a financing statement on June 1 but does not actually advance any funds to the debtor until July 1 (hence, her security interest in the collateral does not attach or become perfected, until that time; *see supra,* §107). B advances value on the same collateral on June 15 (hence his security

EXAMPLE OF PRIORITY BETWEEN PERFECTED SECURITY INTERESTS

Creditor₁ v. Creditor₂

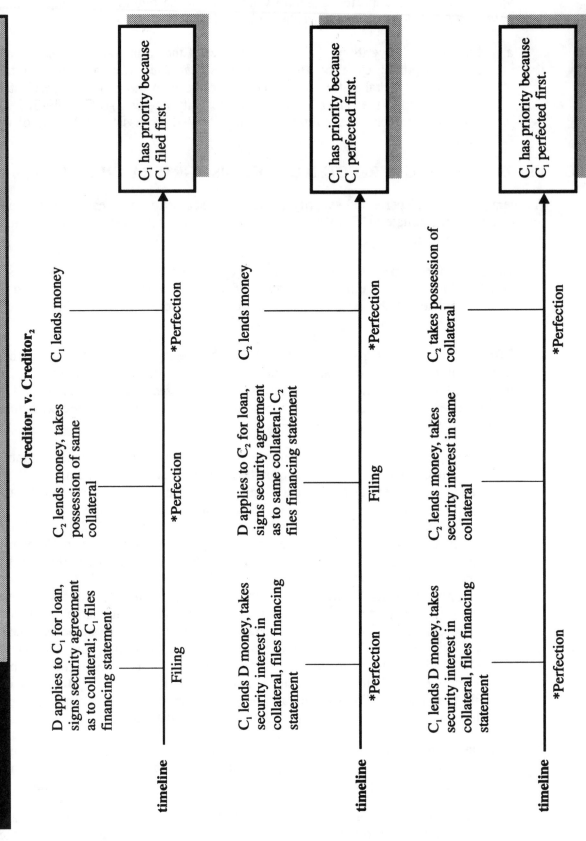

D applies to C₁ for loan, signs security agreement as to collateral; C₁ files financing statement

timeline — Filing

C₂ lends money, takes possession of same collateral

*Perfection

C₁ lends money

*Perfection

C₁ has priority because C₁ filed first.

C₁ lends D money, takes security interest in collateral, files financing statement

timeline — *Perfection

D applies to C₂ for loan, signs security agreement as to same collateral; C₂ files financing statement

Filing

C₂ lends money

*Perfection

C₁ has priority because C₁ perfected first.

C₁ lends D money, takes security interest in collateral, files financing statement

timeline — *Perfection

C₂ lends money, takes security interest in same collateral

*Perfection

C₂ takes possession of collateral

*Perfection

C₁ has priority because C₁ perfected first.

interest attaches on that date), but does not file (perfect) until July 10. A is entitled to priority. Even though B's security interest attached first (June 15), he was not the first to "file *or* perfect."

    (1) **Rationale:** The fact that A's security interest did not arise until after the filing does not affect her priority, because the subsequent creditor (B) was given *constructive notice* by the filing that A might have an interest in the collateral; thus, B has no cause to complain.

   b. **Example:** The result would be the same even if A had perfected by some means other than filing. For instance, suppose B had advanced funds to the debtor on May 15, but had neither filed nor otherwise perfected his security interest at that time. A comes along on June 1 and advances funds to the debtor, taking possession of the collateral (and thus perfecting her interest). If B finally gets around to filing a financing statement on June 15, A prevails. Even though B's interest had attached first (May 15), A was the first to "file *or* perfect."

D. PRIORITY AMONG PERFECTED CREDITORS—SPECIAL RULES FOR PURCHASE MONEY SECURITY INTERESTS [§330]

As indicated previously, the "general rule" of priority (first to file or perfect) is subject to modification where certain types of security interests are involved. In these cases, the Code grants special priority to holders of such interests regardless of whether they would prevail under the general "first-to-file-or-perfect" rule.

1. **Non-Inventory Purchase Money Security Interests:** [§331] A creditor who advances value to a debtor that enables the debtor to acquire an interest in collateral has a "purchase money security interest" (*supra,* §183) and stands in a different position than other creditors. Since the advance is directly related to the collateral, it is right that such a creditor be given additional protection in that collateral over other creditors of the debtor. The Code accomplishes this by declaring that a *purchase money security interest* (in collateral other than inventory) *takes priority* over conflicting security interests in the same collateral if the interest is perfected when the debtor takes possession of the collateral *or within 10 days* thereafter (many states changed this period to *20* days). [U.C.C. §9-312(4)]

   a. **Rationale:** Other creditors of the debtor cannot complain. They are in no worse position than if the debtor had not entered into the purchase money agreement. They may, in fact, be in a better position to the extent the purchase money security interest is less than the value of the collateral.

   b. **Further rationale:** There is an additional pragmatic reason for allowing priority to purchase money interest: The debtor would have no way to finance new purchases if the debtor could not assure the party advancing such funds of priority in the property purchased. The existence of the purchase money priority prevents debtors from being captives of their existing creditors. (This is particularly true in the case of an after-acquired property agreement, discussed *infra,* §§335-341.)

   c. **Effect on general rule of priority:** [§332] This super-priority cuts across the "first-to-file-or-perfect" rule both from the standpoint of time and from the standpoint of method of perfection.

(1) **Example:** A advances purchase money to Debtor to acquire collateral on December 1, and Debtor takes possession of the collateral on that date. On December 5, B advances Debtor value in return for a security interest in the same collateral. B perfects on December 5. A perfects her purchase money interest on December 10, within the 10-day period after possession. A will take priority over B, regardless of the fact that B perfected his interest before A. [U.C.C. §9-312(4)]

(a) **And note:** This result is the same *regardless of the manner* in which the parties perfected. Thus, even if B perfected by taking possession of the collateral on December 5, A wins if she perfects by filing no later than December 10.

d. **Knowledge of prior interest immaterial:** [§333]   The purchase money secured party who perfects within 10 days, as aforesaid, prevails against all conflicting security interests—even interests that were *filed* at the time of sale and of which the purchase money secured party actually *knew*. [Noble Co. v. Mack Financial Corp., 264 A.2d 325 (R.I. 1970)]

e. **Limitation to "purchase money":** [§334]   The priority of the purchase money security interest is limited to the *extent of the "purchase money"* (cash or credit) *used* in acquisition of the collateral.

(1) **Example:** A advances $1,000 to Debtor to purchase collateral worth $5,000 on August 1. On August 5, B advances $3,000 in a nonpurchase money transaction and perfects a security interest in the same collateral by filing on that date. On August 10, A files a financing statement perfecting her security interest, but she also advances another $1,000, taking a security interest in the same collateral and includes this second $1,000 in the financing statement that she files on August 10. Thus, A has a security interest totaling $2,000, and B has interests totaling $3,000. If it is clear that the first $1,000 that A advanced is purchase money (*see supra*, §185), A will have priority even though she filed after B. However, this is the extent of her priority due to purchase money. In weighing A's claim for the second $1,000 against B's claim, B will prevail since the case is governed by the usual rules—here, the "first-to-file-or-perfect" rule.

2. **Purchase Money Security Interests in Inventory:** [§335]   A lender who advances money to a retailer and takes a security interest in the retailer's inventory expects to get top priority as to the debtor's *after-acquired* inventory as well as the existing inventory. If creditors selling inventory to the retailer on credit could get purchase money security interests that prevailed over the first lender's "after-acquired property" interest in the inventory, the first lender's security interest would in time be virtually nonexistent. For this reason, the usual rule of super-priority for purchase money security interests is modified somewhat when the collateral is "inventory" (defined *supra*, §53).

a. **Requirements for priority:** [§336]   A creditor wishing to claim a purchase money security interest in goods that will become inventory in the hands of the debtor is accorded super-priority over other creditors *only if* the following two requirements are first met:

(1) **Perfection requirement:** [§337] The purchase money security interest must already be perfected *at the* time *the debtor receives possession* of the collateral. There is *no 10-day grace period* (as there is for purchase money security interests in non-inventory collateral). [U.C.C. §9-312(3)(a)]

(2) **Notice requirement:** [§338] In addition, the purchase money secured party must give *written* notice to any other security interest holder who has *previously filed a financing statement* covering inventory of the *same type of goods* as those that will be covered in the purchase money security interest (but *not* to persons financing debtor's accounts). The notice must be given *prior* to the date on which the debtor takes possession of the collateral. [U.C.C. §9-312(3)(b)]

  (a) **Contents of notice:** [§339] The notice must state that the person filing has or expects to acquire a purchase money security interest in the debtor's inventory, describing the inventory *by item or type*. [U.C.C. §9-312(3)(d)]

  (b) **Duration of notice:** [§340] Once properly given, the notice lasts for five years (same as the financing statement). If at the end of the five years, the purchase money financing is still continuing, a new notice must be sent to and received by the conflicting interest holder. [U.C.C. §9-312(3)(c)]

b. **Effect of rule:** [§341] By requiring the purchase money secured creditor to perfect and give notice, the Code protects creditors with existing interests in the debtor's inventory. At the same time, the Code preserves the debtor's flexibility in making financing arrangements by giving the purchase money inventory creditor the same super-priority as other non-inventory purchase money creditors if the above requirements are met.

c. **Example:** Retailer owned and ran a book store. She borrowed $20,000 from Bank, which took and filed a security interest in her inventory "now and after-acquired." While selling the original inventory to customers, Retailer bought a new shipment of books from Book Distributors, Inc. ("BDI") on credit, giving BDI a purchase money security interest in the books it sold her. Before delivering the books, BDI filed a financing statement in the proper place and sent written notice of its interest to Bank. Since notice is deemed to give Bank the facts necessary to protect itself (*e.g.,* by cutting off further credit to Retailer and/or repossessing the nonencumbered inventory), BDI takes priority over Bank in the new shipment of books.

3. **Compare—Consignments:** [§342] A similar problem exists where goods end up in a debtor's inventory on consignment from a supplier, and at the same time some prior inventory financer claims an interest in the consignee's (debtor's) inventory under an after-acquired property clause. (*See* discussion of consignments, *supra,* §§79-81.)

a. **"Consignment" in form or substance:** [§343] Of course, if the nominal "consignment" is in fact nothing more than a financing transaction in which

PMSI SUPER-PRIORITY—EXAMPLES

Creditor₁ v. Creditor₂

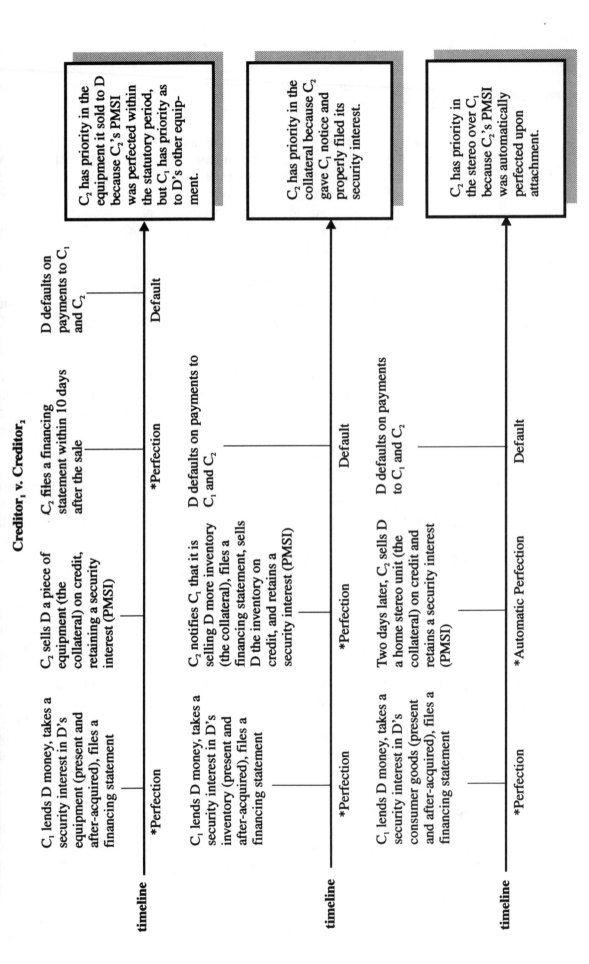

timeline

C_1 lends D money, takes a security interest in D's equipment (present and after-acquired), files a financing statement — *Perfection

C_2 sells D a piece of equipment (the collateral) on credit, retaining a security interest (PMSI)

C_2 files a financing statement within 10 days after the sale — *Perfection

D defaults on payments to C_1 and C_2 — Default

→ C_2 has priority in the equipment it sold to D because C_2's PMSI was perfected within the statutory period, but C_1 has priority as to D's other equipment.

timeline

C_1 lends D money, takes a security interest in D's inventory (present and after-acquired), files a financing statement — *Perfection

C_2 notifies C_1 that it is selling D more inventory (the collateral), files a financing statement, sells D the inventory on credit, and retains a security interest (PMSI) — *Perfection

D defaults on payments to C_1 and C_2 — Default

→ C_2 has priority in the collateral because C_2 gave C_1 notice and properly filed its security interest.

timeline

C_1 lends D money, takes a security interest in D's consumer goods (present and after-acquired), files a financing statement — *Perfection

Two days later, C_2 sells D a home stereo unit (the collateral) on credit and retains a security interest (PMSI) — *Automatic Perfection

D defaults on payments to C_1 and C_2 — Default

→ C_2 has priority in the stereo over C_1 because C_2's PMSI was automatically perfected upon attachment.

the "consignor" has retained title as security for the purchase price—as opposed to a true agency for sale—it will be treated as any other secured transaction. The "consignor's" interest will not be protected against third parties unless perfected in the manner required under Article 9. [U.C.C. §1-201(37)]

b. **Filing and notice required:** [§344]   Where, however, a true consignment is involved, there exists the priority problem noted above. To protect goods on consignment, the consignor is required to comply with the filing provisions of Article 9, **and** to give the same kind of **notice** as a purchase money secured party must give (above) in order to obtain priority over an earlier filed security interest in the debtor's (consignee's) inventory. [U.C.C. §9-114]

(1) **Rationale:** Absent such notice, an inventory financer, relying on the after-acquired property clause and first filed position, could as readily be deceived by consigned merchandise coming into the debtor's inventory as by new inventory subject to a purchase money security interest.

E. PRIORITY AMONG PERFECTED CREDITORS—SPECIAL RULES FOR CERTAIN TYPES OF COLLATERAL

1. **Crop Production Loans:** [§345]   A perfected security interest in crops securing a loan (**new value**) given to enable the debtor to produce the crops during the production season and given not more than three months before the crops were planted, takes priority over an earlier perfected security interest to the extent that such earlier interest secures obligations **due more than** six months before the crops were planted. This special priority holds true even if the lender had **knowledge** of the earlier security interest.

a. **Example:** Bank held a perfected security interest in Farmer's current and future winter wheat crops, payment of which came due on January 25. Farmer failed to pay on that date. On November 1, Farmer borrowed money from Farmer's Co-op to plant a new crop of winter wheat, giving Co-op a security interest in the crop, which Co-op perfected by filing. Farmer planted the crop in November. As to this crop, Co-op has priority over Bank, even if Co-op knew of Bank's perfected security interest when it filed its financing statement.

b. **Compare—other crops transactions:** [§346]   Because of the restrictive time limits in this provision and the facts that the second creditor must give "new value" and the old loan must be "due," section 9-312(2) rarely comes up as a practical matter. If this special section of the Code is not applicable, priority is determined by the usual "first-to-perfect-or-file" rule of section 9-312(5) (*see supra,* §327). [United States v. Minister Farmers Cooperative Exchange, 430 F. Supp. 566 (N.D. Ohio 1977)]

2. **Fixtures:** [§347]   The only circumstance in which Article 9 has major involvement in real property financing arises when the collateral is goods that are currently or are about to become "fixtures"—*i.e.,* personal property attached to real property. Although section 9-313 sets forth special rules dealing with fixtures, the law in this area remains quite complicated since some states adopted nonuniform versions of section 9-313.

a. **"Fixtures" defined:** [§348]   The U.C.C. does not actually define a "fixture." Ordinary building materials that are incorporated into an improvement on land (*e.g.,* bricks, lumber, cement, and the like) are specifically *excluded*, but all other goods become "fixtures" as provided by *local (non-U.C.C.) law.* [U.C.C. §9-313(1), (2)]

   (1) **Under property law:** [§349]   In most states, the notion of what is a "fixture" is intuitive: *permanent attachment of the goods to real property.* (*See* detailed discussion in Property Summary.)

   (a) *Mobile homes* placed on leased land have been involved in a number of cases. Normally, the lessee (debtor) has the right to remove the mobile home, and consequently it is *not* regarded as permanently affixed to the land.

   (b) *Prefabricated buildings* brought onto the land by the owner thereof may be classified as "fixtures" if the owner *intended* a permanent attachment to the land.

   (c) *"Readily removable" factory or office machines* would *hardly ever* be classified as fixtures. However, if they are, a special rule provides that a security interest therein can be perfected by any method permitted under Article 9; *i.e.,* the special fixture filing rules below do *not* apply. This is also true for readily removable *replacements* of domestic appliances that are *consumer goods* (like a window unit air conditioner). [U.C.C. §9-313(4)(c)]

b. **Priority rules**

   (1) **Purchase money security interests—fixture filing required:** [§350] Most security interests in particular fixtures are purchase money security interests (*see supra,* §183). Such interests prevail as against most existing and future interests in the real estate (*see infra,* §354) *provided* the purchase money security interest is *perfected* by a *"fixture filing"* at the time the goods are *affixed* to the realty or within 10 days thereafter. In addition, the "debtor" must be the *owner* of the real estate or someone in possession thereof (*e.g.,* a lessee).

   (a) **"Fixture filing" defined:** [§351]   A "fixture filing" is a perfection of the fixture financer's security interest in the goods that is accomplished by *filing a financing statement* in the place where *real property records* are filed. [U.C.C. §9-313(1)(b)] In addition to the usual requirements for a financing statement (*supra,* §§250-251), a fixture filing financing statement *must recite* that it is to be filed in the real estate records (although if the statement *is* filed in the proper place, the omission of this recital should not destroy perfection), must describe the goods, and must contain a "description of the real estate." [U.C.C. §9-402(5), (6)]

   1) **Description of realty:** [§352]   In most states, the real estate description need only be sufficiently detailed to give *"constructive" notice* of the security interest to those examining the real

estate records. However, some states (*e.g.,* Utah) require the financing statement to contain a technical legal description of the real property.

    2) **Identity of record owner:** [§353]   If the fixture debtor is not the record owner of the realty, but is only in possession, the financing statement must identify the record owner so that it can be indexed under the record owner's name as well (as are most real property recordings). [U.C.C. §§9-402(5), 9-403(7)]

(b) **Limitation—construction mortgages:** [§354]   A lender who finances the construction of a building takes top priority as to *all items that become part* of the building during construction. Thus, when a construction mortgage has been *recorded* against the property, even a perfected purchase money security interest in goods becoming fixtures during construction will be *junior* to the construction mortgage. [U.C.C. §9-313(6), *and see* Comment 4(e)]

    1) **Effect of subordination agreements:** [§355]   However, even where the U.C.C. grants priority to a construction mortgage (or any other prior recorded interest in the real property), the fixture financer will prevail if the real property creditor *agrees* in writing to subordinate its interest to the security interest in the fixture, or if the realty creditor *disclaims* an interest in the goods as fixtures. [U.C.C. §9-313(5)(a)]

    2) **Rationale:** Since the construction mortgagee advanced the money for the whole project, the construction mortgagee should have superior rights to all items that are installed during construction unless the mortgagee agrees to subordinate its interest.

(c) **Right of fixture removal on default:** *See infra,* §§635-636.

(2) **Status of non-purchase money security interests**

(a) **Non-PMSI vs. prior recorded interests in realty:** [§356]   A non-purchase money security interest (or a purchase money security interest perfected *more* than 10 days after the goods become a fixture) *loses* to *prior recorded* interests in the realty even if the fixture financer perfects by a fixture filing. (Conversely, *unrecorded* prior interests in the realty are subordinate to the fixture financer's perfected security interest.)

(b) **Non-PMSI vs. subsequent interests in realty:** [§357]   But the non-purchase money fixture financer can prevail over *subsequent* parties (*i.e.,* later real property mortgagees and buyers) by making a fixture filing before the subsequent parties obtain rights in the realty. [U.C.C. §9-313(4)(b)]

    1) **Subsequent lien creditors:** [§358]   Where the subsequent claimant to the property is a judicial lien creditor (*supra,*

§309), the fixture financer can perfect the security interest by *any* method (not necessarily fixture filing) before the judicial lien attaches to the realty. [U.C.C. §9-313(4)(d)] The avowed purpose of this special rule is to preserve the fixture security interest against invalidation by a trustee in bankruptcy as a hypothetical judicial lien creditor under the Bankruptcy Code (*see infra*, §496).

3. **Accessions:** [§359] Goods that are attached to *other goods* (*e.g.,* a telephone installed in a car) are called "accessions." Since real property is not involved, security interests in accessions fall within the scope of the Code and are governed without undue complexity.

   a. **Where security interest precedes installation:** [§360] In general, a party whose security interest *attaches* before the goods are installed in or affixed to other goods takes priority over a party who has an interest in the whole of the goods. Perfection is *not* required to prevail over prior security interests—even those with "after-acquired property" clauses. [U.C.C. 9-314(1)]

   b. **Where security interest subsequent to installation:** [§361] In the case of a security interest in goods that attaches *after* they have become accessions, the secured party takes priority over those who acquire interests in the whole of the goods *subsequent to attachment*. The secured party takes priority over those who hold interests *at the time of installation or affixation* only to the extent that such parties *consent* to subordination of their security interest or *disdain* an interest in the goods as a part of the whole. [U.C.C. §9-314(2)]

   c. **Exceptions:** [§362] The above priority rules are subject to certain exceptions. These exceptions allow the following persons to *prevail* over an *unperfected* security interest in the accession, unless such persons had knowledge of the unperfected security interest at the time they acquired their interest: a *subsequent purchaser for value* of the whole; a creditor with a *lien* on the whole obtained *subsequent to affixation or installation*; and a creditor with a prior perfected security interest in the whole to the extent that such creditor makes *subsequent advances*. [U.C.C. §9-314(3)]

      (1) **Note:** Purchasers at foreclosure sales may qualify as subsequent purchasers (provided they are not perfected secured parties purchasing at their own foreclosure sales). [U.C.C. §9-314(3)]

4. **Commingled and Processed Goods:** [§363] The Code rules for accessions are closely related to the rules governing processed and commingled goods under section 9-315. Suppose a party takes a security interest in baled cotton that the debtor later spins into thread and then weaves into cloth. The collateral has changed form but is still identifiable, and secured interests need not be affected. But suppose that the cotton is spun into a blend of cotton and rayon. Now, the collateral not only has changed form but also is no longer entirely identifiable.

   a. **Interest extends to ultimate product:** [§364] The Code handles this problem by providing that a perfected security interest in goods that have become part of a product or mass *extends to the product or mass* if they have been manufactured, assembled, or commingled so that they are *no longer identifiable*. [U.C.C. §9-315(1)(a)]

b. **Effect of financing statement:** [§365]   Of course, the same result would follow, regardless of identifiability, if the financing statement specifically provides for extension to a mass or product in which the collateral is subsumed. [U.C.C. §9-315(1)(b)]

    (1) **Note:** Such a contractual provision might also cover accessions that do not lose their identity upon installation or affixation (*e.g.,* a horn installed on an automobile). If so, the secured party would not gain the separate continuing security interest in the accession under section 9-314(1), but would have only an interest in the mass.

    (2) **Compare:** Nevertheless, most commentators urge that if the item is easily traceable and readily removable (*i.e.,* it is not commingled but really is an accession, like tires on an automobile), courts should construe section 9-315 so that the secured party can claim an interest only in the accession and ***not in the whole***. [G. Gilmore, Security Interests in Personal Property §31.5 at 854 (1965)]

c. **Competing interests in ultimate product:** [§366]   It is possible, of course, that more than one secured party may have an interest in a mass of processed or assembled goods (*e.g.,* several types of raw material, each covered by a secured interest, are commingled into one product). The Code ***ranks the interests of such conflicting parties equally***—declaring that each has an interest in the mass or total product in the ratio that the original cost of the goods covered by the security interest of each bears to the cost of the total product or mass. [U.C.C. §9-315(2)]

    (1) **Example:** A takes a security interest in $1,000 of raw cotton, which she perfects, and B takes an interest in $2,000 of raw wool, which he also perfects. Debtor textile producer then spins the raw materials into 50 bolts of glen-plaid, the total cost of which is $6,000. In determining the extent of A's and B's interests in the total product, the Code would give A an interest to the extent of 1/6 (or $1,000/6,000) and B an interest of 1/3.

    (2) **Attachment and perfection irrelevant:** [§367]   Note that it makes no difference when the original interests of A and B attached and were perfected; they are still treated equally.

5. **Proceeds**

a. **Introduction:** [§368]   As will be amplified below, "proceeds" includes anything received by the debtor on the sale or disposition of the collateral, whether or not such disposition was authorized by the creditor.

    (1) **Background:** [§369]   Prior to the Code, if the debtor was allowed to use or to dispose of the collateral or to retain the ***proceeds*** from the sale thereof, the courts treated the security interest as a fraudulent transfer, which could be set aside by a trustee in bankruptcy. [Benedict v. Ratner, *supra,* §30]

        (a) **Code provisions:** [§370]   This rule frustrated the needs of modern commercial financing, and hence was overturned by U.C.C. section

9-205, which specifically provides that a security interest is not invalid or fraudulent against creditors by reason of such permission granted to the debtor. This allows the parties to agree that the debtor may use or dispose of all the collateral and use or dispose of the proceeds obtained thereby.

(b) **Security interest in proceeds:** [§371]   The problem discussed in this section is to what extent the secured party's interest attaches to proceeds.

(2) **"Proceeds" defined:** [§372]   Proceeds includes *whatever is received* on the sale, exchange, or other disposition of collateral or of proceeds (from some previous disposition of collateral). Money, checks, deposit accounts, and the like are *"cash proceeds"*; everything else is *"noncash proceeds."* [U.C.C. §9-306(1)]

(a) **Example:** Secured Party has an interest in Dealer's stock of Hupmobiles. Dealer sells a new Hupmobile for a down payment of $400 cash, a 1909 Stanley Steamer trade-in, and the purchaser's executing a conditional sales contract for the balance. The $400 cash is "cash proceeds"; the Stanley Steamer and the contract ("chattel paper") are "noncash proceeds."

1) **"Second generation" proceeds:** [§373]   If Dealer later resells the Stanley Steamer for $500, the $500 is also "cash proceeds" from sale of the Hupmobile. Such proceeds of proceeds are sometimes called "second generation proceeds."

(b) **Insurance proceeds as "proceeds":** [§374]   Section 9-306(1) expressly states that insurance payable by reason of loss or damage to the collateral *is* "proceeds" (except to the extent that it is payable to a nonparty to the security agreement). However, the fact that insurance proceeds are "proceeds" does not mean that the secured party will automatically get the money. As indicated below, the secured party risks losing the funds to other parties (notably to the trustee in bankruptcy) unless the secured party gets *possession* of the check before others do.

1) **Note—compensation from third parties:** [§375]   Section 9-306(1) does not answer the question of whether money received from *third parties* (other than insurance companies) for damage or destruction of the goods is "proceeds." For example, if a tortfeasor causes injury to the property and pays for it, it will be up to the courts to determine whether such payments—clearly compensation for the destroyed collateral—fall within the meaning of the term "proceeds" so that the secured party can assert a right thereto.

(3) **Express reference to "proceeds" not required:** [§376]   Under the revised Article 9, no express reference to "proceeds" is required in the security agreement *or* in the financing statement. The secured party's rights

with respect to proceeds are deemed to arise by operation of law, in accordance with the parties' *presumed intent*, unless otherwise agreed. [*See* U.C.C. §9-306(2)]

(4) **Secured party's option between proceeds or collateral:** [§377]   It should be emphasized that in many cases the secured party is not limited to asserting an interest in the "proceeds." Wherever the security interest continues in the original collateral notwithstanding transfer thereof to a third person [U.C.C. §9-402(7)], the secured party may claim both the proceeds *and* the original collateral—although the secured party is entitled to but *one satisfaction* of the debt [U.C.C. §9-306(2)].

   (a) **But note:** Of course, in those cases in which the transfer cuts off the security interest, the secured party would be limited to asserting an interest against the "proceeds" (*e.g.,* purchase by buyer in due course from dealer in goods; purchase of negotiable instrument by holder in due course; *see infra,* §§421, 437).

b. **Rules regarding attachment and perfection of security interest in proceeds:** [§378]   As long as the secured party's interest in the original collateral was perfected, that interest normally will continue *automatically* and *permanently* in any *identifiable proceeds* received by the debtor from the sale, exchange, or other disposition of the original collateral; *i.e.,* no new filing is necessary. [U.C.C. §9-306(2)]

   (1) **Security agreement violated:** [§379]   The fact that the "proceeds" were obtained in violation of the security agreement is *immaterial.* For example, Debtor receives payments on accounts receivable already assigned to Lender, but instead of turning the money over to Lender, Debtor puts it in a bank account. Lender's interest in the collateral (accounts receivable) continues in the bank deposits. [Commercial Discount Corp. v. Milwaukee Western Bank, 214 N.W.2d 33 (Wis. 1974)—also holding the creditor's interest in the traceable proceeds superior to any right of set-off in the bank]

   (2) **Limitation—where filing not appropriate means:** [§380]   Where the "proceeds" are the kind of property in which a security interest *cannot be perfected by filing*, the security interest terminates *10 days after the debtor's receipt* thereof (unless extended by a new perfection; *see* below). [U.C.C. §9-306(3)(a)]

      (a) **Example:** Secured Party has a duly filed (perfected) security interest in Debtor's computer.

         1) *If Debtor trades in the computer on a new calculator*, Lender's security interest continues automatically and permanently in the new calculator because filing is an appropriate means of perfection as to the "proceeds" (the calculator).

         2) *However, if Debtor sells the computer for a negotiable promissory note*, Lender's security interest in the note terminates after 10 days, because filing is not an appropriate means of perfection as to negotiable instruments. (To continue the perfection,

Lender would have to take *possession* of the promissory note within the 10-day period.) [U.C.C. §9-304(1); *supra*, §160]

3) *Likewise, if the computer was destroyed by fire*, Lender's security interest in any insurance check payable on account of the loss would depend on getting *possession* of the check. Again, a security interest in insurance proceeds cannot be perfected merely by filing; possession is required. Furthermore, for "cash proceeds" (*see supra*, §372), the 10-day rule does not apply. Common law rules limit the extent of tracing, and they typically permit the creditor to track the cash proceeds through many transactions and transfers and recover them unless the cash has reached the hands of a bona fide purchaser for value. [U.C.C. §9-306(3)(b)]

4) *If Debtor had sold the computer for cash,* perfection would continue only as long as the cash was *identifiable* (*e.g.,* segregated). Once Debtor mingled the cash or used it to buy something else, the security interest in the newly purchased item would terminate after 10 days—*unless* that which Debtor bought was *property of the same type* as that covered under the original financing statement (*i.e.,* another computer). In that case, the new item would be covered by the original filing. Where the new property ("second generation" proceeds, *see supra*, §373) is bought with cash proceeds, perfection will cease after 10 days unless the filed financing statement *already describes* the type of property that constitutes the proceeds or is *amended* to do so within that period. [U.C.C. §9-306(3)]

(3) **Limitation—when filing not in appropriate place:** [§381] Where the place of original filing (covering the original collateral) is *not the appropriate place* for filing as to the "proceeds" received, the security interest also terminates 10 days after receipt thereof by the debtor (unless extended by a new perfection; *see* below). [U.C.C. §9-306(3)(a)]

(a) **Example:** The original collateral was inventory located in State A and was filed against there, but the "proceeds" are accounts payable in State B, where the debtor is located. The filing in State A is not the "appropriate place" to file as to the accounts; hence, the security interest terminates after 10 days unless reperfected in the proper place.

(4) **Extension of security interest by new perfection:** [§382] In the situations noted above (where filing is not an "appropriate means" or not in an "appropriate place" to perfect a security interest in the proceeds received), the secured party has 10 days following the debtor's receipt of such proceeds to protect the secured interest by a new perfection.

(a) **Method of perfecting:** [§383] If the "proceeds" are of a type in which a security interest *can* be perfected by filing a financing statement, a filing must be made within the 10-day period as to the "proceeds." If the proceeds are not susceptible of perfection by filing (*e.g.,* money), the secured party may have to perfect the interest by *taking possession*.

(b) **Time of new perfection:** [§384]   If a new perfection is made within the 10-day period, it "relates back" to the date the original interest was perfected—thus avoiding bankruptcy "preference" problems (*see infra*, §§497-499). [U.C.C. §9-312(6)]

c. **Rules of priority:** [§385]   The usual "first-to-file-or-perfect" rule of U.C.C. section 9-312(5) (*supra*, §327) governs most priority disputes in proceeds. Special statutory variations from this norm are considered in this section.

(1) **Accounts as "proceeds" of inventory:** [§386]   Wherever a security interest·exists in the debtor's inventory and another security interest exists in the debtor's accounts receivable, a conflict will exist if the debtor sells the inventory on credit, since the "proceeds" of inventory will be an account receivable.

(a) **Example:** A files and perfects a security interest in Debtor's inventory on June 1. Debtor sells a portion of his inventory in the ordinary course of business to Purchaser (such sale cutting off the secured interest in the goods) on open account payable within 30 days. Debtor's accounts are subject to a security interest held by B, who had filed a financing statement with regard thereto on May 1.

(b) **Rule:** [§387]   In this case, the accounts receivable financer (B) prevails because he was the "first to file or perfect" *as to the accounts* (the general priority rule of section 9-312(5)).

1) *Even though A may claim the accounts were "proceeds"* of the inventory in which she had a perfected interest, she is not entitled to priority as to the accounts *unless she filed first*.

2) *Where, as here, the accounts receivable financer (B) filed first*, he is entitled to priority. This is true even though, in fact, the inventory financer (A) was the first to extend credit (because the date of *attachment* of the secured interest is *immaterial*; *supra*, §329). It is also true regardless of the purchase money or nonpurchase money nature of the inventory financer's security interest.

(c) **Compare—cash proceeds of purchase money security interests in inventory:** [§388]   The result may be different where the inventory was sold for *cash* and the inventory financer had a *purchase money security interest* in the debtor's inventory. This is because section 9-312(3) provides that the super-priority given a purchase money security interest in new inventory (*see supra*, §335) *continues in the cash proceeds* of sale of such collateral.

1) **Example:** On January 1, A files and perfects a security interest in the inventory of Debtor's hat shop. Debtor's accounts receivable are subject to a perfected security interest in favor of B, who files a financing statement on March 1. On August 1, Debtor orders a shipment of felt hats on credit from C and signs a security agreement giving C a purchase money security interest in the hats. C files a financing statement on August 2

and before delivering the hats to Debtor, C gives written notice to A of its new financing arrangement with Debtor. When the hats are delivered, Debtor sells some for cash and some on credit.

    a)   Since C complied with the early perfection and written notice requirements of section 9-312(3), C's interest in the felt hats prevails over A's existing interest in the general inventory. Also, since C's super-priority *continues* as to cash proceeds resulting from the sale of its collateral, C prevails over B as to the cash traceable from sale of the felt hats.

    b)   However, priority in the *noncash* proceeds (the accounts receivable from the hats sold on credit) depends on the general "first-to-file-or-perfect" rule. Thus, A would have top priority as to the accounts receivable with B and C taking second and third priority, respectively (*i.e.,* their order of filing).

(2) **Promissory notes as proceeds:** [§389] If the sale of collateral generates promissory notes as proceeds, the collateral financer must take possession of the instruments within 10 days to continue the original perfection in the collateral (possession being the only way to perfect a security interest in instruments; *supra,* §160). If, in the meantime, the note is transferred to a holder in due course or to a purchaser for new value in the ordinary course of business without knowledge of the interest, the security interest in the instrument would be *cut off*. [U.C.C. §§9-308, 9-309]

(3) **Chattel paper as proceeds:** [§390] The common method of selling large items such as automobiles and appliances is for the dealer to take a cash down payment for part of the price and chattel paper for the balance. Whoever is financing the dealer's inventory will want its security interest to carry over to the chattel paper since the product is no longer in the inventory as collateral, and the financer's claim to the product sold is cut off by the good faith consumer-buyer. [U.C.C. §9-307(1); *infra,* §421] Some dealers prefer to sell the chattel paper to a second financer, creating conflicting claims between the inventory financer and the chattel paper financer, since a *sale* of accounts or chattel paper is also covered by Article 9 (*supra,* §42).

    (a)   **Where interest in chattel paper claimed as "proceeds" of inventory:** [§391] If the purchaser of chattel paper gives *new value* for it and *takes possession* in the ordinary course of business, the purchaser has a priority over another security interest in the chattel paper that is claimed merely as *proceeds of inventory* subject to a security interest. This is true even though the purchaser of the chattel paper *knows* that the paper being bought is subject to the security interest. [U.C.C. §9-308(b)]

    1)   **Example:** Dealer borrowed money from Bank to finance the purchase of a stock of new cars and gave Bank a security interest in the new cars, which Bank perfected. Dealer then sold a

car to Buyer for cash and chattel paper. Dealer then sold the chattel paper to Discount. Bank had no security interest in the car because Buyer purchased in the ordinary course of business. [U.C.C. §9-307(1)] Bank's security interest in the chattel paper was subordinate to Discount's, because Discount took the chattel paper in the ordinary course of business and gave new value. [Associates Discount Corp. v. Old Freeport Bank, 220 A.2d 621 (Pa. 1966)]

2) **Example:** Financer had a security interest in Dealer's inventory. Dealer was short of cash and sold the chattel paper on 12 recently sold cars to an out-of-town Bank with which Dealer had never done business. Dealer had always carried his own chattel paper previously, so the sale was not in the ordinary course of his business. However, the Bank would still have had priority against Financer, because the Bank took in the ordinary course of *its* business.

(b) **Where chattel paper subject to security interest other than as inventory "proceeds":** [§392]   If the chattel paper is subject to a security interest perfected other than as the proceeds of inventory, a stricter rule is applied. To take priority in this case, the purchaser of chattel paper must not only give new value and take possession in the ordinary course of business, but must also take *without knowledge* of the existing security interest. [U.C.C. §9-308(a)]

1) **Example:** A advances Dealer funds against Dealer's conditional sales contracts, which are assigned to A to secure repayment. However, the contracts themselves are left in Dealer's possession. Dealer then dishonestly obtains new financing from B and transfers possession of the contracts to B. B prevails against A as long as B paid value and took in the ordinary course of business without knowledge of A's interest.

2) **Notice:** [§393]   A secured party claiming an interest in chattel paper other than as a mere claim to proceeds can get protection and still allow the debtor to retain possession of the paper by stamping or marking the paper with a *notice* of the assignment (*e.g.,* "This account has been assigned to XYZ"). This would put any prospective buyer on notice of the prior interest in the paper.

(c) **Effect:** [§394]   The effect of these two sections is to leave open the possibility that a dealer can simultaneously use two sources of collateral financing for the inventory and the chattel paper created by the sale of the inventory. An inventory financer wanting to be protected against the claims of purchasers of the chattel paper must have a claim based on more than the mere "proceeds" of the inventory. One way to do this would be to take a broader security interest in *both* inventory and chattel paper. The secured party could then either take possession of the chattel paper *or* merely mark it with notice of the security interest and be fully protected.

d. **Cash proceeds in insolvency proceedings:** [§395]   In addition to whatever rights to trace assets may be recognized in insolvency proceedings generally (*e.g.,* a creditor's right to trace assets conveyed in fraud), the Code stipulates that in the event of the debtor's insolvency, the secured party has certain rights with respect to the proceeds obtained by the debtor from any disposition of the collateral:

(1) **Secured party's rights:** [§396]   If insolvency proceedings (*e.g.,* bankruptcy) are instituted by or against a debtor, a secured party with a perfected security interest in "proceeds" has a perfected security interest in:

(i) *Identifiable noncash proceeds,* including *separate deposit accounts* containing only such proceeds;

(ii) *Identifiable cash proceeds in the form of money* if the proceeds have not been commingled with other money deposited prior to the insolvency proceedings;

(iii) *Identifiable cash proceeds in the form of checks* and similar items that have not been deposited prior to the insolvency proceedings; and

(iv) *All cash and bank accounts* of the debtor in which proceeds have been *commingled* with other funds, but subject to any right of set-off (below), and (to take priority in this case) limited to the amount of cash proceeds *received by the debtor during the 10 days* before insolvency proceedings and to which the secured party was entitled but was not paid.

[U.C.C. §9-306(4)]

(a) **Example:** Creditor had a perfected security interest in all of the debtor's inventory. In the 10 days before the debtor filed a bankruptcy petition, the debtor sold inventory and received $40,000. Of this amount, the debtor paid $5,000 into a new bank account containing no other funds, and commingled the remaining $35,000 with funds in a bank account containing $6,000 of nonproceeds. Creditor gets $35,000 ($40,000 less the $5,000 already paid to Creditor: $5,000 comes from the noncommingled account [*see* U.C.C. §9-306(4)(a)], and $30,000 from the commingled bank account [*see* U.C.C. §9-306(4)(d)].

(2) **Right of set-off:** [§397]   The right of set-off, which limits the ability of the secured party to trace proceeds commingled in a bank account, does not create any new rights for banks. They can set-off only if they had such a right under previous law. [U.C.C. §9-306(4)(d)]

(3) **Bankruptcy problem:** [§398]   The U.C.C. rule on tracing commingled funds may conflict with the anti-priority provisions of the Federal Bankruptcy Code. Section 545 of the Bankruptcy Code invalidates every "statutory lien" that first becomes effective upon the insolvency of the debtor. Whether U.C.C. section 9-306(4)(d), which creates rights arising only on insolvency, is or is not an invalid "statutory lien" has not been definitely decided.

(a) **Note:** Similar language under the former Uniform Trust Receipts Act was sustained to protect the secured party's interest against the claim of a trustee in bankruptcy. [*In re* Crosstown Motors, Inc., 272 F.2d 224 (7th Cir. 1959)]

(b) **Compare:** Other courts, however, have been hostile to state laws that attempt to give secured creditors a general lien on the insolvent's assets. [Elliot v. Bumb, 356 F.2d 749 (9th Cir. 1966)]

(c) **Comment:** If section 9-306(4)(d) does survive attack, it will be because it establishes only a *tracing* rule and does not give the secured party an interest as such in assets not traceable to proceeds of the sale of the collateral. [*In re* Dexter Buick-GMC Truck Co., 28 U.C.C. Rep. 243 (D.R.I. 1980)]

e. **Returned goods**

(1) **Background:** [§399] Under the rule of *Benedict v. Ratner* (*supra,* §369), whether a secured party could claim any interest in goods that had been sold by the debtor but then had been returned to the debtor for any reason might depend on whether the debtor was required to segregate the returned goods. If the secured party failed to require the debtor to do this, the entire security agreement was sometimes held invalid as against the debtor's trustee in bankruptcy.

(2) **Rule:** [§400] Under the Code, the original security interest in the goods continues (re-attaches) in returned goods. This is true regardless of the reason for their return (voluntary, involuntary, or under seller's repossessing) and whether the claim is asserted against the debtor or the debtor's trustee in bankruptcy. [U.C.C. §9-306(5)(a)]

(a) **Note:** If the original security interest was perfected by a filing that is still effective, nothing further is required to continue the perfection. Otherwise, however, the secured party must take possession of the returned or repossessed goods or must file in order to perfect.

(3) **Rights of third parties:** [§401] Where the sale of the goods has created chattel paper or an account receivable, the purchaser of the chattel paper or account has a security interest in the returned goods—which is good against the debtor (retailer) who sold the chattel paper or account. [U.C.C §9-306(5)(b), (c)]

(a) **Perfection required:** [§402] However, the security interest in returned goods must be *perfected* for protection against creditors of the transferor, as well as purchasers of the returned or repossessed goods. Perfection of the original security interest in the chattel paper or account does *not* carry over automatically to the returned goods, as it does where the secured party originally financed the inventory (above). [U.C.C. §9-306(5)(d)] Rather, the chattel paper or account financer must take steps to get perfection as to the returned goods by filing or by taking possession of them.

(b) **Example:** Dealer sells an automobile to Buyer and transfers the chattel paper to Bank (which had not previously financed the car as inventory). Thereafter, Buyer rightfully rescinds the sale for breach of warranty, and Dealer takes the car back. Bank has a security interest in the car good against Dealer. However, Bank must file a financing statement or possess the car to be perfected against later creditors of Dealer.

1) **Note:** Of course, Bank cannot perfect its security interest against another buyer in the ordinary course of business, so Dealer could still resell the car and an innocent purchaser would prevail against Bank. [U.C.C. §9-307(1); Osborn v. First National Bank, 472 P.2d 440 (Okla. 1970)]

(4) **Conflicting secured interests**

(a) **Inventory financer vs. chattel paper purchaser:** [§403] If a dealer has financing arrangements with two separate parties—a secured party financing inventory and a purchaser of the chattel paper created by sale of the inventory—both may claim a security interest in the returned goods: the inventory financer under subsection 9-306(5)(a) and the purchaser of the chattel paper under subsection 9-306(5)(b). The conflicting claims are resolved under the rules of section 9-308 (*supra*, §391); *i.e.*, the security interest of the purchaser of **chattel paper** has priority over that of the inventory financer if the purchaser of the chattel paper gave value for the paper and took it in the ordinary course of business. [U.C.C. §9-306(5)(b)]

(b) **Inventory financer vs. account assignee:** [§404] A similar conflict may develop between an inventory financer and the assignee of an **account** created upon the sale of goods that are returned. However, in this case, the interest of the account transferee is **subordinate** to that of the inventory financer. [U.C.C. §9-306(5)(c)]

1) **Compare:** If the inventory security interest was **unperfected**, then the security interest of the account transferee would be entitled to priority if it is perfected or filed first under the rule of U.C.C section 9-312(5) (*supra*, §327).

F. PRIORITY AMONG PERFECTED CREDITORS—AS AFFECTED BY TERMS OF SECURITY AGREEMENT

1. **Future Advances:** [§405] Under section 9-204(3) of the Code, a security agreement can create security interests in the collateral covering not only the current loan but also future loans by the same creditor. In this case, a new security agreement is not needed when the future loan is made. The filed financing statement will then perfect the security interest both as originally made **and as expanded** by later advances to the debtor, thereby continuing the original priority. [U.C.C. §9-312(7)]

a. **Example:** Creditor A loans Debtor $10,000 and takes a security interest in Debtor's machinery. The security agreement provides that the machinery is to be collateral not only for this loan but also for any future loans made by A to Debtor. A files a financing statement on January 1. On February 1, Debtor borrows money from Creditor B, who takes a security interest in the same machinery and files a financing statement. On March 1, Creditor A makes another loan to Debtor under the original security agreement. A's security interest in the machinery for the March 1 loan is covered by the original financing statement and so is perfected when the loan is made. Thus, A has priority over B as to both the January and March advances because A filed first.

b. **Compare—advances under later security agreements:** [§406] Sometimes the original security agreement *fails to cover future loans* to the debtor, and the question may arise whether the secured party's priority extends to loans made under *later* security agreements where there are other intervening security interests involved.

  (1) **General rule:** [§407] As long as a secured party had priority over later creditors by *filing or possession*, that party will also prevail as to advances pursuant to a *later* security agreement. This is true even where other Article 9 creditors perfected their security interest in the same collateral *between* the advances. [U.C.C. §9-312(7)]

    (a) **Example:** Sporting Goods Store used its inventory as collateral for a loan of $5,000 from Bank A, which filed a financing statement on March 1, in the proper place. Store repaid this debt in full on September 1. On September 10, Store borrowed $3,000 from Bank B, which also took a security interest in the inventory and filed a financing statement in the proper place. On October 1, Store again borrowed $5,000 from Bank A pursuant to a new security agreement, and again the inventory was used as collateral. As long as Bank A's *original* financing statement is *still on file* (*i.e.,* no termination statement was filed when Store paid off the first loan), Bank A *still* has priority over Bank B—even though its loan was second in time—because Bank A was the first to file.

  (2) **Compare—1962 version of Code:** [§408] Under the 1962 version of Article 9, the result in the last example was debatable. Some courts held that when the first loan was paid off, the financing statement was "spent" and could not serve to continue the priority of future advances made pursuant to later security agreements. [Coin-O-Matic Service Co. v. Rhode Island Hospital Trust, 3 U.C.C. Rep. 1112 (D.R.I. 1966)]

  (3) **Rationale for priority under revised Code:** [§409] By promulgating section 9-312(7), *supra,* the drafters of the 1972 revised Article 9 meant to reject the *Coin-O-Matic* result. The second creditor (Bank B in the above example) has little to complain about: It should have known of Bank A's *superior position* since Bank A's financing statement was still on file when it made its loan; the purpose of a financing statement is to give other creditors *notice* that the secured party claims some interest in the named collateral. (Specific information about the *details* of the underlying agreement—*e.g.,* amount of loan, payment schedule, after-acquired property, etc.—are found in the *security agreement*, which a later creditor can find out about through the debtor.)

    (a) **And note:** The second creditor can always protect itself against future advances by the first creditor to the common debtor, either by insisting that the first creditor's financing statement be removed from the files (a "termination statement"; *see supra,* §292) or by obtaining a *subordination* agreement from the first creditor (*see supra,* §99).

(4) **Limitation—filing or possession required:** [§410]   The first creditor prevails only where its later advance of funds was made while the original security interest was perfected by *filing or possession*. If its interest was perfected in any other way (*e.g.,* "temporary perfection" under section 9-304, *see supra,* §200), the later advance would be junior to a perfected interest arising beforehand. [*See* U.C.C. §9-312, Comment 7]

2. **Dragnet Clauses:** [§411]   A security agreement sometimes provides that the collateral will be security not only for repayment of this loan but also for *any other debts* owed by the debtor to the creditor now or in the future. Such a provision is called a "dragnet clause."

   a. **Validity:** [§412]   Although section 9-204 would appear to authorize dragnet clauses, the courts have refused to enforce them where the other debt is completely *unrelated* to the original transaction so that the parties probably did not intend it to be covered by the dragnet clause. [Kimbell Foods, Inc. v. Republic National Bank, 401 F. Supp. 316 (N.D. Tex. 1975)]

      (1) **Example:** To finance new purchases of cattle for his herd, Farmer borrowed $10,000 from Farmers Friend Bank, giving Bank a perfected security interest in his livestock. The parties signed a security agreement containing a dragnet clause. Six months later, Farmer failed to pay a bill for $300 worth of Christmas presents he had purchased using the credit card Farmers Friend Bank had issued him years before. Bank repossessed his cattle. Most courts would hold Bank guilty of conversion since the *probable intention* of the parties was to have the dragnet clause operate only to secure transactions of the *same class* as the first transaction (*i.e.,* livestock loans).

   b. **Consumer laws:** [§413]   A number of states have enacted special consumer protection statutes designed to prohibit or regulate dragnet clauses and other "cross-collateralization" clauses in consumer transactions. [*See, e.g.,* Uniform Consumer Credit Code §3.303 (1974 version)]

3. **Consent Clauses and Waiver of Security Interests:** [§414]   Security agreements often provide that the debtor may not sell the collateral without the written consent of the secured party. Just as frequently, the debtor continues to sell the collateral on a regular basis anyway. If the secured party finds out about the sales but says nothing and the debtor later defaults on the loan, the question arises as to whether the secured party may follow the collateral into the hands of the debtor's buyer and repossess it; or whether the silence of the secured party constitutes a waiver of the security interest.

   a. **Finding of waiver:** [§415]   Many courts have followed the common law doctrine of waiver (typically defined as "voluntary relinquishment of a known right") and have held that the failure of the secured party to enforce the terms of the security agreement results in a *waiver* of the security interest. [Clovis National Bank v. Thomas, 425 P.2d 726 (N.M. 1967)]

(1) **Statutory basis for waiver:** [§416]   This result has been held supported by U.C.C. section 9-306(2), which states that a security interest continues in collateral notwithstanding the debtor's sale, unless the sale was authorized by the secured party in the security agreement *"or otherwise"*—these last two words being read to include *waiver*.

(2) **Example:** Bank held a perfected security interest in Farmer's cattle. The security agreement provided that the cattle could not be sold by Farmer without the bank's written consent (which it never gave). Nonetheless, over a period of years, Farmer frequently sold the cattle to a meat packing plant, remitting the proceeds of the sales to Bank. Bank knew of all the sales. When Farmer missed three debt repayments in a row, Bank brought a conversion action against the meat packing plant. In jurisdictions following *Clovis,* Bank would probably be held to have waived its security interest in the cattle, and the meat packing plant would win.

b. **No waiver—"course of dealing" theory:** [§417]   Some jurisdictions refuse to find waiver in the above situation, on grounds that by the time the bank learns of the sales, its only recourse is in the proceeds of sale anyway. Therefore, by allowing the security interest to continue in the collateral, such interest also attaches to proceeds of the sale which the creditor can then claim to satisfy the debt. [*See, e.g.,* Wabasso State Bank v. Caldwell Packing Co., 251 N.W.2d 321 (Minn. 1976)]

(1) **Statutory support?** [§418]   Courts following this approach purport to base their finding of no waiver on the language of section 1-205(4) of the Code, which provides that a "course of dealing" between the parties (*i.e.,* the creditor's unspoken acquiescence in the debtor's sales) cannot change the express terms of the security agreement.

(a) **Criticism:** This is an unsound theory. The language of section 1-205 refers to a "course of dealing" occurring *prior* to the agreement. Further, this approach ignores the basic rule of contract law that written conditions in an agreement can be waived by conduct of the parties (*see* Contracts Summary). [*See* U.C.C. §2-208(3)]

c. **"Conditional consent" theory:** [§419]   Finally, some jurisdictions have developed a "conditional consent" test whereby the alleged "waiver" is ineffective to destroy the creditor's security interest if the debtor failed to comply with the implied *condition* in the security agreement that the proceeds of the sale be used to repay the debt to the creditor. If the proceeds are so used, the security interest is waived; if not, the creditor has the option of repossessing the collateral from the buyer or suing the buyer in conversion. [*See* Baker Products Credit Association v. Long Creek Meat Co., 513 P.2d 1129 (Or. 1973)]

G. PRIORITY AMONG ARTICLE 9 PERFECTED CREDITORS AND OTHER CLAIMANTS

1. **Buyers of the Collateral:** [§420]   As discussed earlier (*supra,* §324), a buyer of collateral that is subject to an *unperfected* security interest almost always acquires

the property free of the creditor's right to reclaim it. The discussion below examines the ability of a buyer to purchase the property free of *perfected* security interests.

a. **Buyers in the ordinary course of business:** [§421] A buyer who purchases goods in the *ordinary course of business* from a dealer's *inventory* takes free of perfected security interests held by the dealer's creditors in the inventory. This is true even though the buyer *knows* that the inventory is covered by a security interest, as long as the buyer does not know that the sale is in violation of the terms of the security agreement. [U.C.C. §9-307(1)]

   (1) **Rationale:** The dealer's creditor takes a "floating lien" over the inventory. All parties to the transaction (dealer, creditor, and consumer) *expect* that the particular item sold will be freed from the inventory lien.

   (2) **Example:** Consumer buys a watch from Jeweler knowing that Jeweler's inventory is subject to a perfected security interest in favor of Bank. At the moment of sale, the Bank's security interest *detaches* from the particular watch sold and is transferred to the "proceeds" of the sale (*i.e.,* the money paid by the consumer to the jeweler), and Consumer takes free of the security interest. [U.C.C. §9-306]

      (a) **And note:** The result is the same even if the security agreement between the jeweler and the bank stated that the jeweler was forbidden to sell this particular watch, unless Consumer knew of this particular limitation in the security agreement (most unlikely). [U.C.C. §9-307, Comment 2]

   (3) **Special rules for farm products:** [§422] Under the official version of U.C.C. section 9-307(1), a buyer of farm products from a farmer does *not* take free of existing perfected security interests in the farm products held by the farmer's creditors. *Rationale:* Farmers have so much trouble getting financing that lenders willing to extend credit to farmers are given extra protection. However, this rule proved unpopular with the states, many of which amended the statute to permit buyers of farm products to take free of perfected security interests in certain circumstances. This has all become moot, however, since the federal government now has a special statute on point.

      (a) **Federal statute:** [§423] Under section 1324 of the Food Security Act of 1985 [7 U.S.C. §163], farmers are required to furnish their creditors with a list of buyers of their products. The secured parties then send a notice to these buyers telling them how payment should be made. A buyer who complies with these instructions takes free of the perfected security interest. The Act also encourages the states to set up a central filing system for registry of all the restrictions imposed on selling farmers by their creditors, so that compliance with the central registry restrictions would also protect the buyers of the farm products. Farmers who fail to inform their creditors of the identities of the potential buyers of the farm products are subject to a fine of at least $5,000. [*See* 9 C.F.R. 10795—U.S.D.A. regulations on point]

(b) **Example:** Farmer gave a perfected security interest in his crop to Big Bank and also gave Big Bank a list of buyers to whom Farmer planned to sell his crop. Big Bank sent a letter to all the creditors on the list, telling them that payments for the crop should be made by checks payable to both Farmer *and* Big Bank. Betty Buyer received one of these letters and when she bought part of Farmer's crop, she dutifully made out the check as directed. Paul Purchaser was not on the list, and even though he knew about Big Bank's security interest in the crop, when he bought part of Farmer's crop he paid cash directly to Farmer. Both buyers take free of Big Bank's security interest, Betty because she followed instructions and Paul because he received none. Big Bank's rights are against Farmer alone.

(4) **Buyer must be "in the ordinary course of business":** [§424] The rule of section 9-307(1), above, protects only "buyers in the ordinary course of business," and then only if the security interest in the inventory was "created by the seller." The elements qualifying a buyer for freedom from the security interest in the inventory come from sections 1-201(9) (defining "buyer in the ordinary course of business") and 9-307(1) itself. They are:

(a) **Ordinary purchase:** [§425] The buyer must buy goods out of *inventory* in the "ordinary course of business"—*i.e.*, the transaction must be "run of the mill" purchase and not an extraordinary sale.

   1) **Example:** "Bulk sales" do *not* qualify for section 9-307(1) protection. A "bulk sale" occurs when the buyer buys a "major part" of the dealer's inventory. [U.C.C. §6-102(1)]

(b) **New value:** [§426] The buyer must give *new* value and not just cancel out an old indebtedness. [Chrysler Credit Corp. v. Malone, 502 S.W.2d 910 (Tex. 1973)—holding insurance salesperson's purchase of car from dealer subject to prior security interest because payment for car was cancellation of old insurance debt dealer owed him]

(c) **No knowledge:** [§427] The buyer must buy in *good faith* and not know that the sale is in violation of the terms of a security agreement between the seller and the seller's creditor. [International Harvester Co. v. Glendenning, 505 S.W.2d 320 (Tex. 1974)—no protection to buyer of tractor who went along with dealer's lie to dealer's creditor that buyer had traded in an old tractor as partial payment]

(d) **Interest created by seller:** [§428] Finally, the security interest in the item sold must have been *created by the seller.*

   1) **Example:** Bank had a perfected purchase money security interest in Sailor's yacht. Sailor sold the yacht to Used Boats, Inc., which resold it to Consumer. Consumer does *not* take the yacht free from Bank's security interest because it was not created by Consumer's "seller" (Used Boats, Inc.). [Security Pacific National Bank v. Goodman, 24 Cal. App. 3d 131 (1972)]

2) **Rationale:** If a creditor takes a security interest in inventory, it expects the collateral to be sold and can police the disposition of the proceeds. However, where the debtor sells the collateral to someone who puts it into inventory, as in the last example, the creditor will not know that this has happened and ought not to lose its interest in the collateral simply because the collateral was sold to an innocent buyer. The issue arises most often in the sale of used goods. The disappointed buyer gets relief by suing the used-goods seller for breach of the warranty of good title. [U.C.C. §2-312; *and see* Sales Summary]

(5) **Compare—other collateral:** [§429] Note that a security interest in goods *other than inventory* continues in the collateral even in the hands of a good faith buyer for value. [U.C.C. §9-306(2)]

(a) **Example:** Bank held a perfected security interest in all the *equipment* in Jack's Bar. One night, Jack sold the painting hanging over the bar to a patron. Bank's security interest remains attached to the painting, and if Jack defaults on his loan to the bank, the painting can be repossessed from the patron's home. [I.T.T. Industrial Credit Co. v. H. & K. Machine Service, 33 U.C.C. Rep. 400 (E.D. Mo. 1981)]

b. **Buyers not in the ordinary course of business—future advances:** [§430] If a buyer does *not* qualify for protection against prior security interests under section 9-307, the question arises as to what extent the buyer is subject to expansion of the prior security interest due to future advances.

(1) **Forty-five day rule:** [§431] The U.C.C. provides that a buyer *not* in the ordinary course of business (*e.g.,* a purchaser of non-inventory) takes *free of increases* in the security interest due to future advances, *unless* the advances are made by the creditor in the *45 days* following the sale and are made either *without knowledge* of the sale or "pursuant to a commitment" that was entered into without such knowledge. [U.C.C. §9-307(3)]

(a) **"Pursuant to commitment" defined:** [§432] "Pursuant to a commitment" means an agreement by the secured party to loan money to the debtor in the future. A loan remains "pursuant to a commitment" even if there is an escape clause in the agreement (*e.g.,* "no loan shall be made if the debtor cannot produce financial records demonstrating solvency"), unless the condition excusing the loan promise is completely at the whim of the secured party. [U.C.C. §9-105(1)(k)]

(b) **Example:** On September 30, Lawyer Jones sold a grandfather clock that had been sitting in his office for years to a client who much admired it. He failed to mention to her that all his equipment (worth $50,000) was covered by a perfected security interest in favor of Lawyers Finance Co. ("LFC"), which had loaned Jones $25,000. On October 10, LFC loaned Jones an additional $25,000 (a future advance), which was also collateralized by the office equipment. If LFC had no knowledge of the clock sale at the time of the second loan, *or* if it had such knowledge, but prior to learning of the sale, it had made a commitment to Lawyer Jones to make the second loan, the client would hold the clock subject to LFC's expanded security interest since the sale was within the 45-day period.

(2) **California version:** [§433]   California's version of section 9-307(3) omits the 45-day requirement, making the effect of the future advance depend solely on the creditor's lack of *knowledge* of the sale at the time of the advance or the commitment to make the advance.

c. **Buyers of consumer goods from other consumers:** [§434]   U.C.C. section 9-307(2) provides that a consumer buying consumer goods from another consumer for value takes free of a perfected security interest in the goods unless the buying consumer *knows* of the security interest, or a financing statement covering the goods has been *filed.* Since purchase money security interests in consumer goods are automatically perfected without filing (*see supra*, §181), it would be a rare case in which a filing would exist.

(1) **Example:** Department Store sold Alice a refrigerator on credit, keeping a purchase money security interest therein. Three months later, Alice sold the refrigerator to her next door neighbor Betty. Betty gets the refrigerator free of Department Store's security interest unless she knows of the interest, or unless Store had taken the unusual step of filing a financing statement. [*See* U.C.C. §9-307, Comment 3—suggesting that for motor vehicles, notation on certificate of title is equivalent of filing; *see supra*, §241]

(2) **California:** [§435]   Note that section 9-307(2) was *not* adopted in California.

d. **Buyers of quasi-tangible collateral:** [§436]   Under other Articles of the U.C.C., certain buyers of quasi-tangible paper collateral (instruments, documents, and chattel paper) are given the freedom to purchase such property free of the claims of others—including perfected Article 9 security interests in the paper. [U.C.C. §9-309]

(1) **The protected buyers:** [§437]   The protected buyers are *"holders in due course"* of negotiable instruments [*see* U.C.C. §3-302, *and see* Commercial Paper Summary]; "holders to whom a negotiable *document of title* has been duly negotiated" [U.C.C. §§7-501, 7-505; *and see* Sales Summary]; and "bona fide purchasers" of *investment securities* (*i.e.,* stocks and bonds that, for Article 9 purposes, qualify as "instruments") [U.C.C. §8-302].

(a) **Example:** Karate School pledged all the promissory notes its students had signed to Merchant Finance. When one of the notes fell due, Karate School asked for it back from Merchant Finance so the school could present it to the maker for payment. Merchant Finance released the note to the school, relying on its temporary 21-day period of perfection without possession. [U.C.C. §9-304(5); *see supra*, §206] Instead of presenting the promissory note to the maker, Karate School sold it. If the purchaser qualifies as a holder in due course, it takes the note free of Merchant Finance's security interest.

(2) **Buyers of chattel paper:** [§438]   Where a purchaser of chattel paper (or a buyer of an instrument who for some reason does not qualify as a holder in due course) gives **new value** and takes possession of the collateral in the **ordinary course of business**, the purchaser takes free of a security interest the purchaser does **not know about** at the time of purchase **if** the security interest is only temporarily perfected under U.C.C. section 9-304 or 9-306. (*See supra,* §200.)

(a) **Proceeds—knowledge irrelevant:** [§439]   Further, if the chattel paper or instrument was **not** the original collateral but is claimed merely as proceeds of a sale out of inventory, the purchaser prevails even if the purchaser knows of the prior inventory security interest. [U.C.C. §9-308]

2. **Statutory Lien Holders:** [§440]   Article 9, for the most part, excludes coverage of "statutory" liens (such as tax liens, mechanics liens, etc.). [U.C.C. §9-104(b), (c); *see supra,* §314] However, priority between Article 9 perfected security interests and **possessory** statutory liens (*i.e.,* those arising when the statutory lien holder gets and maintains possession of the collateral) is regulated by Article 9. [U.C.C. §9-310]

a. **Only possessory liens covered:** [§441]   The priority rule of section 9-310 applies only to **possessory** statutory liens. When a statute creates a statutory lien that does **not** require the lien claimant to maintain possession of the collateral to keep the lien, the priority between the nonpossessory statutory lien and an Article 9 security interest is governed by non-U.C.C. law. [Leger Mill Co. v. Kleen-Leen, Inc., 563 P.2d 132 (Okla. 1977)]

(1) **Repeal of nonpossessory lien statutes:** [§442]   Some states have even held that the enactment of section 9-310 impliedly repealed state statutes granting **nonpossessory** statutory liens to people, landlords, etc. [*See, e.g.,* Balzer Machinery Co. v. Klineline Sand & Gravel Co., 533 P.2d 321 (Or. 1975)]

b. **General rule of priority:** [§443]   Under section 9-310, a person who acquires (under separate state law) a lien on goods in that person's possession as a result of materials or services furnished (*e.g.,* repairing a car) prevails over a prior perfected security interest in the goods.

(1) **Example:** Consumer financed the purchase of a car through Consumers Credit Union, which held a perfected purchase money security interest therein. The car broke down, and Consumer took it to Al's Repair Shop. Consumer failed to pay the repair bill, leaving the car at Al's. Consumer then missed two payments to the credit union, which tried to repossess the car. As long as Al's Repair Shop maintains possession of the car, its artisan's lien has priority over the credit union's interest.

(2) **Liens covered:** [§444]   This is true whether the "statutory" lien arises from a statute or the common law (which gave "artisans" a lien for their labors). [National Bank v. Bergeron Cadillac, Inc., 361 N.E.2d 1116 (Ill. 1977)]

(3) **Consent irrelevant:** [§445]   It is also true even if the Article 9 secured creditor did not *consent* to the repair work giving rise to the statutory lien. [General Motors Acceptance Corp. v. Colwell Diesel Service & Garage, 302 A.2d 595 (Me. 1973)]

c.   **Exception—statutory priority:** [§446]   The only exception to the general rule of priority is where the statute creating the lien *expressly* makes the statutory lien junior to prior security interests. [U.C.C. §9-310]

d.   **Compare—consensual liens:** [§447]   In addition to the statutory lien that arises by operation of law, the lienholder sometimes makes the debtor sign an agreement giving the lienholder a *nonpossessory* consensual lien on the debtor's collateral. This agreement *is* an Article 9 security agreement and should be perfected under the Article 9 procedures to be valid against other creditors. However, even if the lienholder fails to perfect, the *statutory lien* may still be available if the lienholder has possession of the collateral.

(1) **Example:** Suppose that when Consumer in the above example took his car in for repair, Al's Repair Shop made him sign a security agreement giving Al's a security interest in the car. A state statute provides that consensual liens are invalid unless noted on the certificate of title; thus, Al's security interest is unperfected. Nonetheless, Al's may still have the benefit of the state's statutory artisan's lien if Al's maintains possession of the car. [*See, e.g.,* Bank of North America v. Kruger, 551 S.W.2d 63 (Tex. 1977)]

3. Federal Tax Lien

a.   **In general:** [§448]   When a taxpayer fails to pay federal taxes, the Internal Revenue Service ("I.R.S.") has the benefit of a federal statute creating a tax lien on *all* of the taxpayer's property, real and personal, now owned or after-acquired, exempt or nonexempt (*i.e., everything the taxpayer owns or hopes to own*). [26 U.S.C. §§6321-6323]

(1) **Creation of lien:** [§449]   The federal tax lien ("FTL") arises at the moment of "assessment"—*i.e.,* the I.R.S.'s determination that the tax is owed, as manifested by a notation of tax liability on a list in the I.R.S.'s district director's office. If the taxpayer does not pay the taxes due, the government will sell the property subject to the lien and pay the taxes from the proceeds.

b.   **Priorities:** [§450]   The FTL is valid against the taxpayer and most other parties at the moment of assessment, even though only the I.R.S. knows about it (*i.e.,* the FTL is a "secret" lien). However, its validity against Article 9 security interests depends on whether such interests are *perfected* before notice of the lien is *filed* in the state. [26 U.S.C. §6323(a); Sams v. New Kensington City Redevelopment Authority, 261 A.2d 566 (Pa. 1970)] The Federal Tax Lien Act ("FTLA") provides that an FTL does *not* prevail over a "security interest" until the FTL is filed. "Security interest" is defined in such a way that only *perfected* Article 9 security interests qualify. [26 U.S.C. §6323(a), (h)(1); Aetna Insurance Co. v. Texas Thermal Industries, Inc., 591 F.2d 1035 (5th Cir. 1979)]

(1) **Unperfected security interests:** [§451] If an Article 9 security interest is unperfected at the time the FTL notice is filed, the federal government has priority over the unperfected creditor. [Fred Kraus & Sons, Inc. v. United States, 369 F. Supp. 1089 (N.D. Ind. 1974)]

(2) **Perfected security interests:** [§452] If an Article 9 security interest is perfected at the time the FTL notice is filed, the secured creditor has priority over the federal government.

(3) **Subsequent purchase money security interests:** [§453] Although the FTLA is silent on the point, the I.R.S. has ruled that the government lien is *subordinate* to a perfected purchase money security interest in property acquired by the taxpayer *after* the FTL filing. [Rev. Rul. 68-57, 26 C.F.R. 301.6321-1 (1968)]

(4) **Security interests in after-acquired property:** [§454] In addition, the FTLA gives limited recognition to security interests that arise automatically in after-acquired property of the debtor ("floating liens"). Such after-acquired security interests in inventory, chattel paper, instruments, and accounts, coming into existence within the *45 days* after the FTL is filed are senior to the FTL, and those arising after the 45-day period are junior to the filed tax lien.

   (a) **Example:** Shoe Store borrowed money from Bank, giving Bank a security interest in the store's inventory. Bank filed a financing statement in the proper place. One year later, on June 15, the I.R.S. filed an FTL against Shoe Store, which had not been paying its taxes. Thereafter, Store received two shipments of new shoes: one on June 20, and the other on September 25. Bank would have priority as to the inventory acquired by the June 20 shipment (within 45 days of the FTL filing), but the I.R.S. would have priority as to the second shipment (which arrived after the 45-day period had expired).

      1) **Note:** The Bank's knowledge of the tax lien filing is irrelevant to its priority as to the collateral acquired during the 45-day period. [Treas. Reg. §301.6323(c)(1), (d)]

(5) **Future advances:** [§455] Where the security agreement covers future advances as well as the original loan (*see supra,* §405), a perfected security interest takes priority over the FTL to the extent enlarged by a future advance only if the advance was made *without knowledge* of the FTL during the 45 days after the FTL filing. [26 U.S.C. §6323(d)]

   (a) **Example:** Bank loaned Smith Machine Co. $20,000, taking a security interest in all of Smith's equipment. The security agreement provided that the equipment would be collateral not only for this loan, but also for any future loans made to Smith by Bank. Bank filed a financing statement in the proper place. One year later, on May 2, the I.R.S. filed an FTL against all of Smith Machine Co.'s property. On May 10, Bank loaned Smith Machine another $20,000. Bank's security interest is superior to the FTL as to all $40,000, as long as Bank did not know of the filed FTL at the time of the second loan. (If it did, Bank's security interest is superior only as to the first $20,000.)

(b) **Other applications of forty-five day rule:** [§456] Similar "45-day" periods apply in determining priorities of future advances over buyers of the collateral [U.C.C. §9-307(3); *supra,* §405] and judicial lien creditors [U.C.C. §9-301(4), below].

4. **Judicial "Lien Creditors"**

a. **General rule of priority:** [§457] While a judicial lien creditor is senior to a security interest that is *unperfected* at the time of the lien creditor's levy (*see supra,* §322), a judicial lien creditor is junior to a *perfected* security interest in the collateral. [U.C.C. §9-301(1)(b)]

b. **Priority of future advances:** [§458] This general rule is modified somewhat where the Article 9 perfected creditor makes future advances to the debtor. In this case, the future advances retain priority if made: (i) within 45 days after the judicial lien is acquired (whether or not the Article 9 creditor knows of the lien); *or* (ii) *after* the 45 days if the creditor either has *no* knowledge of the judicial lien or the advance is made "pursuant to a commitment which was entered into without knowledge of the lien" (*supra,* §432). [U.C.C. §9-105(1)(k)]

(1) **Example:** Debtor's unsecured creditor wins a lawsuit against Debtor and sends out the sheriff, who then levies on (seizes) property subject to a *perfected* Article 9 security interest in favor of Lender. The next day, Lender loans Debtor more money, knowing of the judicial lien but relying on their security agreement stating that the collateral secures future advances as well as the original loan. The second loan (the "future advance") is superior to the judicial lien since the future advance was made within 45 days after the judicial lien was acquired.

(2) **Example:** Bank perfects a security interest in factory equipment used by Smith Machine Co. as collateral for a series of loans from Bank. The parties' security agreement provides that the collateral will also secure future advances made to Smith by Bank and obligates Bank to make loans for one year as long as Smith Machine Co. makes regular repayments of part of the loaned amounts. Pursuant to its "commitment," Bank loans Smith $5,000 on the first of every month starting on January 1. On August 1, Smith Co.'s equipment is seized by the sheriff as part of a judicial action brought against Smith Machine Co. by an unpaid supplier of raw materials. *All* of Bank's loans for the whole year (even those after August 1) are protected by its superior security interest in the equipment because these future advances were made "pursuant to a commitment entered into without knowledge of the lien." [U.C.C. §9-301(4)]

5. **Article 2 Claimants to the Collateral—Buyers and Sellers:** [§459] In addition to the security interest in a seller who "reserves title" to goods sold until the buyer pays for them (a "conditional sale"; *supra,* §14), Article 2 of the U.C.C. (the Sales Article) creates other rights in sellers and buyers of goods that can cause priority problems when those goods are also subject to Article 9 security interests.

a. **Automatic Article 2 security interest:** [§460] On the happening of certain events below), Article 2 of the U.C.C. creates possessory "security interests," or rights very much like security interests, in favor of buyers and sellers of goods.

(1) **Interests of buyers:** [§461]   Under Article 2, a buyer has the right to *reject* defective goods tendered by the seller; or, if a substantial defect is discovered only after "acceptance" of the goods, the buyer may *revoke* acceptance and demand a refund. Upon exercise of either of these rights, the buyer obtains a *possessory* security interest in the goods to secure the return of the price paid for them and other incidental damages. [U.C.C. §§2-602, 2-608, 2-711(3); *and see* Sales Summary]

(2) **Interests of seller:** [§462]   Similarly, a seller's Article 2 "security interest" arises upon exercise of the seller's right to order a carrier of goods sold to stop delivery of the goods (called "stoppage in transit"); or the right of an unpaid seller (or someone in the same position, such as a bank assigned the seller's rights) to *resell* goods the buyer will not accept and *sue* the buyer for the difference between the contract price and the resale price (plus incidental damages, such as the cost of the resale). [U.C.C. §2-706]

(3) **Perfection of Article 2 security interests:** [§463]   To perfect these Article 2 security interests, all that the Article 2 claimant must do is retain *possession* of the goods; no security agreement or filing is required.

    (a) **Rationale:** The Article 2 security interests arise by operation of law. They are not *consensual*, as are Article 9 security interests, and hence no security *agreement* is possible. Furthermore, no filing is required since (as under Article 9) possession fulfills the function of giving notice to others of the Article 2 claimant's interest.

b. **Priorities between Article 2 claimants and Article 9 creditors:** [§464]   The same goods subject to an automatic Article 2 security interest may also be subject to security interests held by Article 9 creditors. U.C.C. section 9-113 provides that security interests arising automatically under Article 2 are governed by Article 9 rules (except that rights on default are controlled by the Article 2 remedy sections). However, the U.C.C. is silent on the resolution of priority disputes between these parties.

(1) **Applicability of general rule of priority:** [§465]   An argument can be made that Article 2 "security interests" are the type of possessory statutory liens that are superior even to perfected Article 9 security interests (*see supra,* §443). However, the better view would seem to be that priority between the Articles 2 and 9 claimants should depend on the usual "first-to-file-or-perfect" rule of section 9-312(5) (*see supra,* §327). There is, however, no case law on point.

    (a) **Example:** Bank had an Article 9 security interest in all the equipment owned by Traveling Circus. The circus sold a wagon to Rube, a wagon collector, but it was defective, and Rube rejected it. Instead of returning the wagon, Rube elected to claim a security interest therein to secure return of its purchase price from Traveling Circus. Under the usual rule, Bank would have the senior interest in the wagon if Bank's Article 9 security interest was perfected prior to Rube's possession. However, if Bank waited to file a financing statement until *after* Rube gained possession, Rube would have the senior interest because he perfected first.

1) **Note:** If the bank's interest had been in "inventory" collateral, a sale of that collateral to a buyer in the ordinary course of business would have freed the collateral from the bank's security interest. [U.C.C. §9-307(1); *see supra,* §421]

(b) **Example:** Buyer ordered goods from Seller. Even before delivery, Buyer gave a security interest in the goods to Bank, which filed a financing statement in the proper place. Before delivery, Buyer repudiated the sale, and Seller resold the goods pursuant to the procedure specified in U.C.C. section 2-706 (*supra,* §462). Seller's interest in the goods would be senior to that of Bank because the goods never left Seller's possession. By the time the bank filed its financing statement and the goods were "identified" so that Buyer had rights in them (a requisite for "attachment"; *see supra,* §148), Seller's possessory rights under Article 2 already existed.

(2) **Special priority rule where buyer insolvent**

(a) **Seller's interest:** [§466]   An insolvent buyer who orders goods on *credit* commits an act regarded as common law *fraud.* Therefore, the Code gives a seller who discovers the buyer's insolvency within *10 days* following delivery of the goods in which to make a demand for their return. However, if the buyer has sent the seller a written misrepresentation of solvency within the three months before delivery, the 10-day limitation does not apply. [U.C.C. §2-702; *and see* Sales Summary]

(b) **Article 9 creditor prevails:** [§467]   However, Article 2 states that the seller's right to reclaim goods from an insolvent buyer is subject to the rights of a "good faith purchaser." Since "purchaser" is defined by the Code to include an Article 9 secured creditor, such a creditor's perfected security interest attaching to goods in the hands of the insolvent buyer is *superior* to the rights of an unpaid seller trying to reclaim the goods under section 2-702. [*In re* Samuels & Co., 510 F.2d 139 (5th Cir. 1975)]

1) **Example:** Bank held a perfected security interest in all of the inventory of Buyer's Clothing Store "now owned or after-acquired." Buyer, while insolvent, ordered new inventory from Seller, who failed to take a security interest in the merchandise it shipped to Buyer's Clothing Store. The day the goods arrived, Seller learned of Buyer's insolvency and demanded return of the goods. Because Bank qualifies as a "good faith purchaser," its interest in the goods is superior to the reclaiming seller.

2) **"Cash sales":** [§468]   Note that the same rule applies even where the buyer pays by check in a transaction that was meant

to have *no credit* involved (at common law, a "cash sale"). Thus, if the buyer's check bounces, the seller still loses to the buyer's perfected creditors. [*In re* Samuels & Co., *supra;* U.C.C. §2-403(a)]

a) **Statutory exception—livestock:** [§469]   An amendment to the Federal Packers & Stockyards Act creates an exception to this rule. If a seller of livestock to a meat packer receives a bad check in return, the seller *prevails* over the packer's creditors if the seller acts quickly after the check is dishonored. [7 U.S.C. §206]

(c) **Buyer's bankruptcy:** [§470]   Under section 546(c) of the Bankruptcy Reform Act, the buyer's trustee in bankruptcy is *subject* to the seller's written demand for return of the goods made within *20* days after their delivery (not just 10, as in U.C.C. section 2-702).

1) **Exception:** [§471]   The Bankruptcy Court may refuse to permit reclamation by the seller if it protects the seller's interest either by giving the seller a priority payment as an administrative expense or by granting the seller a lien in the property.

2) **No three-month exception:** [§472]   The Code provision on which the bankruptcy rule is based [U.C.C. §2-702] provides that the seller is not limited to the 10-day period if the buyer has made a written misrepresentation of solvency within the three months before delivery. The Bankruptcy Act has no such three-month rule; thus, the seller must always make a written demand within 20 days of delivery to prevail over the buyer's bankruptcy trustee.

VII. BANKRUPTCY PROCEEDINGS AND ARTICLE 9

chapter approach

If the debtor suffers financial death and files for bankruptcy, the Bankruptcy Code of 1978 and Article 9 of the Uniform Commercial Code combine to regulate the division of the debtor's property. The key thing to watch for is whether the creditor **perfected** a security interest. If the creditor has done all that the U.C.C. requires to perfect a security interest in the collateral, the collateral can be reclaimed from the bankruptcy estate and used to satisfy the debt. If, however, the creditor has done something wrong, the trustee in bankruptcy will be able to avoid the security interest, add the property to the bankruptcy estate free and clear of the creditor's interest, and relegate the creditor to the pool of "general" (uncollateralized) creditors, who rarely get paid anything.

Even if you find a valid security interest, it may still be subject to attack as a **fraudulent conveyance**. If there has been fraud as to any existing creditor, the trustee in bankruptcy can set aside the transfer. Similarly, the interest may be attacked as a **preference**. Look at **when** the interest was perfected (including the grace period), and whether sufficient **value** was given (remember the special rule as to purchase money security interests).

A. INTRODUCTION [§473]

The acid test of the validity of a security interest is its ability to withstand attack by a trustee in bankruptcy if the debtor goes bankrupt, because a trustee in bankruptcy can assert the rights of almost everyone who can challenge the validity of a security interest. Of course, even if the secured party's interest in the collateral withstands such attack, this is no assurance that the debt will be paid in full. The debtor may have disposed of part of the collateral elsewhere; or, even if the collateral is surrendered intact, its resale may not repay the debt, and a discharge in bankruptcy frees the debtor from further **personal** liability for the deficiency (the amount still owed).

B. BANKRUPTCY CODE PROVISIONS

1. **In General:** [§474]   Bankruptcy is a **federal** procedure for the relief of debtors. It is initiated by the filing of a voluntary or involuntary **petition** in bankruptcy in the local federal district court. Bankruptcy proceedings are tried before a bankruptcy judge. Appeal from the bankruptcy judge's decision is to the federal district court, and from there, through the usual federal appellate process.

   a. **Bankruptcy petition:** [§475]   Along with the petition, which acts as a request for a discharge from the bankrupt's debts, the debtor files schedules of assets, liabilities, and creditors. The creditors are then notified by the court of the need to file a "proof of claim."

      (1) **Timing crucial:** [§476]   The moment of filing of the bankruptcy petition is crucial, because many key bankruptcy issues focus on the status of the parties as of that moment. In addition, control of the debtor's estate passes to the bankruptcy court at the moment of filing the petition.

b. **Receiver:** [§477]   If the debtor's property needs care and management until a trustee can qualify (*see* below), a "receiver" will be appointed. The receiver takes *temporary* custody of the debtor's property. Under the Bankruptcy Code of 1978, the receiver is called an "interim trustee."

c. **Trustee:** [§478]   At the first meeting of the debtor's creditors, the creditors elect a representative called the "trustee." Once the trustee has *qualified, title* to all of the bankrupt's property is vested in the trustee and relates back to the filing of the petition. [Bankruptcy Code §541]

d. **Distribution of debtor's assets:** [§479]   The trustee's first duty is to marshal (gather) the debtor's property, inventory it, and investigate the validity of any claims asserted by the debtor or any third party for release of the property.

(1) **Exempt property released:** [§480]   The trustee is under a duty to release promptly any asset that is exempt from creditor process under section 522 of the Bankruptcy Code (the Code allows the debtor to keep a certain amount of specified property, such as clothes, tools, household goods, etc.).

(2) **Property subject to security interest:** [§481]   Collateral subject to any kind of lien or security interest (whether Article 9 types, real property mortgages, or judicial or statutory liens) that the trustee determines was valid *as of the moment of the filing of the bankruptcy petition* is generally released by the trustee to the lien creditor. Thus, lien creditors get their property *intact*—without any charge or expense of the bankruptcy proceeding being deducted.

(3) **Remaining property sold and proceeds distributed:** [§482]   The debtor's nonexempt property that is free from valid creditor liens or interests is then sold and the proceeds applied as follows:

(a) **"Special" (priority) creditors:** [§483]   The first monies go to any "special" creditors (*i.e.*, those listed in Bankruptcy Code section 507) to cover costs of the bankruptcy proceeding, wages and retirement benefits owing to employees of the bankrupt, certain creditor expenses, and certain tax debts. These are priority debts and must be paid *in full* before any funds are paid to the "general" (unsecured) creditors.

(b) **"General" (unsecured) creditors:** [§484]   Finally, after the priority claims are fully paid, the remaining proceeds are distributed pro rata among the "general" (unsecured) creditors. Often, of course, there is little or nothing left for these creditors.

e. **Discharge:** [§485]   In return for surrendering all nonexempt property, the debtor is usually granted a discharge (a judicial forgiveness) of further personal liability for most debts. [*See* Bankruptcy Code §§523, 524]

2. **Effect of Bankruptcy on Secured Party's Rights—the Automatic Stay:** [§486]   The above discussion makes it clear why it is important for a creditor to have a secured interest in the debtor's property. Even when the secured interest is fully perfected, however, the debtor's bankruptcy may interfere with the secured

party's right to enforce the security interest according to the terms of the contract. The reason is that once a petition in bankruptcy has been filed and the property of the debtor passes into the possession and control of the trustee, a secured creditor *must seek permission* of the court or the trustee to enforce any rights. The filing of the bankruptcy petition creates an *automatic stay* against any creditor collection activity, violation of which leads to contempt of court and damages under Bankruptcy Code section 362.

3. **Trustee's Powers:** [§487]   The trustee in bankruptcy not only succeeds to all of the debtor's rights and interests, but in addition is given various statutory powers under the Bankruptcy Code that enable the trustee to invalidate security interests that would be completely secure outside of bankruptcy.

   a. **All rights and powers of debtor:** [§488]   Upon appointment, the trustee is vested by operation of law with the full *title* the debtor had in the property at the time the petition was filed, *including all rights of action* the debtor had. The trustee also has the benefit of all *defenses* available to the debtor as against third persons. [Bankruptcy Code §541]

      (1) **Example:** The trustee in effect "steps into the shoes" of the debtor. If the debtor could have asserted a right to have a security interest set aside—*e.g.*, for violation of the Statute of Frauds—the trustee may also assert its invalidity.

   b. **Power to set aside fraudulent interests:** [§489]   The trustee can also assert the invalidity of any security interest that is fraudulent as against *any* existing unsecured creditor, or that is otherwise voidable by any creditor under any federal or state law. [Bankruptcy Code §544(b)]

      (1) **"Creditor" defined:** [§490]   The "creditor" must be an actual unsecured creditor with a claim provable under the Bankruptcy Code; hypothetical creditors are ignored. [*But see* Bankruptcy Code §544(a)—discussed below]

      (2) **Effect of setting aside:** [§491]   If a security interest is subject to attack as fraudulent against *any* creditor, then the *entire* security interest is invalid and can be upset by the trustee—thereby benefiting not only the actual creditor as to whom the transaction was fraudulent, but *all creditors*. [Moore v. Bay, 284 U.S. 4 (1931)]

      (3) **"Fraud" defined:** [§492]   The concept of fraud under the Bankruptcy Code is given form by several provisions of the Code. Generally, "fraud" encompasses all transactions that limit a creditor's remedies in an *unlawful manner*.

         (a) **Uniform Fraudulent Transfer Act:** [§493]   The Uniform Fraudulent Transfer Act, in effect in many states, defines some forms of fraud. Bankruptcy Code section 548 is a short form of the Act.

         (b) **Presumption of fraud:** [§494]   Transfers of property (including creation of security interests) made by an *insolvent* for less than "fair consideration" are *presumed* fraudulent. [Bankruptcy Code §548(a)(2)]

(c) **Intent to defraud:** [§495]   In other cases, the concepts of fraud generally apply only where there is actual intent to defraud other creditors of the debtor. [Bankruptcy Code 548(a)(1)]

c. **"Strong arm clause":** [§496]   The trustee also has whatever powers that *could have been exercised* by a creditor with writ of execution returned unsatisfied, or a creditor with a lien on all property of the debtor at the moment the petition for bankruptcy was filed (whether or not such a creditor actually exists), and, for real property (other than fixtures). The trustee also has the rights of a bona fide purchaser of the property. Thus, the trustee is given the powers of real *or hypothetical* creditors. [Bankruptcy Code §544(a)]

(1) **Note:** This is known as the "strong arm clause." It gives the trustee an automatic judicial lien on all property of the debtor so that if a judicial lien creditor *could* have had priority over an Article 9 security interest as of the filing of the bankruptcy petition, the trustee has such priority on behalf of *all* the creditors filing claims. In other words, the trustee will prevail against any claims, liens, or interests that are *not fully perfected* (under applicable state law) *at the time of bankruptcy.*

(2) **Example:** Big Bank took a security interest in Sue Seller's inventory, but, due to malpractice by its attorney, failed to file its financing statement in the appropriate place. Sue filed for bankruptcy, and her trustee in bankruptcy seized and sold the inventory. Under the strong arm clause, the trustee gets whatever rights a levying judicial lien creditor would have, and since such a creditor's levy would cut off unperfected security interests under U.C.C. section 9-301, the trustee has the same ability to take free of Big Bank's security interest.

(3) **But note:** Sometimes even a perfected security interest may be defeated by the trustee if "perfection" occurred within the 90-day period preceding the filing of the petition (*see* "preferences," below).

4. **Preferences:** [§497]   A security interest that is neither fraudulent nor attackable by the trustee asserting the powers of real or hypothetical creditors (above) may still be vulnerable if the perfection of the security interest constitutes a preference.

a. **What constitutes a "preference":** [§498]   A "preference" is:

(i) *A transfer* of any property of the debtor (which includes the *perfection* of an unperfected security interest),

(ii) *Made to or for the benefit of a creditor,*

(iii) *On account of an antecedent debt,*

(iv) *Made by the debtor while insolvent and within 90 days before the filing* of the bankruptcy petition,

(v) *The effect* of which transfer is to allow the creditor *to obtain a greater percentage of the debt* than the creditor could otherwise have received in the bankruptcy proceeding,

(vi) And, in a consumer case only, the **aggregate value of all affected property is greater than $600**.

[Bankruptcy Code §547(b), (c)(8)]

(1) **Result of finding preference:** [§499] If a challenged transaction meets **all** of these qualifications, it is **voidable** by the trustee in bankruptcy. This means that the "preferred" creditor must repay the money to the trustee; or, where **perfection** of a security interest is held "preferential," that the security interest is simply invalid and the creditor becomes a "general" (unsecured) creditor.

   (a) **Example:** Lawyer learned that one of her former clients, Spendthrift, was planning to file a bankruptcy petition. Before filing, Spendthrift paid Lawyer $700 that he owed Lawyer for past services rendered. If Spendthrift then filed a petition within the next 90 days, Lawyer would have to give back the $700 to Spendthrift's trustee and file a proof of claim for $700 as a general creditor.

   (b) **Example:** If Spendthrift had long ago given Lawyer a security interest in his business equipment, but Lawyer had failed to take steps to perfect the interest until the 90-day period before bankruptcy, perfection within that period would be a preferential transfer of property and therefore void. Lawyer would then be an unperfected creditor whose interest is wiped out by the trustee's status as a judicial lien creditor under Bankruptcy Code section 544(a) (*supra*, §496).

(2) **Nonpreferential payments:** [§500] Payments for value and payments made to a fully secured creditor (*i.e.*, with collateral worth as much or more than the debt owed) are **not** voidable as "preferences" even if made on the eve of bankruptcy.

   (a) **Example:** Spendthrift bought $80 worth of groceries the day before filing his petition. This payment is **not** preferential because it is not "on account of an antecedent (old) debt." Rather, it was a **contemporaneous** exchange (*infra*, §506).

   (b) **Example:** Bank held a **perfected** security interest in Spendthrift's car. The amount Spendthrift owed was $1,500, and the car is now worth $3,000. On the day before Spendthrift filed his petition, he paid Bank $200 on the loan. This payment is **not** preferential because it does not diminish Spendthrift's estate. As Spendthrift pays off the debt, the bank's security interest goes down accordingly, and thus more of the car's value is available to the other general creditors.

(3) **Knowledge of insolvency:** [§501] Under the prior Bankruptcy Act, the trustee could not attack a preferential transfer unless it could be shown that the preferred creditor had reasonable cause to believe that the debtor was insolvent at the time of transfer. Except for some transfers to "insiders" (*see infra*, §507), this "knowledge of insolvency" requirement has been dropped from the new Code.

(a) **Presumption of insolvency:** [§502]   The trustee must now demonstrate only that the debtor was *insolvent at the time of the transfer*, but this task is made easier by the Code's *presumption* that the debtor was insolvent during the 90 days preceding the filing of the petition. [Bankruptcy Code §547(f)]

(b) **"Insolvency" defined:** [§503]   The term "insolvency" in a bankruptcy sense means *more debts than assets*. [Bankruptcy Code §101(26)]

(4) **Certain preferences excused:** [§504]   Even if a transfer qualifies as a preference, the trustee may not avoid it if it falls into one of the following categories:

(a) **Substantially contemporaneous exchange:** [§505]   If the parties *intended* a contemporaneous exchange or the transfer was in fact substantially contemporaneous, no preference occurs. [Bankruptcy Code §547(c)(1)]

1) **Example:** Bank loaned debtor money and *two hours* later, the debtor signed the security agreement giving the bank a security interest in the debtor's inventory. There is no preference.

(b) **Routine payments:** [§506]   Payments made in the ordinary course of the debtor's business or financial affairs (if made according to ordinary business terms) are not preferential. [Bankruptcy Code §547(c)(2)] This would exempt routine payments made to all *secured or unsecured creditors*.

1) **Example:** The day before she went bankrupt, debtor paid her monthly phone bill. This is not a preference.

(5) **Special rules for transfers to an "insider":** [§507]   Where the preferred creditor was an "insider" who received a preferential transfer in the period between *90 days and one year before the filing* of the petition, the trustee can recover the property transferred *if* the insider had reasonable cause to believe the debtor was insolvent at the time of transfer. [Bankruptcy Code §547(b)(4)(B)]

(a) **"Insider" defined:** [§508]   An "insider" is someone having a *close connection with the debtor*, such as a relative, a partner, a corporate director, or anyone in control of the debtor. [Bankruptcy Code §101(25)]

(b) **Example:** On January 10, Debtor, who owed $5,000 to Granny, his grandmother, gave her a security interest in his car (worth $2,500). On May 10, he gave her another security interest in his boat (worth $2,500). He was insolvent on both occasions and filed his bankruptcy petition on June 1. His trustee can avoid the May 10 transfer as a preference regardless of Granny's knowledge of Debtor's financial condition, but to avoid the January 10 transfer, the trustee will have to establish that Granny had at that time reasonable cause to believe her grandson was insolvent.

b. **When "transfer" complete:** [§509]   The first key word on which to focus in determining whether a voidable preference has been created is the time of "transfer." For personal property, transfer is complete *when a general creditor of the debtor could no longer have secured a superior lien* to the property by suing the debtor on the debt and levying an attachment on the collateral. For real property, the test is whether a *bona fide purchaser of the property could have obtained rights superior* to those of the secured party. [Bankruptcy Code §547(e)(1)]

(1) **Hypothetical creditor or purchaser:** [§510]   Again, there is no requirement that such a general creditor or bona fide purchaser actually exists—only that a hypothetical one *could* have achieved a higher priority within 90 days of bankruptcy.

   (a) **Note:** The lien of the hypothetical general creditor must be a judicial lien that could be obtained in *the course of proceedings on a simple contract*. It does *not* include statutory liens given preference over earlier security interests; *e.g.*, a mechanic's lien does not qualify.

(2) **Grace periods for transfers of security interests**

   (a) **Purchase money security interests:** [§511]   Where a purchase money secured creditor (*see supra,* §183) perfects within 20 days after the debtor receives possession of the property, no preference occurs even if the creditor gave value prior to the debtor's possession (so that the attachment of the security interest now protects an antecedent debt). [Bankruptcy Code §547(c)(3)]

   1) **Example:** On November 1, Bank loaned Debtor $5,000 to buy a boat, making Debtor sign a security agreement. On November 15, Debtor bought the boat, and Bank filed a proper financing statement on November 20. Even though the *transfer* takes place on November 15 (when attachment occurred because Debtor then acquired rights in the collateral) and, measured at that moment, it secures a loan made *prior in time* (and hence is a preference), since this is a purchase money transaction, no preference occurs.

   2) **Preference excused:** [§512]   Note that in the last example the transfer *is* a "preference" under the usual test. Even the "relation back" to November 15 does not help, since measured as of that date, the transfer is on account of a debt incurred on November 1. The Bankruptcy Code arbitrarily *excuses* this transaction from classification as a "preference" in order to give increased protection to purchase money creditors.

   (b) **Other ten-day grace periods:** [§513]   The Bankruptcy Code gives *all* creditors a 10-day grace period—running from the time the transfer takes effect between the parties—in which to perfect. If perfection is had in that period, the transfer then is judged as of the moment it became effective between the parties (typically the moment of attachment). [Bankruptcy Code §547(e)(2), (3)] Notice that this rule would not help in the last example (*supra,* §511) had the security interest there not been of the purchase money variety, for the reason stated *supra,* §512.

C. AFTER-ACQUIRED PROPERTY IN BANKRUPTCY

1. **Introduction:** [§514]   The major problem encountered in handling security interests in bankruptcy proceedings occurs when the security interest involves *after-acquired collateral* or a *floating lien* on the inventory or accounts receivable of the debtor. The issue arises where inventory or accounts receivable first come into existence and become covered by the perfected security interest within the 90-day period prior to bankruptcy, so that the attachment of the security interest to them is arguably "preferential."

2. **Is Transfer for Antecedent Debt?** [§515]   The Bankruptcy Code, in effect, provides that a transfer for an antecedent debt within 90 days of bankruptcy creates a preference (*see* above). On its face, this would invalidate an after-acquired property clause in a security agreement as to all collateral acquired during the 90 days preceding bankruptcy—since the debt is previously owed and the new collateral gives the secured party a stronger position.

    a. **Code provision:** [§516]   U.C.C. section 9-108 provides a special rule for the after-acquired collateral situation. Under this section, if a secured party makes an advance or incurs an obligation that is to be secured in whole or in part by after-acquired property, the security interest in the after-acquired collateral is deemed to be taken *for new value and not as security for an antecedent debt*—provided the debtor acquires rights in the collateral either (i) in the *ordinary course of the debtor's business,* or (ii) *under a contract of purchase pursuant to the security agreement* within a reasonable time after value is given by the creditor.

        (1) **Example:** The first case covers situations such as inventory financing; the second covers a case where a person borrows cash to buy property and gives the creditor a security interest in the property to be acquired.

    b. **Comment:** The bankruptcy courts have not been enthusiastic about using section 9-108 to avoid preference problems since it is a state statute that tries to dictate federal bankruptcy rules.

3. **Prior Laws:** [§517]   Under the prior Bankruptcy Act (repealed in 1979), the courts strove mightily to find that accounts receivable or inventory first coming into existence during the preferential period before the filing of the bankruptcy petition did *not* constitute a "preference"—although the courts had to concoct a number of artificial theories to save the creditor's perfected interest in this sort of collateral. [*See, e.g.,* Grain Merchants of Indiana v. Union Bank, 408 F.2d 209 (7th Cir. 1969)]

4. **Bankruptcy Code:** [§518]   Under section 547(c)(5) of the 1978 Bankruptcy Code, accounts receivable or inventory falling under a perfected creditor's floating lien are *not* preferential even though first acquired in the 90 days (one year for insiders) prior to the petition.

a. **Example:** Big Bank took a security interest in Retailer's inventory "now owned or after acquired" in return for a loan made on January 3; a proper financing statement was filed on that date reflecting the bank's floating lien on the inventory. On September 8, Retailer purchased new inventory, and since Retailer would not have "rights in the collateral" until then (*see supra,* §144), the bank's security interest could not attach until that time. On September 10, Retailer filed a petition in bankruptcy. Because of the section 547(c)(5) exemption, the September 8 "transfer" of an interest in Retailer's property to the bank is *not* a "preference."

b. **Exception—"build-up" prohibited:** [§519]   If in the 90-day period (one year for transfers to insiders), the secured party has the debtor acquire *more* inventory or accounts receivable than were present at the start of the period (or the bank's first loan if within the period), a preference occurs to the extent of the build-up if unsecured creditors are hurt thereby. [Bankruptcy Code §547(c)(5)]

   (1) **Example:** Bank had a perfected security interest in Debtor's inventory. On January 10, the inventory was worth $20,000. On April 10, when Debtor filed a bankruptcy petition, the inventory was worth $25,000. Bank has received a $5,000 preference. If the bank had loaned the debtor money for the first time on February 10, when the inventory was worth $25,000, no preference would have occurred.

VIII. DEFAULT PROCEEDINGS

chapter approach

If the debtor cannot pay the debt, the creditor must look to the collateral for at least some satisfaction. Debtors, understandably, are reluctant to surrender their property, and heated battles can ensue when the creditor attempts repossession.

This chapter looks at the rights and duties of the parties when repossession threatens. Analyze a question in this area by asking:

1. Has a *default* occurred?

2. What remedies are provided by the *security agreement*?

3. What remedies are provided by the *U.C.C.*?

    (i)   The creditor may *sell* the collateral; if so, discuss the notice requirements, the right of the secured party to bid, the debtor's right to an accounting and to the proceeds after disbursement, and whether the debtor is liable for any deficiency.

    (ii) The creditor may *retain* the collateral in *full satisfaction* of the debt, but remember the limitations as to consumer goods.

    (iii) The creditor may ignore the collateral *and sue on the debt*.

    Watch for any *breach of the peace* by the creditor in taking the property. If there has been such a breach, the creditor loses U.C.C. authorization and is in effect stealing the goods.

4. Has the debtor *redeemed*?

5. What is the effect of the secured party's *failure to comply* with the U.C.C. provisions on disposing of collateral?

A. INTRODUCTION

1. **Default:** [§520]   Regardless of how careful a secured party is in choosing credit risks, there are bound to be cases in which the debtor is unable to meet the obligation set under the security agreement and thereby defaults. Article 9 does not purport to establish what conditions constitute a default; rather, this is to be determined by the provisions of the security agreement. The Code does, however, specify certain remedies for the creditor, although the parties are free to provide other remedies if they choose. [U.C.C. §9-501]

2. **Limitation:** [§521]   Courts are showing increasing concern for protection of consumers' rights. As a result, the secured party's remedies and conduct in event of default are limited by implied standards of *good faith* and by *constitutional due process* requirements (*see* below).

B. OCCURRENCE OF DEFAULT

1. **In General:** [§522]   As noted above, the conditions or events that constitute a default are left to the parties' security agreement. Within limits, the parties are free to establish any conditions that they like. The following clauses, frequently included in such agreements, merit special attention.

2. **Acceleration Clauses:** [§523]   An acceleration clause gives the secured party the option of declaring the *entire unpaid balance* of the obligation *immediately due* upon the occurrence of some default. The Code specifically authorizes such clauses [U.C.C. §1-208], but limits the secured party's right to accelerate to cases "in which he in *good faith* believes that the *prospect of payment or performance* is impaired." Thus, the secured party is prevented from accelerating for trivial or inconsequential defaults. In any event, however, the burden is on the *debtor* to show that the secured party was not acting in good faith. [U.C.C. §1-208; Brown v. Avemco Investment Corp., 603 F.2d 1367 (9th Cir. 1979)]

3. **Insecurity Clauses:** [§524]   Security agreements often accord the secured party the right to *declare the entire obligation due "at will"* or in the event the *secured party "deems himself insecure."* Even so, the standards of *good faith* applicable generally to acceleration apply here as well; *i.e.*, the secured party can accelerate or demand more collateral only if that party in good faith believes the prospects for payment have become impaired. [U.C.C. §1-208]

   a. **Meaning of "good faith":** [§525]   Courts are split as to the standard for deciding whether the creditor exercised "good faith" in accelerating the debt or in "deeming himself insecure."

      (1) **Subjective test:** [§526]   Since "good faith" is defined in section 1-203 of the Code as meaning *"honesty in fact,"* some courts have adopted a purely *subjective* test. Under this approach, the creditor who *in fact* feels "insecure" may accelerate the debt even though no reasonable person in the creditor's position would feel insecure, and even though the creditor is proceeding on the basis of erroneous information that he has made no attempt to verify. [Van Horn v. Van De Wol, Inc., 497 P.2d 252 (Wash. 1972)—creditor who negligently relied on false rumor that debtor had been denied bank loan allowed to accelerate]

      (2) **Objective test:** [§527]   Other courts, following the common law maxim that the "law abhors a forfeiture," do not allow repossession unless the creditor has made a diligent and honest *effort to check* the grounds of insecurity, *and* a reasonable person in the same circumstances would repossess (an "objective" standard). [Black v. Peoples Bank, 437 So. 2d 26 (Miss. 1983)]

4. **Waiver of Defenses Against Assignees:** [§528]   To facilitate financing and negotiability, security agreements frequently contain provisions by which the borrower or buyer agrees to "waive," as against any assignee of the seller or lender, whatever defenses the borrower might have if the seller or lender sued directly. Indeed, where the buyer *signs both a negotiable instrument and a security agreement* as part of a single transaction, the U.C.C. *implies* a waiver of defenses against any assignee of the paper. [U.C.C. §9-206]

a. **Rationale:** This is to assure that the assignee will be able to invoke default remedies if the debtor fails to make the payments due. Otherwise, the debtor could claim there was no default because the debtor's claims against the seller offset any payments due, and the assignee would have "bought a lawsuit" instead of an enforceable security agreement.

b. **Validity of waiver:** [§529]   Except as to consumer goods (below), the Code provides that such waivers are *valid* if the assignee purchased the agreement in *good faith* and *without notice of any defenses* that the buyer or borrower might have against the assignor-seller. [U.C.C. §9-206]

    (1) **"Good faith":** [§530]   "Good faith" is construed narrowly so as to disqualify assignees who are in *collusion* with the assignor. The closer the business dealings between the assignor (*e.g.*, seller) and assignee (*e.g.*, finance company), the more likely the assignee will be denied the "good faith purchaser" status. [Unico v. Owen, 232 A.2d 405 (N.J. 1967)]

    (2) **"Real defenses" not affected:** [§531]   And note that even an otherwise valid "waiver" of defenses does not cut off so-called "real" defenses—defenses that could be raised against a holder in due course of a negotiable instrument (*e.g.*, forgery or unauthorized signatures, fraud as to nature of instrument). [U.C.C. §§9-206, 3-305; *and see* Commercial Paper Summary]

c. **Consumer goods limitation:** [§532]   The validity of waiver-of-defenses-against-assignee provisions in the sale or lease of *consumer goods* must be determined by *other* statutes or decisional laws. (U.C.C. section 9-206 expressly so provides.)

    (1) **Some states uphold:** [§533]   Some states uphold such waivers in favor of "good faith" assignees (*see* above) *provided* the assignee has first *notified* the debtor of the assignment and given a stated period of time (*e.g.*, 10 days) within which to advise of any defenses to the assigned account.

    (2) **Most states prohibit:** [§534]   Most states, such as California, prohibit such waivers altogether in the sale or lease of consumer goods. [Cal. Civ. Code §1804.2—provides that buyer can assert defenses against the seller's assignee "notwithstanding any agreement to the contrary"]

        (a) **And note:** The California statute has been read very broadly so as to permit the buyer not only to defend any action by the assignee, but also *to sue the assignee affirmatively* (for rescission and restitution of the purchase price), at least where the assignee had knowledge of the seller's fraudulent practices. [Vasques v. Superior Court, 4 Cal. 3d 800 (1971)]

    (3) **Federal statutes:** [§535]   Moreover, agreements with "waiver of defenses" clauses, or use of a negotiable note to cut off defenses are now ineffective under a Federal Trade Commission regulation: promissory notes signed after May 14, 1976, by consumers in credit sales or closely connected loans *must* contain a statement preserving the ability of the

consumer to raise defenses against later holders of the note (the assignee). [16 C.F.R. 433 (1976); *see* Commercial Paper Summary]

C. REMEDIES IN GENERAL

1. **Cumulative Remedies:** [§536]   The Code eliminates pre-Code doctrine that required a secured party to make an *election of remedies* between repossession of the goods and an action on the obligation in default. In contrast, the U.C.C. declares that the secured party's rights and remedies are cumulative. [U.C.C. §9-501(1)]

2. **Three Basic Remedies:** [§537]   The three remedies set out in the Code, each of which will be discussed in detail *infra,* §§561 *et seq.,* are:

   (i) *Sale or other disposition* of the collateral [U.C.C. §9-504];

   (ii) *Retention* of the collateral [U.C.C. §9-505]; and

   (iii) *An action for the debt* [U.C.C. §9-501(1)].

   The Code does not allow the secured party to make a profit at the expense of the debtor by compounding remedies, but the pursuit of one remedy does *not* bar pursuit of a subsequent remedy until the secured party is made whole. [Olsen v. Valley National Bank, 234 N.E.2d 547 (Ill. 1968)]

3. **Documents as Collateral:** [§538]   In the event that the collateral consists of documents of title (*e.g.,* warehouse receipt or a bill of lading), the secured party may proceed against either the documents or the underlying goods. [U.C.C. §9-501(1)]

4. **Collateral Involving Real Property Interests:** [§539]   When a security interest applies to collateral that involves both real and personal property—*e.g.,* a security interest in a factory (real property) and its inventory (personal property)—the secured party may proceed against the entire collateral under the procedures governing real property, in which case, the Code does not apply. Or, the secured party may exercise Code remedies with respect to that portion of the collateral that consists of personal property. [U.C.C. §9-501(4)]

D. RIGHT OF POSSESSION UPON DEFAULT

1. **In General:** [§540]   The Code grants the secured party the right to take possession of the collateral upon default, provided that the parties have not agreed otherwise. [U.C.C. §9-503] Repossession of the collateral sets the stage for other remedies, such as sale of the collateral to satisfy the debtor's obligation or extinguishing further rights through continued possession. The provisions for taking possession—often referred to as "self-help measures"—present several innovations.

2. **Is Judicial Process Necessary?**

   a. **No breach of peace:** [§541]   The Code stipulates that as long as possession of the collateral can be obtained *without breach of the peace*, the secured party may proceed to *seize* it without judicial process (*i.e.,* this is "self-help" repossession). Otherwise, legal proceedings are required. [U.C.C. §9-503]

(1) **Rationale:** Forcing the secured party to go to court in every case merely runs up costs, which in turn will be passed on to the debtor. Also, there is no real justification for legal proceedings where the debtor will voluntarily relinquish the collateral or allow the secured party to reclaim it peacefully. Presumably, the fear of a tort action will keep the secured party from taking the collateral by force.

(2) **What constitutes "breach of the peace"**

(a) **Violence or disturbance not required:** [§542] A repossession made over any *protest* by the debtor or anyone present constitutes a "breach of the peace," even though no violence or significant disturbance occurs. [Morris v. First National Bank, 254 N.E.2d 683 (Ohio 1970)—repossession of lawnmower from front yard over protest of debtor's son held to be trespass]

1) **Subsequent attempts not prohibited:** [§543] However, where an attempted repossession is halted upon protest by the debtor, nothing in the Code forbids the creditor from making second, third, or more attempts at repossession. [Ford Motor Credit Co. v. Cole, 503 S.W.2d 853 (Tex. 1974)]

(b) **Constructive force:** [§544] A "peaceful" repossession by a creditor with a *weapon* (although the weapon is not used or even unholstered) constitutes a "breach of the peace," as does a phony show of legal authority (*e.g.,* dressing up as a sheriff). Such actions contain *implied threats* ("constructive force") and hence are not considered "peaceful" repossessions. [Stone Machinery Co. v. Kessler, 463 P.2d 651 (Wash. 1970)—repossession improper where creditor accompanied by off-duty sheriff wearing uniform]

(c) **Breaking and entering:** [§545] Many, but not all, courts hold that breaking and entering the debtor's property is a breach of the peace (and a trespass) even if the security agreement authorizes the same. *Rationale:* Debtors cannot contract away the rights of their families and neighbors to the quiet enjoyment of their surroundings. [*See* Hileman v. Harter Bank & Trust Co., 186 N.E.2d 853 (Ohio 1962)]

1) **Compare—simple trespass:** [§546] Where, however, the creditor comes on the property but does not have to "break and enter," most courts hold that the mere technical trespass is *not* a "breach of the peace." [*See* Raffa v. Dania Bank, 321 So. 2d 83 (Fla. 1975)]

(d) **Trickery allowed:** [§547] Repossessing under false pretenses (*e.g.,* creditor calls debtor to "bring your car in because it's been recalled and we want to fix it up") is perhaps unfair, but the courts have usually held such repossessions valid. [Cox v. Galigher, 213 S.E.2d 475 (W. Va. 1975); *but see* Ford Motor Credit Co. v. Byrd, 351 So. 2d 557 (Ala. 1977)]

(3) **Effect of breach of peace:** [§548]   If the repossessing creditor does breach the peace, the creditor loses the authorization of section 9-503 to repossess without the aid of the courts. Such a creditor is, in effect, *stealing* the debtor's property and is no longer authorized by law to repossess. The debtor may sue for conversion and recover actual (and frequently punitive) damages. [*See* 35 A.L.R.3d 1016]

b. **Requirement of notice:** [§549]   Absent a provision in the security agreement to the contrary, the creditor is *not* required to give the debtor *notice* of a planned repossession. *Rationale:* A debtor given notice might hide the collateral.

(1) **Exception—provision requiring notice:** [§550]   However, where the language of the security agreement *expressly or impliedly* requires the secured party to give a pre-repossession notice, a creditor who seizes the property without first complying is subject to an action for conversion and possibly punitive damages. [Klingbiel v. Commercial Credit Corp., 439 F.2d 1303 (10th Cir. 1971)—security agreement providing for repossession only "on demand" held to require notice]

(2) **Compare—post-repossession notice of resale:** [§551]   *After* repossession, the creditor may wish to resell the collateral and sue the debtor for the amount still due (the "deficiency"). In this situation, the U.C.C. *does* require notice of the time and place of resale. [U.C.C. §9-504; *see infra,* §572]

c. **Constitutionality?** [§552]   Courts today are reassessing all nonjudicial creditor remedies from a due process standpoint—the issue being whether taking a debtor's property without court proceedings of some sort violates the constitutional guarantee that property shall not be taken without due process of law.

(1) **Invalidated remedies:** [§553]   A number of state and federal cases have overturned other creditor remedies instituted without prior court hearings:

(a) **Example:** In *Sniadach v. Family Finance Corp.,* 359 U.S. 337 (1969), the Supreme Court invalidated a state garnishment procedure whereby a debtor's wage could be garnished without prior notice or hearing. The Court stressed that a court hearing at which the debtor is afforded the opportunity to present defenses is required *before* any property can be seized.

(b) **Note:** Similar holdings and reasoning have been applied to all other prejudgment *judicial remedies* (attachments, replevin, claim and delivery). [*See* Fuentes v. Shevin, 407 U.S. 67 (1972)]

(c) **And note:** A number of decisions have extended the rule to the seizure and sale of property under *statutory liens* (*i.e.,* garagemen's liens, innkeepers' liens, etc.), where no court action of any kind was involved. [Adams v. Department of Motor Vehicles, 11 Cal. 3d 146 (1974)]

(2) **Repossession pursuant to security agreement:** [§554] Court decisions have upheld the constitutionality of peaceful creditor repossessions under U.C.C section 9-503. The reasoning is that due process is a limitation only where "state action" is involved, and repossessions by private parties pursuant to the provisions of a security agreement do *not* involve "state action." [74 A.L.R.3d 1030]

(a) **And note:** While the Supreme Court has not resolved this issue, the Court has held that a similar procedure in section 7-210, by which warehousemen sell bailed goods when storage charges have not been paid, was not unconstitutional, since the mere enactment of that section was not sufficient "state action." [Flagg Bros. v. Brooks, 436 U.S. 149 (1978)]

d. **Unconscionability:** [§555] Even if it turns out that private repossessions under U.C.C. section 9-503 are constitutional, the usual fine-print provisions of the security agreement authorizing such repossessions may be subject to attack on grounds of *"unconscionability"*—at least where they involve an unreasonable forfeiture of debtor's equity. [Fontane v. Industrial National Bank, 298 A.2d 521 (R.I. 1973)—where creditor repeatedly accepted debtor's late payments, repossession was not allowed without prior notice; Guzman v. Western State Bank, 540 F.2d 948 (8th Cir. 1976)—punitive damages awarded debtors under Federal Civil Rights Act for repossession of mobile home by creditor using obviously unconstitutional state procedures]

3. **Right of Assemblage:** [§556] The security agreement may require the debtor, upon default, to assemble the collateral at a specified place, reasonably convenient to both parties. Such provisions indicate the parties' intent that the secured party be afforded access thereto in event of default, and are specifically enforceable. [U.C.C. §9-503; Clark Equipment Co. v. Armstrong Equipment Co., 431 F.2d 54 (5th Cir. 1970)—mandatory injunction requiring debtor to assemble and turn over collateral]

4. **Disabling Equipment:** [§557] The Code introduces a new right for the secured party when the collateral consists of equipment. The secured party may render the equipment unusable (*e.g.*, by removing a necessary part) on the debtor's premises and then may dispose of the collateral (*e.g.*, sell it) on the same premises. [U.C.C. §9-503]

a. **Limitation—reasonableness:** [§558] In exercising this right, however, the secured party is still bound by the standard of commercial reasonableness (*infra*, §569)

5. **Duties of Secured Party in Possession:** [§559] After taking possession, the secured party assumes the same duties as a party who perfects by possession; *i.e.*, the possessor must take *reasonable care* of the collateral, maintain it, insure its upkeep, etc. [U.C.C. §9-207]

a. **Duty to return personal items repossessed with collateral:** [§560] If, in repossessing the collateral, the creditor comes into possession of other personal property (*e.g.*, golf clubs in the trunk of a repossessed car), the debtor may be able to sue for conversion. To avoid this problem, most security agreements contain clauses authorizing the secured party to repossess "the collateral and all property contained therein, the property not covered by the security interest to be returned promptly."

(1) **Note:** Where the creditor follows this procedure and behaves fairly, most courts refuse to find the creditor liable for conversion. [Jones v. General Motors Acceptance Corp., 565 P.2d 9 (Okla. 1977)]

(2) **Compare:** Other courts are contra. [Ford Motor Credit Co. v. Cole, *supra,* §543—clause void as against public policy so that creditor liable for conversion of debtor's other property]

b. **Other duties of a party in possession:** *See supra,* §§169 *et seq.*

E. REALIZING UPON THE COLLATERAL

1. **Strict Foreclosure:** [§561]   In lieu of other remedies, the creditor who repossesses goods may elect to *keep* them and forget the rest of the debt. This procedure, called "strict foreclosure," is authorized by section 9-505 of the Code. For obvious reasons, it is used only where the collateral is appreciating in value (*e.g.,* a famous painting) or where the cost of further action is prohibitive.

a. **Exception for consumer goods:** [§562]   Where the repossessed collateral constitutes consumer goods, and the debtor has already *repaid at least 60%* of the cash price or loaned amount, the creditor *must* resell the collateral within 90 days of repossession and turn over any excess to the consumer. Otherwise, the creditor will be liable to the consumer either for conversion or, at the consumer's option, actual damages plus punitive damages in the amount of the finance charge plus 10% of the cash price or loan amount. [U.C.C. §§9-507(1), 9-505(1); *see infra,* §622]

(1) **Rationale:** In this case, the consumer has substantial equity in the collateral, and the value of the collateral may often exceed the balance on the debt. Hence, the Code ensures payment of the surplus to the debtor without requiring any further action on the part of the consumer.

(2) **Waiver after default:** [§563]   Where, however, it is to the debtor's advantage that the secured party keep the collateral in satisfaction of the debt, section 9-505(1) allows the debtor to *waive* the right to sale—but only *after* default has occurred. A waiver contained in the security agreement would therefore have no effect. [Kruse, Kruse & Miklosko, Inc. v. Beedy, 353 N.E.2d 514 (Ind. 1976)]

b. **General notice requirement:** [§564]   Where consumer goods are *not* involved (or where the consumer has not paid 60% of the original amount), the creditor electing strict foreclosure must *send written notice* to the debtor of the creditor's intention to keep the collateral in satisfaction of the debt. In *nonconsumer* goods situations, the creditor must also send such a notice to other secured parties having an interest in the collateral if those creditors themselves have previously sent a written notice to the repossessing creditor of their interests. [U.C.C. §9-505]

(1) **Duty fulfilled when notice sent:** [§565]   Note that the secured party's duty is fulfilled when the notice is sent. The risk of nondelivery of the mails is on the debtor or junior secured party. [U.C.C. §1-201(38)]

(2) **Waiver of notice requirement:** [§566]   Note also that the debtor may waive notice after default under the same rule discussed *supra,* §563.

c. **Effect of objection:** [§567]   If, within *21 days* after the notice is sent, any person entitled to notice (above) *objects* to the secured party's proposal to retain the goods in satisfaction of the debt, the secured party *must* dispose of the collateral by sale. [U.C.C. §9-505(2)]

2. **Disposition of the Collateral by Sale:** [§568]   The U.C.C. provides a great deal of flexibility in the rules governing disposition of collateral by sale. First, under section 9-504, the secured party is not restricted to sale, but is permitted to "*sell, lease or otherwise dispose* of the collateral." Even so, disposition by sale is by far the most common method of realizing on the collateral—particularly because the Code permits either *public or private* sale, and because after sale, the secured party may pursue the debtor for any amount remaining unpaid (the "deficiency").

a. **Commercial reasonableness standard:** [§569]   The only real limitation on the power to sell is that the secured party must act in good faith and in a commercially reasonable manner. Every aspect of the disposition, including the method, manner, time, place, and terms of sale must be *completely reasonable*. [U.C.C. §9-504(3)]

(1) **Time within which sale must occur:** [§570]   No specific time is set within which the secured party must make a disposition of the collateral. The U.C.C. merely requires that the collateral be sold within a "commercially reasonable" time after repossession.

(a) **Note:** A repossessing creditor will not be subject to damages or waive its right to any remedy by retaining possession of the collateral long enough to explore all available avenues for collection of the debt. It need *not* proceed immediately to sell the collateral.

(b) **Compare:** On the other hand, a prolonged interval between the repossession and sale raises at least an inference of commercial *unreasonableness* so that the burden of proof is on the secured party to establish a valid reason for the delay. [Farmers State Bank v. Otten, 204 N.W.2d 178 (S.D. 1973)—13-month delay]

(c) **And note:** Some courts have held that an unreasonable delay in reselling the repossessed collateral results in the loss of the option to do so—in effect a forced "strict foreclosure." [Moran v. Holman, 514 P.2d 817 (Alaska 1973)—creditor's use of possessed truck for personal business for four months held an election of strict foreclosure; *but see* Jones v. Morgan, 228 N.W.2d 419 (Mich. 1975)—contra; debtor's only remedy when this happens is under §9-507(1) (*see infra,* §622)]

(2) **Preparation for sale:** [§571]   Although the Code makes no reference to a duty upon the part of the secured creditor to *advertise or solicit purchasers*

for the sale, failure to do so evidences *lack* of "commercial reasonableness." [Dynalectron Corp. v. Jack Richards Aircraft Co., 337 F. Supp. 659 (W.D. Okla. 1972)]

b. **Notice requirement:** [§572]   Notice must be given to the debtor and certain other persons (below) of the sale of the collateral, except where the collateral is *perishable* (likely to decline speedily in value) or is of a type sold in a *recognized market* (*e.g.*, stocks and bonds). [U.C.C. §9-504(3)]

(1) **Contents of notice**

(a) **Public sales:** [§573]   If the sale is to be *public* (*i.e.*, an auction), the notice must state the *time and place* of the sale. [U.C.C. §9-504(3)]

(b) **Private sales:** [§574]   If the sale is to be *private*, the notice must state the time *after which* the sale will take place. (This gives the debtor a chance to redeem the collateral.) [U.C.C. §9-504(3)]

(2) **Persons to be notified**

(a) **Debtor:** [§575]   Notice of the intended sale is required to be sent by the secured party to the debtor.

1) **Waiver of right to notice before default:** [§576]   Any provision in the original security agreement by which the debtor purportedly waives notice of sale is *void as a matter of law*. Public policy strongly favors the protection of the debtor's rights through such notice. [U.C.C. §9-501(3)(b)]

2) **Waiver after default:** [§577]   The Code specifies that the debtor, *after default*, may sign a statement renouncing or modifying the debtor's right to notice of sale. In such a case, the debtor may be able to extract some concessions from the secured party in exchange for the waiver. [U.C.C. §9-504(3)]

(b) **Sureties:** [§578]   Co-signers, sureties, and guarantors of the debtor's obligation also fall within the U.C.C. section 9-105(1)(d) definition of debtor, and so are entitled to the same notice as the debtor. [McChord Credit Union v. Parrish, 809 P.2d 759 (Wash. 1991)]

(c) **Junior secured parties:** [§579]   In the case of *consumer goods*, notice is *not* required to be given to third persons claiming an interest in the goods. However, as to any other type of collateral, the secured party must send a notice of the sale to all persons who have *notified the secured party* that they claim an interest in the collateral (such persons having given written notice to the repossessing creditor of their security interests before a notice of the sale was sent to the debtor or before renunciation by the debtor of his rights). [U.C.C. §9-504(3)]

1) **Note:** The burden is thus placed on junior secured parties to notify senior secured parties of their existence (rather than forcing the senior party to search the record for juniors).

2) **Comment:** As a matter of routine, therefore, junior secured parties should send notice of their existence to the senior secured party as soon as they acquire their interests (although, as a practical matter, default sales rarely result in any surplus so that in most cases there will be nothing to distribute even if the junior interest holder has given such notice).

(3) **Sufficiency of oral notice:** [§580]   The Code states that notice must be "sent," which suggests that written notice is contemplated. However, several courts have held that oral notice is sufficient, at least where it is clear that the debtor had actual knowledge of the sale. [Bondurant v. Beard Equipment Co., 345 So. 2d 806 (Fla. 1977)]

(4) **Exception as to goods sold in "recognized market":** [§581]   As indicated above, notice is not required where the collateral is sold in a "recognized" market. However, courts have limited the concept of a "recognized market" to *auction markets*, such as grain markets or stock exchanges, where goods are *fungible*. [*See, e.g.*, Norton v. National Bank of Commerce, 398 S.W.2d 538 (Ark. 1966)]

   (a) **Automobiles:** [§582]   The courts are unanimous in holding that automobiles are *not* sold on a "recognized market" because there are so many variables in automobile sales. [*See, e.g.*, Norton v. National Bank of Commerce, *supra*; Nelson v. Monarch Investment Plan, 452 S.W.2d 375 (Ky. 1970)]

   (b) **Caution:** [§583]   If a secured party mistakenly determines that the sale is in a "recognized market" and it is not, the secured party may be liable in damages to the debtor. [*See* U.C.C. §9-507; *and see infra*, §615] Or, the creditor may even be barred from recovering any deficiency against the debtor (below). The safest course, therefore, is to send the notice.

(5) **Timing of notice:** [§584]   The U.C.C. does not say *how far in advance* of resale notice must be sent—although the notice must be timed so as to give the debtor a reasonable chance to redeem the goods (*see infra*, §611) or to attend the sale alone or with bidding friends.

   (a) **Judicial period:** [§585]   Courts in some states have imposed a *three-day notice* period rule whereby the notice is ineffective unless sent in time to give debtors a minimum of three business days to arrange protection of their interests. [First National Bank v. Rose, 249 N.W.2d 723 (Neb. 1977)]

   (b) **Statutory period:** [§586]   Other states have amended section 9-504(3) and added a statutory notice period. For example, California established a five-day period for both a mailed and a *published* notice of sale in its version of section 9-504(3).

c. **Secured party's right to bid for collateral**

(1) **At public sale:** [§587]   The secured party enjoys the right to purchase the collateral at a public sale. [U.C.C. §9-504(3)] Indeed, the secured party is often the only bidder.

(2) **At private sale:** [§588]   Where a *private* sale is involved, the secured party is entitled to bid for the goods only if they are of a type customarily sold in a *recognized market* or are of a type subject to *standard price quotations*. [U.C.C. §9-504(3)]

(a) **Note:** Provisions in the security agreement that would authorize the secured party to buy-in contrary to the above restrictions, have been held *void* as against public policy so that the sale to the secured party is deemed commercially *unreasonable.* [Barber v. Leroy, 40 Cal. App. 3d 336 (1974)]

d. **Application of proceeds:** [§589]   The Code establishes a strict priority for application of the proceeds of a sale of collateral. In general, proceeds are applied in turn to (i) the *expenses* of the secured party in connection with the default; (ii) the *debt owed* the secured party; and (iii) the indebtedness owed to *other* secured parties having interests in the collateral. [U.C.C. §9-504(1)]

(1) **Expenses:** [§590]   The secured party is first reimbursed for the expenses incurred in the sale, including legal expenses and reasonable attorneys' fees (*if* provided for in the security agreement) and any costs in taking or holding the collateral. Also, the secured party is entitled to be reimbursed for any improvements in or processing of the collateral undertaken to make it more marketable. [U.C.C. §9-504(1)(a)]

(2) **Debt:** [§591]   After initial expenses, the proceeds are applied to the obligation upon which the debtor has defaulted and under which the disposition of the collateral is made. [U.C.C. §9-504(1)(b)]

(3) **Other debts:** [§592]   Finally, the proceeds go to satisfy the interests of other secured parties in the collateral, provided that such subordinated holders advise the secured party of their intention to participate before the proceeds are disbursed. The secured party may demand proof of the interest of other parties prior to disbursing the proceeds. [U.C.C. §9-504(1)(c)]

e. **Surplus and deficiency:** [§593]   The secured party is required to turn over to the debtor any proceeds that are left after the disbursements. Conversely, the debtor will be liable for any *deficiency*—the amount by which the proceeds failed to cover the expenses of sale and the indebtedness—unless the debtor is specifically exempted from this obligation under the terms of the security agreement or by some other state law. [U.C.C. §9-504(2)]

(1) **Computing amount of surplus or deficiency**

(a) **Sale price:** [§594]   Absent fraud in the sale, the amount bid or received on the sale of the collateral is usually accepted as the basis for determining the amount of the surplus or deficiency. [Schabler v. Indianapolis Morris Plan, 234 N.E.2d 655 (Ind. 1968)]

      1) **Low price not determinative:** [§595]   The mere fact that the amount realized at the sale is substantially below the fair market value of the collateral is *not enough* by itself to render the sale commercially *unreasonable*—at least where the secured party has otherwise acted reasonably to attract prospective purchasers and bidding. [Sierra Financial Corp. v. Brooks-Farrer Co., *supra*, §68—where collateral worth $27,000 sold to secured party for $500, sale upheld; *see* U.C.C. §9-507(2)]

      2) **Effect of fraud:** [§596]   However, the result is clearly contra where the secured party is guilty of *fraud or bad faith*—e.g., conspiring with others to depress the bidding at the sale in order to minimize the surplus (or increase the deficiency). In such a case, the courts will disregard the sale price and order the secured party to account in accordance with the *fair market value* of the collateral.

  (b) **Expenses:** [§597]   Again, absent fraud or bad faith, the secured party's expenses in retaking and reselling the goods (above) are usually accepted as proper charges in computing the amount of the surplus or deficiency.

      1) **Reasonableness not required:** [§598]   Courts have generally rejected claims that the secured party's expenses must be shown to have been "reasonable." Rather, the secured party is held entitled to recover expenses as long as *incurred in good faith*, and the mere fact that the charges are high is not enough by itself to show bad faith. [John Deere Co. v. Catalano, 525 P.2d 1153 (Colo. 1974)—legal fees of $1,500 in reselling a tractor worth $3,000 held not excessive]

  (2) **Penalties for noncomplying resale**

  (a) **Flaws in resale:** [§599]   The cases are *split* on the effect of flaws in the repossession or resale proceedings where there is otherwise no fraud or bad faith involved. The two flaws that most often give rise to this issue are failure to give the debtor a proper *notice* of the resale and failure of the creditor to conduct a *commercially reasonable resale*.

      1) **"Absolute bar" rule:** [§600]   Many courts hold that *any defect* in the repossession or in the notice of sale, or in the time or conduct of the sale, etc., *bars* the secured party from any deficiency against the debtor. The creditor either dots every "i" and crosses every "t" in the repossession and resale or loses the chance for a deficiency. [Atlas Thrift Co. v. Horan, 27 Cal. App. 3d 999 (1972)]

      2) **"Rebuttable presumption" rule:** [§601]   Other jurisdictions indulge in a *presumption* in the first instance that the collateral was worth at least the amount of the debt and thereby shift to the creditor the burden of proving that any lesser amount obtained through the sale was a fair price and was not colored by

the flaw in the repossession or sale. [Rushton v. Shea, 423 F. Supp. 468 (D. Del. 1976)]

 3) **"Damages only" rule:** [§602] Still other courts hold that these *flaws do not affect* the secured party's right to a deficiency. The secured party is, of course, liable for whatever *damages* resulted from the improper notice or sale procedure (under U.C.C. section 9-507, *infra*); and such damages can be asserted as a setoff to the secured party's deficiency. [United States v. Whitehouse Plastics, 501 F.2d 692 (5th Cir. 1974)]

  a) **Comment:** This position has been the most criticized, because it is usually very difficult for the debtor to prove any damages resulting from improper notice; the effect therefore is to allow the secured party to recover in full. [59 A.L.R.3d 401]

 (b) **Consumer protection statutes:** [§603] Article 9 defers to local consumer protection legislation. [U.C.C. §9-201—"Nothing herein validates any practice illegal under any statute or regulation governing retail installment sales or the like"] Hence, where deficiency judgments are barred under local law, they cannot be recovered under the U.C.C. Since consumer protection statutes often radically alter the U.C.C. rules on repossession and resale, they must be carefully studied where consumer goods are the collateral.

(3) **Exception as to sales of accounts and chattel paper:** [§604] Where the collateral in question consists of *accounts* or *chattel paper* in the possession of the secured party, the Code rules for deficiency and surplus are just the opposite: Unless the security agreement states otherwise, the *debtor is neither entitled to any surplus, nor liable for any deficiency*. [U.C.C. §9-504(2)]

 (a) **Rationale:** The collateral here involves rights to *payments owed by a third person*, and the price that a purchaser is willing to pay upon sale of these rights may reflect the *willingness of the seller to guarantee* and make good the performance of the third party in the event that party defaults.

  1) *When accounts or chattel paper are sold*, they are sold either "with recourse" or "without recourse." (If no mention, it is presumed they are sold "without recourse.")

  2) *When sold "with recourse,"* the seller *guarantees* the obligation in the event the account-debtor fails to pay, thus allowing the creditor *recourse* to the seller. If the sale is made *"without recourse,"* there is no such guarantee.

  3) *Since a sale "without recourse" is generally more risky* for the purchaser, that party usually pays a somewhat *lower price* for the rights involved than would have been paid if the seller had been willing to sell "with recourse."

> 4) ***In any event, because the purchase price depends on the seller's*** (secured party's) willingness to guarantee the obligations, the U.C.C. rule is to ***exclude*** any right to either surplus ***or*** deficiency—unless the parties ***expressly*** provide otherwise.

    f.   **Rights of purchaser of collateral:** [§605] The purchaser of the collateral at the secured party's sale takes all rights the debtor had in the collateral, together with the interest of the secured party and ***all interests subordinate thereto.*** [U.C.C. §9-504(4)]

        (1) **As to junior creditors:** [§606] This means that the purchaser takes ***free*** from the secured interests of all creditors lower in priority than the seller; *i.e.*, the purchaser "steps into the shoes" of the secured party with respect to all other security interests in the collateral.

        (2) **As to senior creditors:** [§607] Strangely enough, the Code does not expressly state what happens to the rights of a ***senior*** creditor if a junior creditor repossesses and resells the goods. Some courts in this situation would make the junior creditor use the proceeds to pay off the senior debt, but others simply hold that the purchaser at the resale takes subject to the security interest of the senior creditor, who would have to be paid off by the purchaser; otherwise the senior creditor could repossess the collateral from the purchaser. [*See* Starnes, U.C.C. Section 9-504 Sales By Junior Secured Parties: Is a Senior Party Entitled to Notice and Proceeds?, 52 U. Pitt. L. Rev. 563 (1991)]

        (3) **Effect of defects in sale:** [§608] Even if the secured party has failed to comply with the default provisions of Article 9, at least with respect to junior interests, the purchaser's interest is still protected as long as the purchaser was acting in good faith. In the case of a ***public*** sale, the purchaser need only show no knowledge of any defect in the sale proceedings and that there was no collusion with the secured party, those conducting the sale, or other bidders. [U.C.C. §9-504(4)(a), (b)]

  3. **Allowing Debtor to Retain Collateral and Suing on Debt:** [§609] The secured party may allow the collateral to remain with the debtor and sue upon the debt, thereby reducing the claim to a judgment. Any lien that the secured party subsequently acquires through a levy upon the collateral (*e.g.*, by writ of execution) ***dates back to the date of perfection of the original security interest.*** [U.C.C. §9-501(5)]

    a. **Example:** Creditor perfected a security interest in Debtor's factory equipment on May 1, 1996. Debtor defaulted in loan repayment on September 1, 1996. Creditor did not repossess the collateral, but instead ***sued*** Debtor and recovered a judgment in the amount owed. The sheriff, pursuant to writ of execution, levied on (seized) Debtor's factory equipment on October 1, 1996. Debtor filed a bankruptcy petition the next day. Creditor's lien on the factory equipment dates from May 1, 1996, ***not*** October 2, 1996—an important distinction since the trustee in bankruptcy can attack liens arising in the 90-day period prior to bankruptcy as preferences (*see supra,* §497).

    b. **Judicial sale:** [§610] In most jurisdictions, the secured party may purchase at a ***judicial sale***, in which event that party takes the collateral free from any provisions of the U.C.C.

F. DEBTOR'S RIGHT OF REDEMPTION

1. **In General:** [§611] The fact that the debtor has defaulted does not irreversibly set in motion the provisions for the disposition and retention of collateral by the secured party under sections 9-504 and 9-505(2). The debtor may exercise the *right of redemption* at any time prior to the time the secured party has disposed of the collateral or entered into a contract for its disposition, or before the debtor's obligation has been discharged by the secured party's retention of collateral (*supra*, §561). [U.C.C. §9-506; Old Colony Trust Co. v. Penrose Industries Corp., 398 F.2d 310 (3d Cir. 1968)]

2. **Tender:** [§612] To redeem, the debtor must tender the *entire* obligation due, *plus* any expenses incurred by the secured party in taking or caring for the collateral, along with any expenses already incurred in connection with the sale of the collateral. [U.C.C. §9-506]

    a. **Acceleration clause:** [§613] If the agreement contains an acceleration clause, the debtor must be prepared to tender the *entire* debt, not just the delinquent installments. However, courts *may* read in "unconscionability" or "public policy" limitations to prevent unjust results so that the debtor need do no more than pay the expenses of repossession and the debt currently due *without acceleration*. [*Compare* U.C.C. §9-506, Comment, *with* Urdang v. Muse, 276 A.2d 397 (N.J. 1971); Robinson v. Jefferson Corp., 4 U.C.C. Rep. 15 (N.Y. 1967); Street v. Commercial Credit Corp., 281 P. 46 (Ariz. 1929)]

3. **No Waiver Prior to Default:** [§614] A debtor *cannot* validly waive the right of redemption *prior* to default. This is specifically prohibited in the Code [U.C.C. §9-501(3)(d); *infra*, §628] and reflects basic public policy of protecting debtors' rights [Indianapolis Morris Plan v. Karlen, 28 N.Y.2d 30 (1971)]. The common law maxim is that "nothing can clog the equity of redemption."

    a. **Note:** The right of redemption may be waived *after* a default (*infra*, §629).

G. EFFECT OF FAILURE TO COMPLY WITH DEFAULT PROVISIONS

1. **In General:** [§615] If the secured party does not comply with the default provisions of the Code in proceeding against the debtor, the debtor may seek *judicial direction* as to the type of disposition or may wait until after the goods have been disposed of and then proceed against the secured party for *damages*. [U.C.C. §9-507(1)] The provisions of the section are very general, and when combined with the exculpatory language in subsection 9-507(2), below, the standard of recovery appears to be very strict.

2. **Standards for Reviewing Secured Party's Conduct:** [§616] As indicated previously, *"commercial reasonableness"* is the basic requirement. Since the Code contains few rules as to what is and is not "commercially reasonable," much is left to the courts and to the changing standards of the business community itself.

    a. **U.C.C. standards:** [§617] The Code does set three standards that, if met, do establish a "commercially reasonable" disposition [U.C.C. §9-507(2)]:

        (i) *Sale in the usual manner in any "recognized market"* (*supra*, §581) is commercially reasonable.

(ii) *Sale at a price current* in a recognized market, regardless of how the sale is made, will also be free from attack.

(iii) *Sale of the collateral in accordance with practices common* among those who are *dealers* in the collateral will also be deemed to be a commercially reasonable disposition.

(1) **Higher price obtainable:** [§618]   The fact that the secured party could have obtained a higher price in the sale of the collateral by selling it at a different time or by using a different method is *not* sufficient by itself to establish that the disposition was commercially *unreasonable*. [U.C.C. §9-507(2)]

b. **Approval of disposition:** [§619]   A disposition will also be held "commercially reasonable," regardless of whether it has met one of the above standards, if the disposition has been approved by a judicial proceeding, by a bona fide creditor's committee, or by representatives of the debtor's creditors. [U.C.C. §9-507(2)]

(1) **Rationale:** The reason for upholding the validity of the disposition in these cases is simply that the parties whose interests are most vitally affected have either had their rights determined judicially or they have voluntarily expressed their approval of the disposition arrangements. In either case, they have no cause to challenge the secured party's disposition.

(2) **Lack of approval not determinative:** [§620]   Note, however, that the lack of judicial approval or the absence of consent of creditors does *not* mean that the transaction is automatically commercially *unreasonable*.

3. **Penalties for Secured Party's Noncompliance:** [§621]   Increasingly, courts have shown a willingness to develop appropriate remedies to insure the "commercial reasonableness" of the secured party's conduct. Such remedies may include the denial of a deficiency; shifting the burden to the secured party to prove that the sale price *was* fair; crediting the debtor with a fair price, as determined by the court; and, of course, awarding *damages* measured by any loss resulting from the noncompliance (presumably the difference between the sale price and market value). (*See supra*, §599.)

4. **Penalty Where Collateral Is Consumer Goods:** [§622]   Since the extent of harm to the consumer may not merit the costs of litigation, the Code establishes a *minimum recovery* when the failure to observe the default provisions prejudices the consumer debtor. The debtor has a right to *damages* not less than the *credit service charge plus 10% of the principal amount due on the debt*. [U.C.C. §9-507(1)— not in effect in California] Alternatively, the debtor may be awarded the *time price differential plus 10% of the cash price*. The standard of damages depends on how the transaction is structured.

a. **Example:** Suppose Debtor purchased a 1996 Wombat automobile. The price was $2,500. Debtor paid $500 down, plus a credit service charge of $200, and agreed to pay the remaining $2,000 over the next two years. In effect, the credit service charge represents prepaid interest. Suppose Secured Party makes a fraudulent sale upon Debtor's default in payment. Debtor's minimum damages would be $400: $200 for the credit service charge plus 10% of the principal, or $200.

b. **Example:** Suppose the same sale of the Wombat had been structured without a service charge; instead, the secured party computes a "time sale price," being the total amount of the principal and interest to be paid under the transaction. If the same rate of interest is used as in the foregoing example, the time sale price will be $2,700. Thus, the time price differential, or the difference between the cash sale price and the total credit price (*i.e.*, the "interest" or "finance charge"), is $200. Should Secured Party violate the default provisions, Debtor's minimum recovery would be $450: $200 for the time price differential plus 10% of the *cash* price, or $250.

c. **Comment:** One of the weaknesses of the Code damage determination in the case of consumer goods is the difficulty of reducing the transaction to hard figures, and the fact that the minimum recovery under the Code often turns out to be the maximum.

H. NONWAIVABLE RIGHTS UNDER THE SECURITY AGREEMENT

1. **In General:** [§623]   As has been stressed, the default provisions of the Code invite flexibility, and the parties are encouraged to tailor their security agreement to the facts of their case. However, this is not an invitation for the parties to evade the Code through clever private draftsmanship, because the standards specified by the parties cannot be manifestly unreasonable. Moreover, the Code declares that a number of rights may *not* be waived, although parties may specify their own standards for the performance of these rights (*see* below). [U.C.C. §9-501(3)]

2. **Accounting for Surplus:** [§624]   When the security agreement secures an indebtedness, the parties may not dispense with the obligation to account for any surplus that accrues from the disposition of the collateral. [U.C.C. §9-501(3)(a)]

3. **Notice Requirements:** [§625]   The secured party must comply with the notice requirements for disposition and/or retention of the collateral (above). These *cannot be waived*. [U.C.C. §9-501(3)(b)]

   a. **Compare—manner of notice:** [§626]   The parties can, by agreement, however, alter the Code provisions regarding the *manner* of notice. Moreover, the debtor may, *after* default, effectively waive the right to notice of sale. [U.C.C. §9-504(3); *supra*, §577]

4. **Discharge Upon Retention:** [§627]   Retention of the collateral under section 9-505 discharges the debtor's obligation (*supra*, §561), and the parties may not contract otherwise. [U.C.C. §9-501(3)(c)]

   a. **Rationale:** The Code's policy here does not conflict with its promotion of alternative and cumulative remedies. When the secured party has retained the collateral, there has been no public or even third-party determination of its value. If the secured party wants the collateral *and* also wants to be able to sue the debtor for any possible deficiency, the party can always buy the collateral at public sale or under certain conditions at private sale (*supra*, §§587-588). The Code protects a debtor in a weak bargaining position from being forced to bargain away the protection of an external valuation of the collateral if the secured party wishes to retain it *and* exercise the right to proceed further.

5. **Right of Redemption:** [§628]   Neither may the parties contractually eliminate the debtor's right to redeem the collateral under section 9-506 (*supra,* §614). [U.C.C. §9-501(3)(d)]

   a. **Waiver after default:** [§629]   However, section 9-506 *allows* the debtor to waive the right to redemption *after default*. At this point, the secured party theoretically has no advantage over the debtor, and the debtor may be willing to sign a waiver if the debtor does not intend to redeem in order to give the secured party more flexibility in his disposition arrangements. Also, the debtor may be able to bargain for a release of personal liability on any deficiency.

6. **Liability for Failure to Comply:** [§630]   The secured party may not disclaim or reduce liability under section 9-507 for failing to comply with the default provisions of the Code. [U.C.C. §9-501(3)(e)] Here again, the Code protects the debtor in a weak bargaining position from negotiating away essential rights in order to obtain credit.

7. **Waiver of Rights by Guarantor:** [§631]   The common law clearly allowed guarantors of the debt to sign a guarantee agreement in which the right to object to improper resales of the collateral was waived. The definition of "debtor" in section 9-105(d), however, as a "person who owes payment . . . of the obligation" seems to include the guarantor. So read, section 9-501 would then make *invalid* a pre-default waiver by the guarantor of the right to notice and a commercially reasonable resale of the collateral, and almost all courts considering the issue have reached this result. [*See* Dakota Bank & Trust v. Grinde, 422 N.W.2d 813 (N.D. 1988); *but see* Stenberg v. Cinema N'Drafthouse Systems, Inc., 28 F.3d 23 (5th Cir. 1994), predicting that the Texas Supreme Court would allow a pre-default waiver]

I. SPECIAL DEFAULT RULES FOR INTANGIBLES AND FIXTURES

1. **Intangibles:** [§632]   Where the financing transaction involves accounts or chattel paper—either through the sale of such rights or through their use as collateral—the secured party may wish to collect directly from the underlying obligors, rather than by taking payment through the debtor or seller of the rights. Where the debtor-seller's financing arrangements are kept concealed from the debtor's customers, the customers may not know that the right to their payments has been assigned; they will continue to pay the debtor, who then remits to the secured party. This is known as *"nonnotification financing"* of accounts receivable (*supra,* §26).

   a. **Rights of notification:** [§633]   In the event of default, the secured party is *entitled* to notify the underlying account debtors or obligors of the secured party's interest and to collect directly from them. [U.C.C. §9-502(1)]

      (1) **Note:** Of course, if the parties agree, the secured party may also exercise the right of notification prior to any default.

      (2) **And note:** If the financing is on a "with recourse" basis (the debtor being liable for any ultimate deficiency; *see supra,* §604), the secured party may charge the debtor for the reasonable expenses incurred in notifying the debtor's customers and collecting the accounts. [U.C.C. §9-502(2)]

b. **No rights to surplus or deficiency:** [§634]   And remember the special rules governing *surplus and deficiency* on sale of contract rights, accounts, and chattel paper; the debtor is neither entitled to any surplus nor liable for any deficiency. [U.C.C. §9-504(2); *see supra*, §604]

2. **Fixtures and Related Interests:** [§635]   In the case of fixtures and accessions, there is an obvious problem in taking the collateral for retention or sale since it is attached to either real property or to other goods. The Code protects the rights of the secured party in fixtures and accessions by declaring that *when the secured party has priority* over other interests in the real property or the mass of goods (*supra*, §350), the secured party is entitled *to remove* the collateral. [U.C.C. §§9-313(8), 9-314(4)]

a. **Damages caused by removal:** [§636]   The secured party must reimburse the encumbrancer or owner of the underlying property (*other than the debtor*) for any *damages or repair* necessitated by the removal. The owner or encumbrancer may demand adequate security of such reimbursement before allowing removal. However, the secured party is *not* liable for any diminution in the value of the property caused by removal. [U.C.C. §9-313]

b. **Example:** Secured Party has a perfected interest in Debtor's built-in television and decides to remove the television upon default. It costs $100 to repair the hole in the wall, but the house is worth $500 less because it has no built-in TV. If the only person suffering a loss here is Debtor, Secured Party owes nothing and may repossess freely (Debtor has only himself to blame if repossession causes damage). But if another creditor has an interest in the realty (a mortgage, for example), Secured Party is responsible to the other creditor for the $100 repairs but not for the diminution in the value of the underlying property.

J.   RELATION OF DEFAULT PROVISIONS TO OTHER STATE LEGISLATION

1. **Special State Legislation:** [§637]   Although the Code provisions offer a complete system governing default, special legislation is often adopted to cover default in cases of *retail sales* and default in *credit auto purchases*.

a. **Example:** In California, the Unruh Act [Cal. Civ. Code §§1801 *et seq.*] governs general consumer financing, and the Rees-Levering Automobile Financing Act [Cal. Veh. Code §§11713 *et seq.*] provides the principal statutes in consumer auto transactions. The provisions of the U.C.C. are made subordinate to these provisions.

b. **Comment:** As a matter of practice, when dealing with these two areas of financing in any jurisdiction, it is important to check for additional legislation covering consumer transactions and to determine whether specific legislation entirely supersedes the Code or whether it merely takes precedence when in conflict with the Code.

IX. BULK TRANSFERS

chapter approach

On your exam, whenever you see a transfer of *inventory*, be sensitive to the possibility of bulk transfer issues. Determine whether the transfer was *in bulk* and *not in the ordinary course* of the transferor's business. If so, be sure that all Article 6 rules have been met. Remember that these rules are to protect unsecured creditors, and that *both* the transferor and transferee have duties intended to give notice to the transferor's creditors. You should also be aware that some states have repealed Article 6 altogether or have adopted the 1988 revised version of Article 6. Make sure you find out what your state has done.

A. INTRODUCTION

1. **Basic Problem:** [§638]   Official Comment 2 to U.C.C. section 6-101 explains that bulk sales laws aim to correct the situation where the seller of an inventoried business sells that inventory to someone else at a low price and then disappears, leaving behind unpaid creditors. The innocent buyer of the inventory, a bona fide purchaser, arguably takes free of the claims of unsecured creditors, and so the unpaid creditors have no recourse against the buyer or the inventory itself.

2. **Common Law Solution:** [§639]   The common law solved this problem, in part, through the law of fraudulent conveyances, holding that a sale for less than fair consideration was fraudulent, as well as one in which the buyer understood there was an actual fraud on creditors. [Uniform Fraudulent Transfer Act §§4, 5]

3. **Article 6:** [§640]   Article 6 of the Uniform Commercial Code is the latest in a series of state statutes dealing with the problem more directly. Under Article 6, the buyer of an inventoried business is required to give the seller's creditors *notice* prior to the sale. The notice informs the creditors of what is going on, thus giving them time in which to object (file suit, levy on the property, make threats, etc.). The idea is that creditors having notice of the sale have the chance to protect their interests. The penalty for failing to give notice (*see infra,* §668) usually involves giving the creditors the ability to go after the inventory (and, in some instances, against the buyer directly).

4. **The 1988 Revision of Article 6:** [§641]   Recognizing that it is rarely wise to impose penalties on innocent purchasers, as bulk sales laws do, the Uniform Law Commissioners recommended in 1988 that Article 6 be repealed in its entirety. The problems leading to the enactment of the original Article 6 can be better handled by requiring major creditors to get a perfected Article 9 security interest in the inventory (which would then prevail over a buyer in bulk [U.C.C. §§9-301, 9-306(2)]). For states unwilling to repeal Article 6 (or politically unable to do so), the Commissioners have proposed adoption of a revised version of Article 6, referred to below by the use of the letter "R" in the citation, *e.g.*, "§6R-101." Generally speaking, the revision narrows the scope of Article 6 and makes compliance easier.

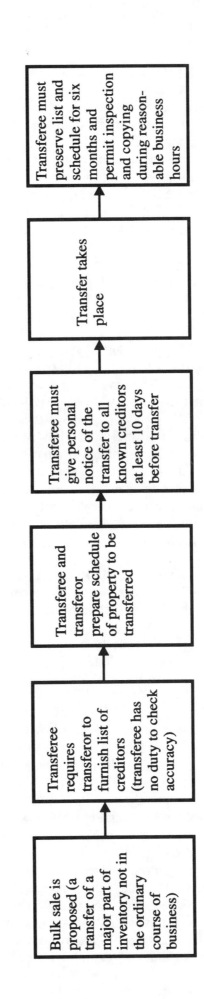

A TYPICAL BULK TRANSFER

Bulk sale is proposed (a transfer of a major part of inventory not in the ordinary course of business)

→

Transferee requires transferor to furnish list of creditors (transferee has no duty to check accuracy)

→

Transferee and transferor prepare schedule of property to be transferred

→

Transferee must give personal notice of the transfer to all known creditors at least 10 days before transfer

→

Transfer takes place

→

Transferee must preserve list and schedule for six months and permit inspection and copying during reasonable business hours

B. SCOPE OF ARTICLE 6

1. **In General:** [§642]   Article 6 applies to "bulk transfers" *not in the ordinary course of the transferor's business* of a *major part* of the materials, supplies, or other inventory. [U.C.C. §6-102(1)] Thus, if the seller routinely transfers a major part of the business inventory every year to clean it out, a bulk transfer is not involved, and no Article 6 notices need be given. [*In re* Curtina International, Inc., 23 B.R. 969 (S.D.N.Y. 1982)] Under the revision, a bulk sale is defined as a sale of *more than half* of the seller's inventory where the buyer knows that the seller will not continue to operate a similar business after the sale. [U.C.C. §6R-102(1)(c)]

2. **Sale of Inventory Required:** [§643]   A sale "in bulk" is the sale of an inventoried business, one whose principal activity is the sale of merchandise from stock. The sale of a business that has no stock on hand (*e.g.,* a health spa) is not a "bulk transfer," and Article 6 may be safely ignored.

   a. **Sale of equipment:** [§644]   U.C.C. section 6-102(2) provides that the sale of *equipment* is not a bulk transfer unless the equipment is sold along with the inventory. The revision has the same rule. [U.C.C. §6R-102, Official Comment 1(c)]

   b. **Restaurants and bars:** [§645]   Courts have split on the issue of whether the sale of a restaurant or a bar is the sale of an inventoried business, although Official Comment 2 to section 6-102 (Comment 1 to section 6R-103) clearly states that a restaurant is not covered because it is not the type of business for which unsecured credit is commonly extended on the faith of a stock of merchandise. Some states have special statutes including restaurants and bars under Article 6.

3. **Excluded Transfers:** [§646]   U.C.C. section 6-103 (section 6R-103(2)) contains a list of bulk transfers that would normally trigger the need to comply with Article 6, but which are nonetheless excluded for various policy reasons.

   a. **Transfer of security interest:** [§647]   The creation of a security interest in the inventory, while technically a "transfer," is not a sale of that inventory and does not require the sending of Article 6 notices. [U.C.C. §§6-103(1), 6R-103(3)(a)]

   b. **Transfers to creditors:** [§648]   All other transfers to creditors to create or realize upon a lien (*e.g.,* a repossession or a transfer to an assignee for creditors) are also excluded because they are not true sales. [U.C.C. §§6-103(2), (3), 6R-103(3)]

   c. **Transfers to transferee who assumes all debts:** [§649]   If the transferee (i) maintains a known place of business in the state (ii) decides to assume the transferor's debts in full, and (iii) gives public notice of this fact, Article 6 may be ignored on the theory that the creditors of the transferor are not prejudiced by the sale. Public notice may be given by publishing once a week for two consecutive weeks an advertisement in a local newspaper giving the names of the parties and the effective date of the transfer. [U.C.C. §6-103(6), *see* last paragraph] Under the revision, Article 6 does not apply if a solvent buyer assumes all of the debts of the seller and either gives notice of the sale to the seller's creditors within 30 days thereof or files a notice of the sale in the office of the secretary of state. [U.C.C. §6R-103(3)(i), (j)]

d. **Transfer to new business:** [§650]   If a business changes form of ownership (*e.g.*, a partnership becomes a corporation) and the new business assumes the debts of the old, and public notice (as in the last section) is given, no Article 6 notices need be sent as long as the new business gets no rights that are superior to those of the old business's creditors. [U.C.C. §§6-103(7), 6R-103(3)(k)]

e. **Transfer exempt from execution:** [§651]   If the bulk sale is of assets that are exempt from execution, Article 6 may be ignored. Where this happens, the transferor's creditors are not hurt because they could not have seized the property in any event. [U.C.C. §6-103(8)]

f. **Price range:** [§652]   In the revised version of Article 6, a bulk sale must transfer assets valued between $10,000 and $25 million, or the Article does not apply. [U.C.C. §6R-103(3)(1)]

C.   COMPLIANCE PROCEDURE—ORIGINAL VERSION OF ARTICLE 6

1. **Schedules:** [§653]   U.C.C. section 6-104 requires the *transferor* to prepare a list of existing creditors and *both parties* to prepare a schedule of the property to be transferred. Note the division of duties here.

2. **List of Creditors:** [§654]   The transferor's list of creditors must be signed and sworn to, contain the names and business addresses of the creditors plus the amount owed to them, and include the names of those holding what the transferor resists as disputed claims. [U.C.C. §6-104(2)]

   a. **Errors on list of creditors:** [§655]   If the list is incomplete or contains errors, the transferee may nonetheless rely on it (and is not subject to attack by omitted creditors) *unless the transferee knows of the error or omission*. [U.C.C. §6-104(3)]

   b. **Affidavit of no "creditors":** [§656]   If the transferor furnishes an affidavit stating that there are no creditors, may the transferee believe this? It is a rare business that has no creditors at all. The leading case [Adrian Tabin Corp. v. Climax Boutique, Inc., 313 N.E.2d 66 (N.Y. 1974)], held that the transferee who has no actual knowledge that the affidavit is wrong is not required to investigate, and may continue with the sale without giving notices.

3. **Preservation of the List and Schedule:** [§657]   The transferee must preserve the list of creditors and schedule of property for six months after the sale and permit creditors to examine and copy these items. [U.C.C. §6-104(1)(c)]

4. **Notice:** [§658]   U.C.C. section 6-107 lists two different forms of the required notice to creditors, the so-called "long" and "short" forms. The short form is used where the debts of the transferor are to be paid in full. If this is not the case, or the transferee is unsure as to this, the long form must be used.

   a. **Short form:** [§659]   The short form notice states that a bulk transfer is about to be made, gives the names and addresses of the parties (including other business names and addresses used by the transferor in the past three years), states whether the debts of the transferor are to be paid in full, and, if so, the address to which creditors should send their bills. [U.C.C §6-107(1)]

b. **Long form:** [§660]   In addition to the above, the long form *also* requires the location and description of the property to be transferred, the estimated total of the transferor's debts, the address where the list and schedule may be inspected, what debts will be paid, and a description of the consideration to be paid. [U.C.C. §6-107(2)]

c. **Delivery of notice:** [§661]   The notice may be hand delivered to the transferor's creditors or sent by registered or certified mail. It should be given to all creditors on the list, plus those known by the transferee to be creditors. [U.C.C. §6-107(3)]

d. **Auctions:** [§662]   Where the bulk transfer is by an auction, the auctioneer must perform the duties of the transferee as described above. [U.C.C. §6-108]

e. **Timing of the notice:** [§663]   An important rule, found in U.C.C. section 6-105, is that the notice must be given at least *10 days* before the transferee takes possession of the goods or pays for them. There is no case law on the issue of whether a down payment given prior to the sending of notice violates this rule.

5. **Paying the Creditors:** [§664]   Some states have adopted optional U.C.C. section 6-106. This section requires the *transferee* to make sure that the consideration for the transfer is paid, *pro rata*, to all creditors shown on the list of creditors or who file their claim in writing within 30 days after the mailing of the notice. A transferee who trusts the transferor to fulfill this duty will remain liable if the money is not so paid. [Darby v. Ewing's Home Furnishings, 278 F. Supp. 917 (W.D. Okla. 1967)]

D. COMPLIANCE PROCEDURE—REVISED ARTICLE 6

1. **Notice of Filing:** [§665]   The usual method of compliance under revised Article 6 is for the buyer to send the seller's creditors a notice 45 days in advance of the bulk sale stating that it is going to occur. [U.C.C. §6R-104] However, where the seller has 200 or more creditors, the buyer gives sufficient notice by *filing* the written notice of bulk sale with the secretary of state's office not less than 45 days before the sale. [U.C.C. §6R-105]

2. **Distribution Schedule:** [§666]   The above notice must state how the proceeds of the sale will be distributed. [U.C.C. §6R-105(3)] The schedule of distribution must comply with the requirements of section 6R-106, which include rules concerning the amendment of the schedule of distribution where the original schedule becomes impossible.

E. RIGHTS OF CREDITORS

1. **Omitted Creditors:** [§667]   If the transferee sent proper Article 6 notices, an omitted creditor of whom the transferee had no actual knowledge has no rights against the transferee or the property (unless there was a valid security interest therein, *see infra*, §672). Such a creditor must look to the transferor for relief.

2. **Noncompliance with Original Article 6:** [§668]   If the transferee did not comply with the Article 6 rules (no notice sent, or defective notice sent), the transferor's creditors may take legal action. The original version of Article 6 did not specify the exact remedy, and the courts reached different results.

   a. **Rights against the property:** [§669]   All courts agreed that the transferor's creditors may proceed to seize the property transferred, and some courts also permitted the creditors to reach the proceeds of the property transferred (the money or checks received for it, or even subsequent property purchased with the proceeds of the sale of the original property).

   b. **Rights against the transferee:** [§670]   A large number of courts also permitted the transferor's creditors to maintain a personal action against the transferee where the Article 6 rules had been violated. [*See discussion in* Bill Voorhees Co. v. R&S Camper Sales, Inc., 605 F.2d 888 (5th Cir. 1979)]

3. **Liability Under Revised Article 6:** [§671]   The revision is a lot clearer about remedies, with the key section being section 6R-107, providing for damages to be paid by the noncomplying buyer for any loss caused by the noncompliance. There is a good faith effort defense in section 6R-107(3), and a cap on the liability of the buyer limiting exposure to twice the value of the contract. [U.C.C. §6R-107(4)]

4. **Rights of Secured Creditors:** [§672]   Only unsecured creditors get the benefits of bulk sales laws. The rights of secured creditors are governed by Article 9 of the U.C.C. If a secured creditor's security interest is *perfected* at the time of the bulk transfer, the creditor may seize the transferred property or the proceeds thereof, even though the transferee has carefully complied with Article 6. [U.C.C. §§9-201, 9-306(2)] On the other hand, *unperfected* security interests are cut off by a bulk transfer to a transferee who has no knowledge of the security interest and who gives value and receives delivery of the property prior to perfection of the security interest. [U.C.C. §9-301(1)(c)]

5. **Statute of Limitations:** [§673]   Under the original version of Article 6, an action to attack a bulk transfer must be brought within *six months* after the transferee's taking of possession, or the creditors lose their rights under Article 6. Where, however, the transaction was *concealed*, the six-month period starts to run after the transfer is discovered. [U.C.C. §6-111] Courts have split on the issue of whether mere noncompliance with Article 6, without more, is a "concealment" so as to trigger the longer limitations period. [*Compare* Columbian Rope v. Rinek Cordage Co., 461 A.2d 312 (Pa. 1983)—is concealment; *with In re* Del Norte Depot, Inc., 716 F.2d 557 (9th Cir. 1983)—is not concealment] In the revision, the statute of limitations period has expanded to one year. [U.C.C. §6R-110] The period runs from the date of the sale, but if the sale has been concealed, then the period begins to run when the person bringing the action should have discovered the sale (in no event more than two years after the sale). On the concealment issue, section 6R-110(2) flatly states that complete noncompliance with the bulk sales laws does not of itself constitute concealment so as to trigger the longer statute of limitations.

6. **Subsequent Transfers by Transferee:** [§674]   If the transfer is defective because of failure to comply with Article 6, a subsequent purchaser of the property from the transferee who gives value and buys without knowledge of the defect takes free of the rights of the original transferor's creditors. [U.C.C. §6-110] The revision does not speak to this issue.

REVIEW QUESTIONS

COVERAGE OF ARTICLE 9

1. Farmer executes a chattel mortgage on his crops to Bank as security for a loan. Is the transaction subject to Article 9? _____

2. Architect has a contract under which she is to receive $25,000 from Builder upon completion of a design for a new office building. Because she is short of funds, she borrows money from Lender and, as security for repayment, assigns the fee that she is to receive. Is the transaction subject to Article 9? _____

   a. Assume Architect also delivered to Lender as security the research studies, blueprints, and preliminary design work she had done on the building. Would this transaction be subject to Article 9? _____

3. Professor assigns to Lender, as security for a loan, the salary that he is to earn from University during the forthcoming year. Is the transaction subject to Article 9? _____

4. Manufacturer sells to X all of his outstanding accounts receivable, for which X pays face value less 10%.

   a. Assume the purpose of the sale was to enable Manufacturer to raise needed cash for expansion purposes. Is the transaction subject to Article 9? _____

   b. Assume the assignment was part of Manufacturer's sale of his entire business (along with his equipment, inventory, etc.). Would the transfer of his accounts be subject to Article 9? _____

   c. Assume the assignment was made to satisfy a *preexisting* indebtedness owed by Manufacturer to X (rather than for new consideration). Would the assignment be subject to Article 9? _____

5. As security for a loan, Manufacturer executes a promissory note and assigns to Lender his leasehold interest in the premises where he conducts business. Is the transaction subject to Article 9? _____

   a. Assume that Lender, to secure its own line of credit, then assigns Manufacturer's note and the assigned leasehold interest to Bank. Is the transaction between Lender and Bank subject to Article 9? _____

CREATION OF SECURITY INTEREST

6. Debtor executed a valid security agreement with Lender covering Debtor's machinery and equipment. However, Lender fails to perfect her security interest by filing or in any other manner. If Debtor defaults, can Lender enforce the interest? _____

7. Jeweler pledges a bag of diamonds worth $50,000 as security for repayment of a loan from Lender. Assume no written security agreement is ever executed and

no financing statement is ever filed. Does Lender have an enforceable security interest in the diamonds? _____

8. Manufacturer borrows $100,000 from Lender and executes a financing statement (but not a security agreement) covering all of its inventory, equipment, accounts, etc. Does Lender have an enforceable security interest in the described collateral? _____

9. If a security agreement describes the collateral as "all machinery and equipment located at. . . [debtor's address]," is the description sufficient to create a security interest in machinery and/or equipment having license or serial numbers for identification? _____

10. As security for a loan, Merchant conveys to Lender a security interest in his "inventory and stock on hand" at a designated location.

   a. Does such description confer upon Lender a security interest in the cash and accounts that Merchant will obtain when he sells the inventory? _____

   b. Is the description sufficient to confer upon Lender a security interest in items that become part of Merchant's inventory *after* the date of the security agreement, in the absence of any "after-acquired property" clause? _____

   c. Assume Merchant has signed the security agreement and financing statement, but Lender has not. Does this affect the validity of Lender's interest? _____

11. Debtor executes a security interest on certain collateral in reliance on Lender's promise to loan $10,000. Can Lender claim an enforceable interest in the collateral *before* paying over the $10,000? _____

12. Printer borrows $50,000 from Bank to purchase a printing press to be manufactured to his specifications by Pressco. The security agreement describes the press as being in the process of manufacture. Does Bank have any security interest in the press during the several months that it takes to complete manufacture and prior to its delivery to Printer? _____

PERFECTION

13. As security for a loan, Debtor delivers to Lender several bags of "junk silver coins." No financing statement is filed but Lender has signed a receipt for the coins, stating that they will be returned on repayment of the loan.

   a. Does Lender have a perfected security interest in the coins? _____

   b. Is Lender entitled to add insurance and storage costs to the amount of the loan and retain the coins until these are paid? _____

   c. If the coins are stolen from Lender and insurance does not cover the full loss, who bears the loss? _____

   d. If Lender fails to exercise reasonable care for the coins, does Lender lose her security interest? _____

14. Hi-Fi Store sells and delivers a $5,000 stereo system to Buff, who pays $2,000 down and agrees to pay the balance in monthly installments plus interest. Buff subsequently defaults.

    a. If Store's invoice to Buff states, "Seller reserves title to all merchandise sold until paid in full," can Store assert a valid security interest against Buff? _____

    b. Assume there is a valid security agreement, but no financing statement is ever filed. Can Store assert a security interest in the stereo system against *other creditors* of Buff? _____

    c. Assume that Store did not finance the purchase. Rather, Buff went to his Bank, where he borrowed the $3,000 necessary to pay off Store and executed a valid security agreement. Can Bank assert a security interest in the stereo system against Buff's other creditors *without filing* a financing statement? _____

    d. Same facts. Assume that Buff's security agreement with Bank expressly stated that the interest would extend to "all debts and obligations now or hereafter owed" to Bank. Assume further that Buff then owed Bank $2,000 on an *unrelated* debt. Can Bank assert a perfected security interest as to the $2,000 debt *without filing* a financing statement? _____

15. Grimm is in the business of buying hard-to-collect accounts at a discount. Grimm purchases from Manufacturer all of its "bad" accounts (those 180 days or more past due) at 50% of face value. Grimm neither notifies the account-debtors nor files a financing statement as to his purchase. Does Grimm have a perfected security interest in the accounts (so as to be protected against later assignments by Manufacturer)? _____

16. Bank lends money to Processor to enable it to purchase a boatload of raw material. As security for the loan, Processor signs a security agreement with respect to the shipment and assigns to Bank the bill of lading covering the shipment. Before the shipment arrives, Bank releases the bill of lading to Processor to enable it to make arrangements for delivery. If Other Creditor levies a writ of attachment while the bill of lading is in Processor's possession, who prevails? _____

17. Bank lends money to Printer to enable Printer to purchase a new printing press, which is installed in Printer's plant in State X. Printer signs a security agreement and financing statement covering the press, and Bank's interest is perfected by filing in State X. Later, however, Printer moves the press to a new plant site in State Y, without Bank's knowledge or consent. Would the unauthorized removal of the press operate to jeopardize Bank's perfected security interest? _____

    a. Assume that Bank *knew* at the time of the loan that Printer planned to move the press to State Y after purchase. Under which state's laws would Bank's security interest have to be perfected *originally*? _____

18. Sly purchases a used car from Seller in State A on a conditional sale contract. Seller's interest is noted on the certificate of title as required by State A law, and Seller retains the certificate. Sly moves his residence to State B without advising Seller and makes no further payments on his contract.

a. If it takes Seller *six months* to locate Sly in State B, can Seller still claim an enforceable security interest in the car? _____

b. Would the answer be the same if, in the interim, Sly had registered the car in State B (which does not require the surrender of the certificate of title) and had obtained a clean registration showing him as the owner? _____

c. Would the answer be the same if, after obtaining the clean registration in State B, Sly had sold the car to Dealer in State B, who had no knowledge of Seller's interest? _____

FILING

19. Debtor has executed a valid security agreement, but failed to sign a financing statement at the time of the loan.

   a. If Lender files a financing statement bearing only Lender's own signature, is the filing sufficient to perfect the interest? _____

   b. If Lender files a copy of the security *agreement* in lieu of a financing statement, will the filing perfect Lender's interest? _____

20. Which, if any, of the following facts *must* be shown in the financing statement to perfect the security interest? _____

   a. The amount of the debt or obligation.

   b. Due date of debt or obligation.

   c. Intended use of collateral.

   d. Whether after-acquired collateral is also covered.

   e. Whether proceeds are covered.

21. A filed financing statement lists the debtor as "Minerva Schwartz." Several months later, the debtor marries and changes her name to "Minerva Jones." Is the filed statement effective to perfect the secured party's interest in *after-acquired collateral*? _____

   a. If an amended filing is required, is it valid if signed only by the secured party? _____

22. A filed financing statement lists the debtor's address as "407 Fillmore Street, San Francisco." Later, the debtor moves to Los Angeles. Is the filed statement effective to perfect the secured party's interest in *after-acquired* collateral? _____

23. A filed financing statement describes the collateral as "machinery and equipment located at 407 Fillmore Street, San Francisco." Later, the debtor acquires *other* machinery and equipment at a *different* address in the same city. Is the filed statement effective to perfect the secured party's interest in the other collateral? _____

   a. If an amended filing is required, must it be signed *both* by debtor and secured party? _____

24. Regardless of the nature of the collateral, is a secured party automatically protected by filing the financing statement in the appropriate *state* office (as opposed to any local or county filing)? _____

25. Lender filed a copy of the security *agreement* in lieu of a financing statement. The agreement shows that the loan is due in 12 months. For how long a period is the filing effective? _____

26. If a loan remains unpaid at the end of the effective period of the original filing, can the secured party *unilaterally* obtain an extension? _____

27. Can a prospective lender force the secured party to divulge the amount and extent of its interest in order to evaluate whether to make a further loan to the debtor? _____

PRIORITIES

28. On March 1, Lender A files a financing statement covering Jeweler's inventory, but does not actually make the loan until March 15. Meanwhile, on March 10, Jeweler pledges a bag of diamonds to Lender B, who advances funds immediately. Who is entitled to priority as to the bag of diamonds? _____

29. Lender A advances funds to Debtor on April 1, but inadvertently fails to file a financing statement until April 10. Meanwhile, on April 5, Lender B advances funds and takes possession of the collateral. Who is entitled to priority? _____

    a. Would it make any difference whether B *knew* of A's interest when B made the loan on April 5? _____

30. Bank loans money to Debtor on May 1, to enable Debtor to purchase a new stereo set: Debtor signs a security agreement with Bank covering the stereo but no financing statement is ever filed. On June 1, Debtor borrows money from Lender, signing a security agreement and financing statement covering the same stereo. Lender's financing statement is promptly filed. Who is entitled to priority? _____

31. On January 1, Computer Store borrows from Bank and executes a security agreement and financing statement. The security agreement creates an interest in Computer Store's "existing inventory of office machines, as well as any and all such items hereafter acquired." When Bank files the financing statement, it describes the collateral only as "inventory located at. . . (store address)."

    a. Is the filing sufficient to constitute a lien on office machines later acquired by Computer Store as part of its inventory? _____

    b. Assume that on June 1, Computer Store borrowed from Lender and gave a security interest on its entire inventory as of that date. Who would be entitled to priority as to office machines acquired between January 1 (date of Bank's filing) and June 1? _____

32. Bank has a perfected security interest in Printer's machinery and equipment, pursuant to a security agreement that expressly covers "all items of press equipment now located at (printing plant) as well as any such equipment hereafter acquired and installed at such location." Printer buys a new press from Press Co.

who perfects a security interest in the press to secure payment of the purchase price. Who is entitled to priority in the new press—Bank or Press Co.?

33.   Bank loans Printer funds on May 1 to purchase a new printing press. Printer signs a security agreement with Bank covering the printing press, but no financing statement is ever filed. On June 1, Printer borrows money from Lender, signing a security agreement and financing statement covering the printing press. Lender's financing statement is promptly filed. Who is entitled to priority?

34.   On May 1, Bank loans Printer funds to purchase a new printing press, and Printer obtains delivery of the press on the same date. On May 3, Printer borrows from Lender, who immediately files a financing statement covering the press. On May 8, Bank files a financing statement covering the press. Who is entitled to priority?

      a.   Would the result be the same if Lender had perfected its interest by obtaining *possession* of the printing press on May 3?

      b.   If Printer sold the press for cash, who would have priority as to the cash proceeds?

35.   On May 1, Bank loans Liquor Distributor funds to purchase a truckload of liquor, which is to be received on May 5. Bank is *aware* that Lender has previously filed a security interest covering all of Liquor Distributor's existing and after-acquired inventory. Can Bank attain priority over Lender's interest as to the truckload of liquor? How?

36.   Homeowner purchases a new furnace from Appliance Co., and the furnace is installed in Homeowner's house. Appliance Co. has retained a security interest in the furnace to secure payment of the purchase price. Homeowner's house is already subject to a mortgage that constitutes a lien on any fixture therein. As between Mortgage-Holder and Appliance Co., who is entitled to priority with respect to the furnace?

37.   Motor Co. has supplied Lawnmower Co. with gasoline motors for installation in its lawnmowers. At the same time of sale, Motor Co. perfected a security interest in the motors to secure payment of the purchase price. At all times, Lawnmower Co.'s finished goods inventory was subject to a security interest held by Lender, which covers both existing and after-produced inventory. In the event of default, who is entitled to priority as to the motors?

      a.   In the event that Lawnmower Co. sells a portion of its inventory to Dealer, who pays value and takes without knowledge of Motor Co.'s security interest, does the sale cut off Motor Co.'s interest?

38.   Produce Co. supplies a carload of potatoes to Chip Co. and perfects a security interest in the shipment to secure payment of the purchase price. Chip Co. uses the potatoes to manufacture 500 cases of potato chips. At all times, Chip Co.'s finished goods inventory was subject to a perfected security interest held by Lender, which covered both its existing and after-produced inventory for regular financing purposes.

a. Does Produce Co. have any enforceable interest in the potato chip inventory? _____

b. As between Produce Co. and Lender, who is entitled to priority? _____

39. Lender has filed a financing statement perfecting its security interest in the inventory of Hi-Fi Store. Hi-Fi sells a stereo set for $5,000 to Purchaser, who pays for it as follows: $1,000 credit for trade-in on old equipment (added to Hi-Fi's inventory); $1,000 cash, balance of $3,000 to be paid on a "conditional sale" installment contract.

a. Does Lender have a security interest in the stereo system sold to Purchaser? _____

b. Does Lender have a security interest in the old equipment traded in by purchaser and added to Hi-Fi's inventory? _____

c. Does it make any difference that *neither* the security agreement nor financing statement signed by Hi-Fi Store mentioned any security interest in "proceeds"? _____

d. Does it make any difference that Hi-Fi Store's sale of the stereo system *violated* a term of the security agreement (which provided that no system selling for more than $1,000 would be sold without Lender's express consent)? _____

e. Assume that Hi-Fi deposited the $1,000 down payment received from Purchaser in its checking account, along with other funds. Will Lender's security interest continue in Hi-Fi's checking account for any amount? _____

f. Assume that Hi-Fi discounted and assigned Purchaser's $3,000 installment contract to Bank, who is *aware* that Lender had a security interest in Hi-Fi's inventory. As between Lender and Bank, who is entitled to priority in Purchaser's obligation? _____

g. Assume that Purchaser returned the stereo system to Hi-Fi because he realized he would be unable to pay for it. As between Lender and Bank, who is entitled to priority in the returned stereo system? _____

40. On October 1, Jeweler borrows $10,000 from Bank and executes a security agreement and financing statement covering Jeweler's entire inventory. Bank files the financing statement immediately. On October 15, Jeweler takes from inventory a bag of diamonds and pledges this to Lender as security for a $25,000 loan. On November 1, Bank lends Jeweler an additional $50,000 without knowledge of the interim transaction with Lender. Who is entitled to priority and in what amount? _____

a. Would the answer be the same even if the financing statement filed by Bank made *no mention* of the fact that future advances would be made? _____

b. Would the answer be the same if Bank was *not obligated* under the security agreement to make the $50,000 loan on November 1? _____

c. Would the answer be the same if Bank *knew* about the intervening transaction with Lender?   _____

41. Lender has a perfected security interest in Manufacturer's machinery and equipment to secure repayment of a loan. Manufacturer sells its entire business, including the machinery and equipment, to Purchaser. Purchaser paid full value and had no knowledge of Lender's security interest. Manufacturer's loan from Lender remains unpaid.

   a. Assume that Manufacturer had falsely stated to Purchaser that there were no security interests outstanding in its machinery and equipment and Purchaser relied in good faith in purchasing the equipment. Does the sale to Purchaser cut off Lender's security interest?   _____

   b. Assume that Purchaser, as security for its own financing, conveys a security interest in the machinery and equipment to Bank. Is Bank's interest subject to Lender's security interest?   _____

42. Lender has a perfected security interest in the inventory of Liquor Distributor. Distributor makes an unauthorized sale of 200 cases of whiskey to Purchaser, who pays full value, and who has no knowledge of Lender's security interest. Does Purchaser take subject to Lender's interest?   _____

   a. Would Purchaser take subject to Lender's interest if Purchaser *knew* of Lender's interest when the purchase was made?   _____

43. Lender has filed and perfected a security interest in the inventory and equipment of Liquor Distributor. Included in its equipment is an expensive camera that Distributor uses for advertising purposes. Distributor makes an unauthorized sale of the camera to Purchaser, who buys the camera for personal use, pays full value therefor, and has no knowledge of Lender's security interest. Does Purchaser take subject to Lender's interest?   _____

44. On June 1, Jeweler borrows $10,000 from Bank and executes a security agreement and financing statement covering Jeweler's entire inventory. Bank files the financing statement immediately. On June 15, in an effort to streamline inventory, Jeweler sells to Liquidator all silverware and related items in inventory. Liquidator paid $25,000 (a fair price) and had no knowledge of Bank's interest. On October 1, Bank loaned Jeweler an additional $50,000 without knowledge of the intervening sale of the silverware inventory. What is the extent, if any, of Bank's security interest in the silverware following the sale?   _____

   a. Could Bank also claim a security interest in the $25,000 received by Jeweler from Liquidator?   _____

45. Carl became insolvent and could not afford to get his car out of Auto Fix-It Shop where he had taken it for repairs. A month later, Carl persuaded Auto Fix-It to let him borrow his car for a few hours to visit his father in a local hospital. While the car was parked at the hospital, it was seized by the county sheriff, who was executing a judgment acquired by Carl's landlord for $460 back rent owed by Carl. Both Crunch Credit Union (which had a perfected security interest in the car when it was seized) and Auto Fix-It Shop seek to have the car turned over to them. Who wins?   _____

46. Bank has a perfected security interest in Jeweler's inventory to secure payment of a $10,000 loan. Creditor levies a writ of execution on the inventory, which is actually worth $50,000. The following day, Bank loans Jeweler an additional $40,000 pursuant to the security agreement and files a third-party claim proceeding for release of the inventory, asserting the amount of its lien as $50,000. Creditor resists on the ground that Bank's lien is limited to $10,000. In whose favor should the court rule in the third-party claim proceeding?

_____

47. Local Bank holds a perfected security interest in the inventory of Great Gift Shoppe ("GGS"). Emma Hobby sells GGS 50 ceramic objects that she made in her basement and receives in return a check for $150. The check bounces. When Emma returns to GGS, the store has gone out of business and its inventory (including her ceramic pieces) has been seized by Local Bank. May Emma reclaim her ceramics from GGS?

_____

BANKRUPTCY PROCEEDINGS

48. Lender loaned money and obtained a valid security interest on Debtor's inventory one week before Debtor filed for bankruptcy. Debtor was adjudicated a bankrupt *before* Lender filed its financing statement. Will Lender's security interest be set aside because not fully perfected at the time of bankruptcy?

_____

49. On June 1 and while clearly insolvent, Debtor gives a security interest in Debtor's inventory to Lender as security for an account past due. Lender delays filing the financing statement until June 9. On October 15, Debtor files bankruptcy. Can Lender's security interest be set aside as a "preference"?

_____

50. On June 1, Lender loans money to Debtor whom Lender knows is insolvent, and obtains a security interest in Debtor's inventory. On July 1, Lender files a financing statement. On August 1, Debtor files bankruptcy. Can Lender's security interest be set aside as a "preference"?

_____

51. On March 1, Lender perfects a security interest in Debtor's "existing and after-acquired" inventory as security for a loan made on that date. On August 1, Debtor makes a bulk purchase of a competitor's inventory assets and adds these to Debtor's own inventory, even though Debtor was then clearly insolvent. On September 1, Debtor files for bankruptcy. Lender claims an interest in the assets acquired by Debtor on August 1 as "after-acquired property." The trustee in bankruptcy moves to set aside the interest as a "voidable preference." Who wins?

_____

DEFAULT PROCEEDINGS

52. Pressco sells a printing press to Printer, for which Printer signs a negotiable promissory note and security agreement. Pressco discounts these documents to Bank for cash. Printer refuses to pay the note, claiming that the printing press is defective. If Printer's claim is valid, does this affect Bank's right to enforce its interest?

_____

53. Pressco sells a printing press to Printer, retaining a valid security interest to secure payment of the purchase price, which is payable in installments over five years. Printer defaults in payment of one installment, whereupon Pressco enters

Printer's plant and removes a key part of the press rendering it inoperative. Can Printer recover damages against Pressco?

54. Jeweler pledges a bag of diamonds worth $100,000 with Lender as collateral for a $25,000 loan. If Jeweler fails to repay the loan within the time agreed, does Lender have the right to **retain** the diamonds in satisfaction of the loan (*i.e.,* without selling them and accounting to Jeweler for any excess)?

   a. Assume that Jeweler had repaid all but $5,000 of the loan before defaulting. Would this affect Lender's right to retain the diamonds?

55. Having perfected its security interest, Hi-Fi Store repossesses a stereo system upon default of Purchaser. After notifying Purchaser in writing of its intent to do so, it places the stereo on its showroom floor, and several days later sells it to another customer for $3,000, although it had been sold to Purchaser several months earlier for $5,000. Purchaser sues for damages (amount of the down payment). Will Purchaser prevail?

   a. Was notice to Purchaser required to be sent, since Hi-Fi intended to dispose of the goods at **private sale**?

   b. Assume that Hi-Fi had received written notice from Lender claiming that Lender had a junior secured interest in Purchaser's stereo system. Was it required that Hi-Fi send written notice to Lender before selling the stereo?

56. Pursuant to its security agreement, Seller validly repossesses an auto following Purchaser's default in payment. Seller sends written notice to Purchaser that Seller intends to sell the automobile to itself at a designated time and place for "low blue book" price. Does Seller have a right to do so?

57. Collateral that has an actual fair market value of $100,000 is sold at a properly noticed public sale in good faith to an arm's-length purchaser for $10,000.

   a. If the obligation in default is $25,000, is the secured party entitled to sue for a $15,000 deficiency?

   b. In the absence of agreement, are expenses incurred by the secured party in **repossessing** the collateral proper charges in computing the amount of any deficiency?

   c. If there was some defect in the notice or conduct of the sale, could Debtor move to set aside the sale to Purchaser?

58. Debtor defaults on an obligation for which a valid security interest is held by Secured Party. To facilitate immediate disposition of the collateral, Secured Party pays Debtor $100 to sign a document that purports to "waive" the following rights: (i) right to compel public sale of collateral; (ii) right to notice of public sale; (iii) right to any surplus from proceeds of public sale; and (iv) right to redeem collateral prior to public sale. Is the "waiver" valid in whole or in part?

59. Purchaser defaults on her contract to purchase a stereo system, upon which Hi-Fi Store has a perfected security interest. Hi-Fi repossesses and conducts a public sale, but fails to notify Purchaser in writing of the time and place of sale. The original cost of the stereo was $5,000, and Purchaser had paid $2,000 as down

payment and signed a contract to pay $3,800 over three years (the $800 reflecting interest on the unpaid balance). What is the minimum amount of damages to which Purchaser is entitled?　　　　　　　　　　　　　　　　　　_____

BULK TRANSFERS

60. Movie Studio was sold for $30 million. Along with the goodwill of the business, the sale included all assets, real and personal. The prop department alone contained 50,000 items. Is this a bulk transfer so as to trigger the necessity of compliance with Article 6?　　_____

61. Bank took a security interest in the inventory of Appliance Store so it could seize the appliances if the store failed to repay the loan Bank made to it. Is this a bulk transfer?　　_____

62. When Appliance Store was sold, the new buyer was careful to comply with all the rules of Article 6. Nonetheless, unknown to the buyer, the seller's list of creditors omitted one creditor: the seller's mother, to whom the seller owed $23,000. Within six months of the sale, the seller's mother filed a lawsuit in which she tried to attach the transferred inventory, now in the hands of the buyer. Will she succeed?　　_____

ANSWERS TO REVIEW QUESTIONS

1. **YES** A security interest in any kind of "goods" is subject to the U.C.C. (and "goods" includes crops growing on land). [§54]

2. **YES** A security interest can be created in "accounts" or contract rights whether or not yet earned by performance. [§§64-65]

  a. **YES** As a pledge of "general intangibles." [§66]

3. **NO** Assignment of wage claims is excluded from Article 9. [§91]

4.a. **YES** The sale of accounts (or chattel paper) is as much a financing transaction as borrowing on the security of such accounts. It makes no difference whether the assignment is with or without reserve. [§§42, 93]

  b. **NO** Here, it is clearly not for financing purposes and is covered by a specific exclusion. [§94]

  c. **NO** Again, a specific exclusion applies. [§97]

5. **NO** Leaseholds in real property are excluded from the U.C.C. [§86]

  a. **YES** As a financing transaction involving *existing instruments*; it is immaterial that the original obligation giving rise to the instrument was exempt from the U.C.C. [§100]

6. **YES** Failure to perfect a security interest does not affect the validity of the interest as against the debtor. [§§104-105]

7. **YES** Where the collateral is in the *possession* of the secured party, no formal security agreement is required for the interest to attach, and the interest is perfected upon possession. [§§111, 157]

8. **PROBABLY NOT** A financing statement *by itself* is not enough to create a security interest. But, if there is any other evidence of Manufacturer's intent to create a security interest in favor of Lender, the result would be contra. [§§115-116]

9. **YES** A reasonable identification is all that is required; description by category and location is generally enough. [§125]

10.a. **YES** Unless otherwise agreed, proceeds of described collateral are covered as a matter of law. [§129]

  b. **YES** Although there is some authority contra, the word "inventory" is usually sufficient to create an interest in after-acquired items. [§133]

  c. **NO** Neither the security agreement nor the financing statement depends for its validity on the secured party's signature. The debtor's signature alone is sufficient. [§§139-140, 268]

11. **YES** The interest attaches when "value" is given; and the commitment to make the loan is "value" under the U.C.C. [§143]

12.	**PROBABLY**	A security interest attaches as soon as the debtor acquires rights in the collateral. [§144] Printer's right to possession (enforceable through replevin or specific performance) would arise as soon as goods had been identified to the contract. Bank's interest would attach at this time (subject to Pressco's right to withhold to complete production and to obtain payment, etc.).
13.a.	**YES**	The security interest was perfected by taking *possession*. [§§157-158]
b.	**YES**	Lender is entitled to reimbursement for reasonable expenses. [§174]
c.	**PROBABLY LENDER**	Debtor bears the loss unless attributable to Lender's failure to exercise reasonable care. Failure to insure to full value would probably constitute unreasonable care. [§§176-177]
d.	**NO**	The secured party is liable for any loss resulting from such breach of duty of care but does not forfeit the interest. [§170]
14.a.	**NO**	Where debtor has possession of goods, there must be a signed security agreement. [§112]
b.	**YES**	Because in consumer goods transactions, the seller can perfect a purchase money security without filing. [§182]
c.	**YES**	A purchase money security interest can be perfected either by the seller or any lender who supplies the funds used to purchase the collateral in question. [§184]
d.	**NO**	A security interest can be perfected without filing only to the extent of the value advanced for the *purchase* of collateral. [§185]
15.	**DEPENDS**	On whether the "bad" accounts were a "significant portion" of Manufacturer's receivables. If not, no filing is required; the interest is perfected on sale or assignment. (Remember, however, that some states have rejected this exemption from the filing requirement.) [§§196-198]
16.	**DEPENDS**	On whether Bank filed a financing statement within 21 days after release of the bill of lading. Having possession of the bill of lading, Bank's interest was perfected *without filing*; but upon releasing the bill of lading (a negotiable instrument), Bank's interest would become unperfected *after 21 days* unless Bank filed a financing statement in the interim. If Bank failed to do so, Other Creditor would prevail. [§§205-207]
17.	**YES**	Unless a new financing statement is filed *within four months*, Bank's interest would become unperfected, and hence subject to being cut off by sale to a good faith purchaser or intervening liens. [§221]
a.	**DEPENDS**	If taken into State Y *within 30 days* after Printer receives the press, State Y's laws would apply. Otherwise, State X's. [§228]
18.a.	**YES**	The rule requiring a reperfection within four months does not apply to a security interest in an automobile that has been perfected by notation on the certificate of title, until reregistered in a new state. [§§243-245]

b.	**YES**	As long as no innocent purchaser is involved, Seller's interest would still be enforceable. [§246]
c.	**NO**	Because if Seller's interest was not reperfected *within four months* after the car entered State B, it ceases to be perfected as against all subsequent purchasers having no knowledge of the unperfected interest. [§246]
19.a.	**NO**	A financing statement must generally be signed by the debtor. [§250]
b.	**YES**	The agreement gives even more complete notice than would the financing statement. [§247]
20.	**NONE**	A financing statement is complete if it is signed by the debtor, contains the names and addresses of both debtor and secured party, and contains a description of the collateral. No further details are required. [§250]
21.	**DEPENDS**	A new filing within four months is required whenever debtor's name is changed so as to be "seriously misleading." (Note that this impairs only after-acquired collateral, however.) [§257]
a.	**YES**	This is one of the exceptional situations where debtor need not sign. [§269]
22.	**YES**	In most states a change of address within the same state does not require refiling. [§258]
23.	**NO**	The designation of location would not constitute reasonable notice of interest claimed at other locations. [§254]
a.	**YES**	Both parties must sign an amendment to the financing statement. [§271]
24.	**NO**	In all states, there are exceptions in which only a local filing will perfect the interest—*e.g.*, fixtures, farm products, timber, etc. [§§274-280]
25.	**5 YEARS**	The loan period (if shown) is irrelevant. [§287]
26.	**YES**	Secured party may file a *continuation* statement for an additional five years (debtor's signature not required). Must be filed within six months prior to expiration. [§291]
27.	**NO**	No third party has the right to compel the secured party to release this information; but the secured party must give a written statement upon request of the *debtor*. [§§303-305]
28.	**A**	The first to file or perfect wins. Filing on March 1 protects A even though his interest was not actually perfected until he made the loan (March 15). *Rationale:* B could have protected himself by checking the filings before lending money. [§§327-329]
29.	**B**	B is first to file *or perfect*. (A's interest *attached* first, but that does not count.) [§§327-329]
a.	**NO**	Where interests have been perfected, priority is *not affected* by actual knowledge of competing interests. [§§327-329]

30.	**BANK**	A purchase money interest in consumer goods is perfected *without* filing and is entitled to priority as the "first to file or *perfect*." [§§182, 327]
31.a.	**YES**	The financing statement need not mention the after-acquired property agreement. [§265]
b.	**BANK**	After-acquired property clause in security agreement gives Bank priority as to such property over subsequent interest holders. [§329]
32.	**PRESS CO.**	A purchase money security interest takes priority over an after-acquired property clause. [§331]
33.	**LENDER**	A purchase money security interest in *non-consumer* goods must be perfected by filing. [§§182, 331]
34.	**BANK**	A purchase money security interest can be perfected *within 10 (and in many states 20) days* after debtor obtains possession; if so perfected, it takes priority over any intervening interests. [§331]
a.	**YES**	The method by which the intervening interest was perfected is immaterial. [§332]
b.	**BANK**	The purchase money secured party is entitled to the same priority in proceeds as in the original collateral. [§388]
35.	**YES**	By giving Lender *written notice* before the shipment is received that Bank expects to acquire a purchase money security interest therein; and by actually *perfecting* (*e.g.*, by filing) its interest *before* the shipment is received (no 10-day grace period). [§§335-340]
36.	**DEPENDS**	Appliance Co. would win as long as its security interest had *attached* before the furnace was installed, *provided* Appliance Co. *perfects* its interest through a special *fixture filing* (in real estate records) within 10 days after installation. [§350]
37.	**MOTOR CO.**	Where the security interest *precedes* installation, it takes priority over the claims of any other person in the finished goods inventory. [§360]
a.	**DEPENDS**	If the sale was "in the ordinary course of business," it would cut off all security interests. [U.C.C. §9-307(1); *see* §421] If it was not, then it would not cut off Motor Co.'s interest because the interest was *perfected before* the sale (*i.e.,* constructive notice given). [§362]
38.a.	**YES**	As long as Produce Co.'s interest was *perfected* prior to processing, its interest continues in the finished product. [§363]
b.	**LENDER**	Produce Co. would prevail over Lender's perfected interest in the inventory only if it gave the section 9-312(3) notice and perfected prior to delivery. [§§335-341]
39.a.	**NO**	Sale in ordinary course of business by dealer cuts off prior secured interest of Lender. [§§421-429]

b.	**YES**	Trade-in is "proceeds" of inventory item sold. [§372]
c.	**NO**	The secured party's right arises by operation of law. [§376]
d.	**NO**	The fact that the "proceeds" were obtained in violation of the security agreement is immaterial. [§379]
e.	**NO**	Where the proceeds are cash, the secured party's interest terminates **10 days after receipt** unless in the interim there has been a new perfection. Where the cash has been commingled, filing is not an appropriate means of perfection, so that even if Lender filed, it would not do any good. [§380]
f.	**BANK**	Party who gives value and takes possession of chattel paper cuts off security interest claimed merely as "proceeds" of inventory. Bank's knowledge of Lender's interest is immaterial. [§391]
g.	**BANK**	Purchaser of chattel paper (conditional sales contract) is entitled to priority over financer of inventory as to returned goods. [§403]
40.	**BANK— $60,000**	Under the Code, future advances relate back to the date of original perfection (Bank filed October 1), so as to take priority over all later interests— even where the later interest is perfected by possession. [§§407-410]
a.	**YES**	This need not be disclosed in the financing statement. [§409]
b.	**YES**	Because the filing on October 1 constitutes constructive notice that Bank had some sort of interest; it would be up to Lender to find out. [§409]
c.	**YES**	Because the "first-to-file-or-perfect" rule applies regardless of knowledge of competing interests. [§329]
41.a.	**NO**	A perfected security interest in machinery and equipment is **not** cut off by a sale to a bona fide purchaser. Filing constitutes constructive notice. [§§421-429]
b.	**YES**	Lender's interest attaches to the **collateral** regardless of who is the owner. Bank is charged with notice of any interest conveyed by any prior owner in Purchaser's source of title. [§§327, 429]
42.	**NO**	A buyer **in ordinary course of business** from a dealer in such goods cuts off even a perfected security interest. [§421]
a.	**NO**	Mere knowledge of Lender's interest would not invalidate the sale, but knowledge that the sale to Purchaser was **unauthorized** under the security agreement would. [§421]
43.	**YES**	Seller here was **not** a dealer in the goods sold, and hence the purchaser is not protected under U.C.C. section 9-307(1). [§§421-425]
44.	**ONLY $10,000**	Sale to Liquidator was **not** "in ordinary course of business" and hence did not cut off Bank's interest. But Bank's interest is limited to the original advance because the subsequent advance occurred **more than 45 days** following sale. [§§430-431]

a. **YES** As "proceeds" of the collateral originally covered. The fact that Bank's security interest also continued in the silverware (to the extent of $10,000) is immaterial; it **can claim both**. [§379]

45. **CRUNCH CREDIT** Fix-It is a statutory lien holder with a possessory lien. [*See* U.C.C. §9-310] Since it parted with possession (regardless of how meritorious its reason for doing so), it lost its lien. [*See* §441] As between Crunch and the landlord, the former prevails since a judicial lien creditor (the landlord) is junior to a **perfected** security interest. [§457]

46. **BANK** Advances made within 45 days of levy by a lien creditor are protected even where secured party **had knowledge** of the lien. [§458]

47. **NO** Emma's sale to GGS was a "cash sale" and so not covered by U.C.C. section 2-702. Moreover, under section 2-403(1), a seller's right to repossess goods from an insolvent buyer is subject to the rights of a good faith purchaser for value. Since "good faith purchaser" includes a secured party and value includes satisfaction of a security interest, Local Bank's rights are superior to those of Emma. [§§467-468]

48. **NO** Lender has 10 days in which to perfect. [§512]

49. **NO** Bankruptcy Code gives secured interest holder 10 days within which to perfect by filing, in which event transfer dates from when interest was created rather than from filing. Accordingly, Lender's interest dates from June 1, and the 90-day preference period expired September 1. [§§498, 513]

50. **YES** Because filing occurred beyond the 10-day grace period. Hence, "transfer" took place only on July 1. At that time, it was for an **antecedent** debt (loan made June 1); hence, a preference. [§§497 *et seq.*]

51. **TRUSTEE** "Transfer" is deemed made on August 1 when assets became subject to Lender's after-acquired property clause. At that time, the transfer was for an **antecedent debt** (the loan was made on March 1). It **cannot** be saved as a transfer for value under U.C.C. section 9-108 because debtor did **not** acquire these items in the **ordinary course** of business (bulk purchase). [§§515-519]

52. **NO** There is no indication that Bank is so intimately involved with Pressco's affairs as to be chargeable with knowledge of its business practices. The U.C.C. implies a **waiver** of defenses in favor of **good faith** assignees. [§§528 *et seq.*]

53. **PROBABLY NOT** As long as a **default** exists (even one installment missed), the secured party is entitled to the remedies provided under the U.C.C. One of these is to **disable** the collateral on the debtor's premises, provided the secured party acts in a commercially reasonable manner. [§§552, 556-557]

54. **YES** Provided Jeweler complies with the notice requirement. [§§564-565]

a. **NO** The "60%" rule applies only to consumer goods; Jeweler can force resale by objecting to strict foreclosure by notice in writing. [§§564-567]

55. **PROBABLY NOT** Assuming the repossession was proper (and no constitutional objection), Hi-Fi was entitled to dispose of collateral in any "commercially reasonable manner"—

including private sale (especially since it was a dealer in such merchandise). Lower sale price is not enough by itself to show resale was commercially unreasonable. [§§568-569, 594-595]

a. **YES**   The notice requirement applies whether a public or private sale is contemplated. [§§572-574]

b. **NO**   Where consumer goods are involved (stereo sold for Purchaser's personal use), notice to debtor alone is sufficient. [§579]

56. **PROBABLY NOT**   A secured party is not entitled to sell to itself at a *private sale* except if the goods are of a type customarily sold in a recognized market or at widely distributed standard price quotations. "Low blue book" would probably *not* qualify. [§§582, 588]

57.a. **YES**   Absent fraud in the sale, the *sale price* (not market value) is used to compute any deficiency. [§594]

b. **YES**   All expenses incurred in good faith in retaking and disposing of the collateral may be included. [§§597-598]

c. **NO**   The purchaser's title cannot be set aside for defects in the sale unless the debtor can prove that the purchaser was in collusion with the secured party or had knowledge of the defect. [§608]

58. **IN PART**   (i), (ii), and (iv) *can* be "waived" by the debtor *after* default, as here. Not so, however, as to (iii). [§§623-624]

59. **$1,300**   Consumer goods penalty measure: *i.e.,* the time-price differential ($800) plus 10% of the original cash price ($500). [§622]

60. **NO**   The principal business of the enterprise sold was making movies and not the sale of merchandise from stock. [§643]

61. **NO**   The creation of a security interest is exempted from the need to comply with the bulk transfer laws. [§647]

62. **NO**   The buyer is entitled to rely on the seller's list of creditors, and unless the buyer has actual knowledge that the list is in error, the buyer is not liable to an omitted creditor, who must look to the seller for relief. [§§655, 665, 667]

SAMPLE EXAM QUESTION I

Pecos Bill was a financial speculator. Early this year, he purchased the favorite guitar of a famous late rock and roll star, planning to hold on to the guitar as its value appreciated, and eventually sell it at a tremendous profit. In the meantime, Pecos Bill used the guitar as collateral for a $10,000 loan from Antitrust National Bank ("ANB"), which had him sign a security agreement and a financing statement. The financing statement was filed by the bank in the county in which Pecos Bill lived. This filing was in error, as the state's version of U.C.C. section 9-401 required that all financing statements of this kind be filed in the office of the secretary of state. Pecos Bill then asked Nightflyer Loan Company ("NLC") to lend him $5,000, giving the guitar as collateral. NLC agreed, but before lending the money, it had its attorney check the files. In the course of doing so, the attorney stumbled across ANB's misfiled financing statement; however, seeing it was misfiled, the attorney ignored it. NLC went through with the loan, keeping the guitar in its possession. No security agreement was signed, and no financing statement was ever filed on this transaction. Pecos Bill failed to repay either debt, and ANB sued NLC to recover the guitar.

(a)   How would the guitar be classified as collateral using Article 9 terminology?

(b)   Does NLC have a valid security interest in the guitar?

(c)   Which creditor, ANB or NLC, has the senior interest in the guitar?

SAMPLE EXAM QUESTION II

Mortar Construction Company was incorporated under the laws of the State of Delaware and had its main offices in Chicago, Illinois. Mortar was awarded the job of building a civic center for the City of Thebes, Utah. To finance the construction, Mortar borrowed $500,000 from Builders State Bank of Smalltown, West Virginia. While in West Virginia negotiating the loan, Moe Mortar, president of the construction company, signed a security agreement and a financing statement giving the bank a security interest in the money Mortar expected to receive from the City of Thebes for constructing the civic center project. Builders State Bank seeks advice as to where it should file the financing statement. Advise.

SAMPLE EXAM QUESTION III

Nancy Chef owned a cooking utensils store in Big Red, California. Her inventory was encumbered by a perfected security interest in favor of the Big Red State Bank. In January, Nancy bought a snowmobile for her personal use from Snowfun Vehicles, which had her sign a security agreement in its favor to secure the unpaid portion of the purchase price. She also owned a car that was subject to a security interest in favor of Big Red State Bank (this interest being noted on the car's certificate of title as required by California law).

On February 28, Nancy moved her whole business to Apple Valley, Oregon. On March 1, she signed a security agreement in favor of the Oregon Valley Bank ("OVB") giving OVB a security interest in the store's inventory; OVB filed a financing statement in the proper place. In September, Nancy went bankrupt. She still had the store, the snowmobile, and the car (for which she had the original California title, not having reregistered the car in Oregon). Both banks claim the inventory; Snowfun Vehicles wants the snowmobile (which is worth no more than the debt still owed it); and Big Red State Bank claims a senior interest in the car. Nancy's trustee in bankruptcy would like to keep these items in the estate if possible.

Who has the senior rights as to each of the above items?

SAMPLE EXAM QUESTION IV

The inventory of Arabian Rug Company "now owned or after-acquired" is subject to a perfected (filed) security interest in Retailer Bank. Arabian Rug Company is contacted by Ornate Rugs of Persia, a rug manufacturer, which asks Arabian's owner if the company would be willing to act as Ornate's selling agent in the United States in return for a 30% commission on each rug sold. Ornate and Arabian sign a contract containing a clause providing that Arabian is only a selling agent and that title to the rugs will at all times remain in Ornate. Before shipping the rugs to Arabian, the president of Ornate seeks advice. Are there any other steps Ornate should take before shipment?

SAMPLE EXAM QUESTION V

In January, White Truck Ice Cream Company granted a security interest in all its equipment to Tenacles National Bank ("TNB"), which perfected its interest by filing. TNB committed itself to loan White Truck $10,000 each month as long as White Truck repaid a certain portion of the debt monthly. These loans were made on the first of every month. On May 10, White Truck sold one of its ice cream making machines to a competitor, Blue Truck Ice Cream Company. TNB knew nothing about this sale. On September 1, TNB made its usual loan to White Truck. On September 25, the federal government filed a tax lien in the proper place against White Truck, which had somehow neglected to pay its taxes for the past year. On October 1, November 1, and December 1, TNB made its usual loans, but the day before Christmas, TNB discovered the tax lien. TNB wants to find out what its rights are against Blue Truck, and which, if any, of its loans to White Truck has priority vis-a-vis the government. Discuss.

SAMPLE EXAM QUESTION VI

Music, Music, Music Co. ("MMMC") sold musical instruments. Its inventory was subject to a security interest in favor of Local Bank, which had filed a financing statement in the proper place on April 1. When MMMC sold a piano on credit, it made the buyer sign a promissory note payable to MMMC, plus an agreement giving MMMC a security interest in the piano. MMMC never filed financing statements for these transactions. The resulting notes and security agreements were sold to Merchants Finance Company with an agreement to buy them back should they prove uncollectable. In January of the next year, MMMC contracted to buy 50 fancy black walnut pianos from Black Walnut Piano Company. Black Walnut agreed to sell them to MMMC on credit, reserving (pursuant to agreement) a security interest in the pianos to secure their purchase price. Prior to delivering the pianos to MMMC, Black Walnut filed a financing statement in the appropriate place and sent a letter to Local Bank (but not to Merchants Finance) describing the deal. Cathy Consumer bought a black walnut piano from MMMC on credit, signing the usual documents, which MMMC sold to Merchants Finance. Assuming MMMC repays none of its debts:

(a) Can Black Walnut or Local Bank get back the piano sold to Cathy Consumer?

(b) Which creditor, Local Bank or Black Walnut, has the superior interest in the black walnut pianos in MMMC's inventory?

(c) Which creditor, Local Bank, Merchants Finance, or Black Walnut, has the superior interest in the rights represented by the documents Cathy Consumer signed?

SAMPLE EXAM QUESTION VII

Helene Houseowner decided to build her dream house. To do the job, she borrowed $80,000 from Sharksteeth Finance Company ("SFC"), giving SFC a mortgage on the property and all additions thereto, which SFC properly recorded. When the dream house was almost complete, Helene bought a large exercise machine designed to be built into her exercise room from Muscles, Inc. on credit. Muscles, Inc. had Helene sign a security agreement and a financing statement.

Muscles, Inc. now seeks advice. On previous sales transactions, Muscles, Inc. was advised that it need not go through the expense of filing a financing statement to preserve its purchase money security interest in consumer goods. Is there any reason why it should file in this case? If so, where should it file? Are there any other steps it should take before installing the machine in Helene's exercise room?

SAMPLE EXAM QUESTION VIII

Farmer MacDonald put his crop in a grain elevator and received in return a negotiable warehouse receipt. MacDonald took the receipt to Antitrust National Bank ("ANB") and asked to borrow money on the strength of it. ANB loaned MacDonald $5,000 and had him sign a security agreement and a financing statement in its favor, but left the warehouse receipt with Farmer MacDonald. ANB filed the financing statement in the proper place. Farmer MacDonald then took the receipt to Farmers Friend State Bank ("FFSB") and pledged it to them for a loan of $7,000. Farmer told FFSB nothing about the ANB deal, and FFSB did not check the filing records. Two months later, when it came time to sell the grain, MacDonald retrieved the warehouse receipt from the possession of FFSB so that he could get the grain from the elevator. The next day, Farmer filed a voluntary bankruptcy petition and turned the receipt over to his trustee in bankruptcy. Both ANB and FFSB claim the receipt, and the bankruptcy trustee now seeks advice, stating that the financing statement filed by ANB failed to mention ANB's address. Who is entitled to the grain: the trustee or one of the banks?

SAMPLE EXAM QUESTION IX

On June 10, Mary Shrub borrowed $8,000 from Consumers Bank and signed a security agreement and financing statement giving the bank a security interest in her very valuable china collection. On November 8, Mary bought furniture for her law office on credit, signing a security agreement and financing statement in favor of the seller, Office Furnishings. On November 12, Consumers Bank filed its financing statement in the proper place. On November 15, Mary filed a voluntary bankruptcy petition. On November 16, Office Furnishings filed its financing statement in the proper place.

Which of these transactions is valid against Mary's bankruptcy trustee? Explain.

SAMPLE EXAM QUESTION X

After Tim Isle had paid back $900 of a $1,000 debt owed on his automobile to the Repossession Finance Company, he missed the final $100 payment. A clause in the security agreement gave Repossession the right to break into Tim's home to retrieve the car. Pursuant to this clause, Repossession sent out a repo-man named Sam Price, who jimmied open a window in Tim's garage, hot wired the car, and drove it off in the middle of the night. At the time of repossession, the car had several of its parts removed because Tim was tuning the engine. Four months after the repossession, the finance company sold the car for $40 to Sam Price, who paid this low amount because the car "wasn't running right." No one had checked the car to discover the source of its mechanical difficulties. Repossession gave no notice to Tim of the private sale to Price, so that the first Tim knew of the sale was when he received notice of a lawsuit Repossession was bringing against him for $360—the $60 remaining on the debt, plus the costs of repossession and resale. What arguments can Tim Isle raise in defense of this suit?

ANSWER TO SAMPLE EXAM QUESTION I

(a) The guitar is obviously "goods." [U.C.C. §9-105(h)] The question is into which of the four categories of goods defined in U.C.C. section 9-109 does it fall. The guitar is probably not "consumer goods" because of its business purpose (although one court has held a coin collection to be "consumer goods." [*In re* Midas Coin Co., 264 F. Supp. 193 (1967), *aff'd,* 387 F.2d 118 (8th Cir. 1968)] The guitar could be termed "inventory" since it is being held for eventual resale. However, Comment 3 to section 9-109 states that "inventory" must be held for sale in the "ordinary course of business," and it seems unlikely that sale of this guitar would be considered to be in the ordinary course of Pecos's business. Thus, the guitar is most likely to fall into the catch-all category of "equipment" since it does not fit into any of the other categories. [*See* U.C.C. §9-109(2), Comment 5; *and see* §55]

(b) NLC does have a valid security interest in the guitar. An oral security agreement is permissible whenever the secured party has possession of the collateral (a "pledge") [*see* U.C.C. §9-203(1)(a); *and see* §112], and possession is one method of perfection.

(c) Priority is based on the "first-to-file-or-perfect rule" of U.C.C. section 9-312(5)(a). [*See* §327] Although ANB misfiled, it did file first. And because NLC's agent discovered the misfiled statement before NLC perfected, the misfiling perfects ANB against NLC. [U.C.C. §9-401(2); *and see* §§281, 313] ANB therefore has the senior interest in the guitar.

ANSWER TO SAMPLE EXAM QUESTION II

U.C.C. section 9-103, governing multiple state transactions, controls here. To use that section, the collateral must first be classified under its proper Article 9 label. Here the collateral is a right to payment not evidenced by chattel paper or an instrument, and so is classified as an "account." [*See* §64] Therefore, perfection is to be accomplished in the state of the *debtor's* location, meaning place of business (chief executive office). [U.C.C. §9-103(3)(b), (d); *and see* §§232-235] Since Mortar Construction Company is borrowing the money, it is the "debtor." And since its place of business (main offices) is in Chicago, Illinois is the appropriate state in which to file the financing statement.

ANSWER TO SAMPLE EXAM QUESTION III

The "four-month" rule of U.C.C. section 9-103 requires that a security interest be reperfected in the new state within four months after the collateral is moved into that state or else perfection lapses. Since Big Red State Bank ("BRSB") failed to reperfect in Oregon, its security interest in the inventory became unperfected four months after Nancy's move. [*See* §221]

On the other hand, Snowfun Vehicles did not lose its perfection because its purchase money security interest in consumer goods (the snowmobile) was perfected "automatically" as soon as its security interest attached. [*See* §181] Since a purchase money creditor of consumer goods does not have to file, the four-month rule of section 9-103(1)(d) does not apply, and Snowfun remained perfected in both states. The same is true regarding Big Red State Bank's interest in Nancy's car. As long as the California certificate of title with BRSB's security interest noted thereon is outstanding, BRSB maintains its perfection despite the usual four-month rule until the car is registered in the new state. [U.C.C. §9-103(2)(b); *and see* §§245-246]

Thus, the trustee gets none of the property, Oregon Valley Bank has a perfected interest in the inventory, and the original security interests in the snowmobile and the car retain their initial perfections in spite of the move.

ANSWER TO SAMPLE EXAM QUESTION IV

Consignment transactions such as the one between Ornate and Arabian are treated by the U.C.C. as secured transactions. [*See* §79] For this reason, Ornate Rugs will lose its ownership rights in the rugs, which will fall under Retailer Bank's floating lien [*see* §136] unless Ornate takes the steps specified by U.C.C. section 9-114—namely, filing a financing statement [*see* U.C.C. §9-408] in the appropriate place *before* delivering the rugs to Arabian, and giving a written notice to Retailer Bank describing the transaction (which notice must then be renewed every five years). [*See* §344]

ANSWER TO SAMPLE EXAM QUESTION V

Unless the secured party authorizes the sale or waives its security interest, the collateral is not freed from the security interest by the debtor's sale. [U.C.C. §9-306(2)] Thus, Tenacles National Bank can repossess the truck from Blue Truck Ice Cream Company. (Blue Truck would, however, have an Article 2 breach of warranty of good title action against its seller, White Truck. [U.C.C. §2-312])

TNB's competition with the federal tax lien looks less promising. [*See* §448] Future advances by a creditor to a debtor are protected against a filed federal tax lien only if made without knowledge of the lien and within 45 days of the tax lien filing. Here, TNB's security interest protects the loans TNB made prior to 45 days after September 25 (when the tax lien was filed). Thus, the October and November loans (and the ones prior thereto) are superior to the I.R.S., but the December advance is not. [*See* §455]

ANSWER TO SAMPLE EXAM QUESTION VI

(a) No. Buyers out of inventory who buy in the ordinary course of business are protected by U.C.C. section 9-307(1), which allows them to take the product they purchase free of preexisting security interests created by their seller. [*See* §421] Thus, Cathy Consumer gets the piano free of the security interests in both Local Bank and Black Walnut.

(b) Black Walnut has the senior interest in the black walnut pianos since it complied with the steps that U.C.C. section 9-312(3) requires be taken by those creditors claiming a purchase money security interest in goods about to become part of the debtor's inventory—*i.e.,* perfection prior to debtor's possession and written notice of the transaction to the existing inventory lienor. [*See* §§336-341]

(c) These documents (an instrument plus a security interest agreement) constitute "chattel paper." [U.C.C. §9-105(1)(b); *and see* §61] U.C.C. section 9-308(b) provides that a purchaser of chattel paper (here Merchants Finance Company) prevails over previous financers of the inventory who are claiming the chattel paper as proceeds of the inventory.

ANSWER TO SAMPLE EXAM QUESTION VII

A purchase money secured creditor usually does not have to file to perfect a purchase money security interest in consumer goods. [*See* §182] However, where, as here, the goods are to become *fixtures,* automatic perfection rules do not apply, and Muscles, Inc. must make a *fixture filing* of a financing statement in the real estate records. [*See* U.C.C. §9-402(5),(6); *and see* §§350-351] Moreover, even if Muscles, Inc. makes such a filing, it will still be junior to the preexisting perfected interest of Sharksteeth Finance Company which has a "construction mortgage" on the property. [U.C.C. §9-313(1)(b), (6)] Muscles, Inc. could try to convince a court that the exercise machine qualifies as "readily removeable replacements of domestic appliances which are consumer goods" since a security interest in such goods, if perfected before affixation, is senior even to a construction mortgage. [U.C.C. §9-313(4)(c); *and see* §349] However, since no attorney would counsel a client to rely on such a chancy argument, the best course for Muscles, Inc. to follow would be to get an agreement by SFC to *subordinate* its interest to Muscles, Inc. [U.C.C. §9-313(5)(a); *see* §355]

ANSWER TO SAMPLE EXAM QUESTION VIII

A financing statement must state the secured party's address. [U.C.C. §9-402(1)] While some courts have held that this omission is an excusable "minor error, not seriously misleading" [U.C.C. §9-402(8); *and see* §252], most courts would not excuse the error and would hold that Antitrust National Bank is unperfected and thus, loses out to the bankruptcy trustee (who has the status of a judicial lien creditor who has levied on the collateral). [U.C.C. §9-301; *and see* §496]

This leaves only Farmers Friend State Bank for the trustee to contend with. FFSB's interest arose from a pledge of the warehouse receipt (a "document of title," called simply a "document" by Article 9). [*See* U.C.C. §9-105(1)(f); *and see* §60] Even though FFSB surrendered the document to the debtor, U.C.C. section 9-304(5)(a) continues FFSB's perfection for a 21-day period following the surrender, so that FFSB remains perfected against the debtor's trustee in bankruptcy whose interest arose in that period. [*See* §§204-206, 217]

Actually, however, the trustee might still prevail under section 544 of the Bankruptcy Code, because the trustee has the power to step into the shoes of the holder of any interest the trustee has invalidated. Since ANB had a superior position to FFSB, the trustee steps into ANB's position and is therefore superior to FFSB.

ANSWER TO SAMPLE EXAM QUESTION IX

If Consumers Bank had filed its financing statement immediately after the loan (which it was required to do since it did not have a *purchase money* security interest in these consumer goods), it would have had no problems. Instead, however, it waited and filed during the 90-day period prior to the debtor's filing of a bankruptcy petition. This effected a transfer of the debtor's property to itself to secure an antecedent debt, thereby creating a *preference* and enabling the bankruptcy trustee under section 547 of the Bankruptcy Code to avoid the security interest. [*See* §§497-499]

In comparison, Office Furnishings *does* have a purchase money security interest and, thus, has the benefit of a 20-day grace period after Shrub receives possession in which to file its financing statement. (Note that Office Furnishings must file since the collateral is not consumer goods.) [U.C.C. §9-301(2); *and see* §511] This 20-day period is *not* cut short by the filing of the bankruptcy petition, so the filing of the financing statement on November 16 perfected the interest against the attack of Shrub's bankruptcy trustee.

ANSWER TO SAMPLE EXAM QUESTION X

The actions of Repossession violated almost every relevant provision of Article 9. Section 9-503 permits self-help repossession" of the sort undertaken here only if it can be accomplished without a "breach of the peace." Most courts would hold the peace breached by Price's breaking and entering, even though the security agreement gave the creditor this right. [*See* §545] A repossession without the authority of U.C.C. section 9-503 is *stealing*—the tort of conversion—for which the debtor may recover actual and punitive damages. (The latter may be measured by the U.C.C. section 9-507(1) formula of 10% of the cash price plus the finance charges; *see* §622.)

In addition, the consumer-debtor who has paid 60% or more of the cash price (as Isle did here) is entitled by section 9-505(1) to have the collateral *resold* within 90 days of the repossession (here the creditor waited four months), or the debtor may sue in conversion or under section 9-507(1). [*See* §§561-564]

Finally, U.C.C. section 9-504 requires that the resale be commercially reasonable in all aspects and that the debtor be sent a pre-sale notice. [*See* §575] Selling repossessed cars without repairing minor problems (like replacing engine parts that the debtor had removed for maintenance purposes) has been held to be commercially unreasonable. Of course, Isle received no notice here of the resale. In this situation, some courts have denied the creditor any right to sue for the deficiency (the amount still owing). Other courts have indulged in the presumption that *had* the sale been commercially reasonable, the collateral would have been sold for the amount still owing (thus putting the burden on the creditor to prove otherwise). Still other courts have left the debtor only with the statutory remedy provided by section 9-507(1). [*See* §§616-622]

TABLE OF CITATIONS
TO UNIFORM COMMERCIAL CODE
(All Article 9 Citations are to the Revised 1972 Article 9)

TABLE OF CASES

INDEX

Notes

Publications Catalog

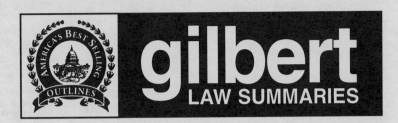

Gilbert Law Summaries are the best selling outlines in the country, and have set the standard for excellence since they were first introduced more than twenty-five years ago. It's Gilbert's unique combination of features that makes it the one study aid you'll turn to for all your study needs!

Accounting and Finance for Lawyers
TBA
Basic Accounting Principles; Definitions of Accounting Terms; Balance Sheet; Income Statement; Statement of Changes in Financial Position; Consolidated Financial Statements; Accumulation of Financial Data; Financial Statement Analysis.
ISBN: 0-15-900382-2   Pages: 136 $16.95

Administrative Law
By Professor Michael R. Asimow, U.C.L.A.
Separation of Powers and Controls Over Agencies; (including Delegation of Power) Constitutional Right to Hearing (including Liberty and Property Interests Protected by Due Process, and Rulemaking-Adjudication Distinction); Adjudication Under Administrative Procedure Act (APA); Formal Adjudication (including Notice, Discovery, Burden of Proof, Finders of Facts and Reasons); Adjudicatory Decision Makers (including Administrative Law Judges (ALJs), Bias, Improper Influences, Ex Parte Communications, Familiarity with Record, Res Judicata); Rulemaking Procedures (including Notice, Public Participation, Publication, Impartiality of Rulemakers, Rulemaking Record); Obtaining Information (including Subpoena Power, Privilege Against Self-incrimination, Freedom of Information Act, Government in Sunshine Act, Attorneys' Fees); Scope of Judicial Review; Reviewability of Agency Decisions (including Mandamus, Injunction, Sovereign Immunity, Federal Tort Claims Act); Standing to Seek Judicial Review and Timing.
ISBN: 0-15-900000-9   Pages: 300 $19.95

Agency and Partnership
By Professor Richard J. Conviser, Chicago Kent
Agency: Rights and Liabilities Between Principal and Agent (including Agent's Fiduciary Duty, Principal's Right to Indemnification); Contractual Rights Between Principal (or Agent) and Third Persons (including Creation of Agency Relationship, Authority of Agent, Scope of Authority, Termination of Authority, Ratification, Liability on Agents, Contracts); Tort Liability (including Respondeat Superior, Master-Servant Relationship, Scope of Employment). Partnership: Property Rights of Partner; Formation of Partnership; Relations Between Partners (including Fiduciary Duty); Authority of Partner to Bind Partnership; Dissolution and Winding up of Partnership; Limited Partnerships.
ISBN: 0-15-900327-X   Pages: 142 $16.95

Antitrust
By Professor Thomas M. Jorde, U.C. Berkeley, Mark A. Lemley, University of Texas, and Professor Robert H. Mnookin, Harvard University
Common Law Restraints of Trade; Federal Antitrust Laws (including Sherman Act, Clayton Act, Federal Trade Commission Act, Interstate Commerce Requirement, Antitrust Remedies); Monopolization (including Relevant Market, Purposeful Act Requirement, Attempts and Conspiracy to Monopolize); Collaboration Among Competitors (including Horizontal Restraints, Rule of Reason vs. Per Se Violations, Price Fixing, Division of Markets, Group Boycotts); Vertical Restraints (including Tying Arrangements); Mergers and Acquisitions (including Horizontal Mergers, Brown Shoe Analysis, Vertical Mergers, Conglomerate Mergers); Price Discrimination — Robinson-Patman Act; Unfair Methods of Competition; Patent Laws and Their Antitrust Implications; Exemptions From Antitrust Laws (including Motor, Rail, and Interstate Water Carriers, Bank Mergers, Labor Unions, Professional Baseball).
ISBN: 0-15-900328-8   Pages: 193 $16.95

Bankruptcy
By Professor Ned W. Waxman, College of William and Mary
Participants in the Bankruptcy Case; Jurisdiction and Procedure; Commencement and Administration of the Case (including Eligibility, Voluntary Case, Involuntary Case, Meeting of Creditors, Debtor's Duties); Officers of the Estate (including Trustee, Examiner, United States Trustee); Bankruptcy Estate; Creditor's Right of Setoff; Trustee's Avoiding Powers; Claims of Creditors (including Priority Claims and Tax Claims); Debtor's Exemptions; Nondischargeable Debts; Effects of Discharge; Reaffirmation Agreements; Administrative Powers (including Automatic Stay, Use, Sale, or Lease of Property); Chapter 7- Liquidation; Chapter 11- Reorganization; Chapter 13-Individual With Regular Income; Chapter 12- Family Farmer With Regular Annual Income.
ISBN: 0-15-900245-1   Pages: 356 $19.95

Business Law
By Professor Robert D. Upp, Los Angeles City College
Torts and Crimes in Business; Law of Contracts (including Contract Formation, Consideration, Statute of Frauds, Contract Remedies, Third Parties); Sales (including Transfer of Title and Risk of Loss, Performance and Remedies, Products Liability, Personal Property Security Interest); Property (including Personal Property, Bailments, Real Property, Landlord and Tenant); Agency; Business Organizations (including Partnerships, Corporations); Commercial Paper; Government Regulation of Business (including Taxation, Antitrust, Environmental Protection, and Bankruptcy).
ISBN: 0-15-900005-X   Pages: 295 $16.95

California Bar Performance Test Skills
By Professor Peter J. Honigsberg, University of San Francisco
Hints to Improve Writing; How to Approach the Performance Test; Legal Analysis Documents (including Writing a Memorandum of Law, Writing a Client Letter, Writing Briefs); Fact Gathering and Fact Analysis Documents; Tactical and Ethical Considerations; Sample Interrogatories, Performance Tests, and Memoranda.
ISBN: 0-15-900152-8   Pages: 216 $17.95

Civil Procedure
By Professor Thomas D. Rowe, Jr., Duke University, and Professor Richard L. Marcus, U.C. Hastings
Territorial (personal) Jurisdiction, including Venue and Forum Non Conveniens; Subject Matter Jurisdiction, covering Diversity Jurisdiction, Federal Question Jurisdiction; Erie Doctrine and Federal Common Law; Pleadings including Counterclaims, Cross-Claims, Supplemental Pleadings; Parties, including Joinder and Class Actions; Discovery, including Devices, Scope, Sanctions and Discovery Conference; Summary Judgment; Pretrial Conference and Settlements; Trial, including Right to Jury Trial, Motions, Jury Instruction and Arguments, and Post-Verdict Motions; Appeals; Claim Preclusion (Res Judicata) and Issue Preclusion (Collateral Estoppel).
ISBN: 0-15-900272-9   Pages: 447 $19.95

Commercial Paper and Payment Law
By Professor Douglas J. Whaley, Ohio State University
Types of Commercial Paper; Negotiability; Negotiation; Holders in Due Course; Claims and Defenses on Negotiable Instruments (including Real Defenses and Personal Defenses); Liability of the Parties (including Merger Rule, Suits on the Instrument, Warranty Suits, Conversion); Bank Deposits and Collections; Forgery or Alteration of Negotiable Instruments; Electronic Banking.
ISBN: 0-15-900367-9   Pages: 222 $17.95

Community Property
By Professor William A. Reppy, Jr., Duke University
Classifying Property as Community or Separate; Management and Control of Property; Liability for Debts; Division of Property at Divorce; Devolution of Property at Death; Relationships Short of Valid Marriage; Conflict of Laws Problems; Constitutional Law Issues (including Equal Protection Standards, Due Process Issues).
ISBN: 0-15-900235-4   Pages: 188 $17.95

1

LAW SCHOOL LEGENDS SERIES

America's Greatest Law Professors on Audio Cassette

Wouldn't it be great if all of your law professors were law school legends? You know — the kind of professors whose classes everyone fights to get into. The professors whose classes you'd take, no matter what subject they're teaching. The kind of professors who make a subject sing. You may never get an opportunity to take a class with a truly brilliant professor, but with the Law School Legends Series, you can now get all the benefits of the country's greatest law professors…on audio cassette!

Administrative Law
Professor Patrick J. Borchers
Albany Law School of Union University

TOPICS COVERED: Classification Of Agencies; Adjudicative And Investigative Action; Rule Making Power; Delegation Doctrine; Control By Executive; Appointment And Removal; Freedom Of Information Act; Rule Making Procedure; Adjudicative Procedure; Trial Type Hearings; Administrative Law Judge; Power To Stay Proceedings; Subpoena Power; Physical Inspection; Self Incrimination; Judicial Review Issues; Declaratory Judgment; Sovereign Immunity; Eleventh Amendment; Statutory Limitations; Standing; Exhaustion Of Administrative Remedies; Scope Of Judicial Review.
3 Audio Cassettes
ISBN 0-15-900189-7 $45.95

Agency & Partnership
Professor Richard J. Conviser
Chicago Kent College of Law

TOPICS COVERED: Agency: Creation; Rights And Duties Of Principal And Agent; Sub-Agents; Contract Liability–Actual Authority: Express And Implied; Apparent Authority; Ratification; Liabilities Of Parties; Tort Liability–Respondeat Superior; Frolic And Detour; Intentional Torts. *Partnership:* Nature Of Partnership; Formation; Partnership By Estoppel; In Partnership Property; Relations Between Partners To Third Parties; Authority Of Partners; Dissolution And Termination; Limited Partnerships.
3 Audio Cassettes
ISBN: 0-15-900351-2 $45.95

Bankruptcy
Professor Elizabeth Warren
Harvard Law School

TOPICS COVERED: The Debtor/Creditor Relationship; The Commencement, Conversion, Dismissal and Reopening Of Bankruptcy Proceedings; Property Included In The Bankruptcy Estate; Secured, Priority And Unsecured Claims; The Automatic Stay; Powers Of Avoidance; The Assumption And Rejection Of Executory Contracts; The Protection Of Exempt Property; The Bankruptcy Discharge; Chapter 13 Proceedings; Chapter 11 Proceedings; Bankruptcy Jurisdiction And Procedure.
4 Audio Cassettes
ISBN: 0-15-900273-7 $45.95

Civil Procedure
By Professor Richard D. Freer
Emory University Law School

TOPICS COVERED: Subject Matter Jurisdiction; Personal Jurisdiction; Long-Arm Statutes; Constitutional Limitations; In Rem And Quasi In Rem Jurisdiction; Service Of Process; Venue; Transfer; Forum Non Conveniens; Removal; Waiver; Governing Law; Pleadings; Joinder Of Claims; Permissive And Compulsory Joinder Of Parties; Counter-Claims And Cross-Claims; Ancillary Jurisdiction; Impleader; Class Actions; Discovery; Pretrial Adjudication; Summary Judgment; Trial; Post Trial Motions; Appeals; Res Judicata; Collateral Estoppel.
5 Audio Cassettes
ISBN: 0-15-900322-9 $59.95

Commercial Paper
By Professor Michael I. Spak
Chicago Kent College Of Law

TOPICS COVERED: Introduction; Types Of Negotiable Instruments; Elements Of Negotiability; Statute Of Limitations; Payment-In-Full Checks; Negotiations Of The Instrument; Becoming A Holder-In-Due Course; Rights Of A Holder In Due Course; Real And Personal Defenses; Jus Teril; Effect Of Instrument On Underlying Obligations; Contracts Of Maker And Indorser; Suretyship; Liability Of Drawer And Drawee; Check Certification; Warranty Liability; Conversion Of Liability; Banks And Their Customers; Properly Payable Rule; Wrongful Dishonor; Stopping Payment; Death Of Customer; Bank Statement; Check Collection; Expedited Funds Availability; Forgery Of Drawer's Name; Alterations; Imposter Rule; Wire Transfers; Electronic Fund Transfers Act .
3 Audio Cassettes
ISBN: 0-15-900275-3 $39.95

Conflict Of Laws
Professor Richard J. Conviser
Chicago Kent College of Law

TOPICS COVERED: Domicile; Jurisdiction; In Personam, In Rem, Quasi In Rem; Court Competence; Forum Non Conveniens; Choice Of Law; Foreign Causes Of Action; Territorial Approach To Choice/Tort And Contract; "Escape Devices"; Most Significant Relationship; Governmental Interest Analysis; Recognition Of Judgments; Foreign Country Judgments; Domestic Judgments/Full Faith And Credit; Review Of Judgments; Modifiable Judgments; Defenses To Recognition And Enforcement; Federal/State (Erie) Problems; Constitutional Limits On Choice Of Law.
3 Audio Cassettes
ISBN: 0-15-900352-0 $39.95

Constitutional Law
By Professor John C. Jeffries, Jr.
University of Virginia School of Law

TOPICS COVERED: Introduction; Exam Tactics; Legislative Power; Supremacy; Commerce; State Regulation; Privileges And Immunities; Federal Court Jurisdiction; Separation Of Powers; Civil Liberties; Due Process; Equal Protection; Privacy; Race; Alienage; Gender; Speech And Association; Prior Restraints; Religion—Free Exercise; Establishment Clause.
5 Audio Cassettes
ISBN: 0-15-900319-9 $45.95

Contracts
By Professor Michael I. Spak
Chicago Kent College Of Law

TOPICS COVERED: Offer; Revocation; Acceptance; Consideration; Defenses To Formation; Third Party Beneficiaries; Assignment; Delegation; Conditions; Excuses; Anticipatory Repudiation; Discharge Of Duty; Modifications; Rescission; Accord & Satisfaction; Novation; Breach; Damages; Remedies; UCC Remedies; Parol Evidence Rule.
4 Audio Cassettes
ISBN: 0-15-900318-0 $45.95

Copyright Law
Professor Roger E. Schechter
George Washington University Law School

TOPICS COVERED: Constitution; Patents And Property Ownership Distinguished; Subject Matter Copyright; Duration And Renewal; Ownership And Transfer; Formalities; Introduction; Notice, Registration And Deposit; Infringement; Overview; Reproduction And Derivative Works; Public Distribution; Public Performance And Display; Exemptions; Fair Use; Photocopying; Remedies; Preemption Of State Law.
3 Audio Cassettes
ISBN: 0-15-900295-8 $39.95

Corporations
By Professor Therese H. Maynard
Loyola Marymount School of Law

TOPICS COVERED: Ultra Vires Act; Corporate Formation; Piercing The Corporate Veil; Corporate Financial Structure; Stocks; Bonds; Subscription Agreements; Watered Stock; Stock Transactions; Insider Trading; 16(b) & 10b-5 Violations; Promoters; Fiduciary Duties; Shareholder Rights; Meetings; Cumulative Voting; Voting Trusts; Close Corporations; Dividends; Preemptive Rights; Shareholder Derivative Suits; Directors; Duty Of Loyalty; Corporate Opportunity Doctrine; Officers; Amendments; Mergers; Dissolution.
4 Audio Cassettes
ISBN: 0-15-900320-2 $45.95

Criminal Law
By Professor Charles H. Whitebread
USC School of Law

TOPICS COVERED: Exam Tactics; Volitional Acts; Mental States; Specific Intent; Malice; General Intent; Strict Liability; Accomplice Liability; Inchoate Crimes; Impossibility; Defenses; Insanity; Voluntary And Involuntary Intoxication; Infancy; Self-Defense; Defense Of A Dwelling; Duress; Necessity; Mistake Of Fact Or Law; Entrapment; Battery; Assault; Homicide; Common Law Murder; Voluntary And Involuntary Manslaughter; First Degree Murder; Felony Murder; Rape; Larceny; Embezzlement; False Pretenses; Robbery; Extortion; Burglary; Arson.
4 Audio Cassettes
ISBN: 0-15-900279-6 $39.95

Criminal Procedure
By Professor Charles H. Whitebread
USC School of Law

TOPICS COVERED: Incorporation Of The Bill Of Rights; Exclusionary Rule; Fruit Of The Poisonous Tree; Arrest; Search & Seizure; Exceptions To Warrant Requirement; Wire Tapping & Eavesdropping; Confessions (Miranda); Pretrial Identification; Bail; Preliminary Hearings; Grand Juries; Speedy Trial; Fair Trial; Jury Trials; Right To Counsel; Guilty Pleas; Sentencing; Death Penalty; Habeas Corpus; Double Jeopardy; Privilege Against Compelled Testimony.
3 Audio Cassettes
ISBN: 0-15-900281-8 $39.95

Evidence

By Professor Faust F. Rossi
Cornell Law School

TOPICS COVERED: Relevance; Insurance; Remedial Measures; Settlement Offers; Causation; State Of Mind; Rebuttal; Habit; Character Evidence; "MIMIC" Rule; Documentary Evidence; Authentication; Best Evidence Rule; Parol Evidence; Competency; Dead Man Statutes; Examination Of Witnesses; Present Recollection Revived; Past Recollection Recorded; Opinion Testimony; Lay And Expert Witness; Learned Treatises; Impeachment; Collateral Matters; Bias, Interest Or Motive; Rehabilitation; Privileges; Hearsay And Exceptions.

5 Audio Cassettes
ISBN: 0-15-900282-6 $45.95

Family Law

Professor Roger E. Schechter
George Washington University Law School

TOPICS COVERED: National Scope Of Family Law; Marital Relationship; Consequences Of Marriage; Formalities And Solemnization; Common Law Marriage; Impediments; Marriage And Conflict Of Laws; Non-Marital Relationship; Law Of Names; Void And Voidable Marriages; Marital Breakdown; Annulment And Defenses; Divorce — Fault And No-Fault; Separation; Jurisdiction For Divorce; Migratory Divorce; Full Faith And Credit; Temporary Orders; Economic Aspects Of Marital Breakdown; Property Division; Community Property Principles; Equitable Distribution; Marital And Separate Property; Types Of Property Interests; Equitable Reimbursement; Alimony; Modification And Termination Of Alimony; Child Support; Health Insurance; Enforcement Of Orders; Antenuptial And Postnuptial Agreements; Separation And Settlement Agreements; Custody Jurisdiction And Awards; Modification Of Custody; Visitation Rights; Termination Of Parental Rights; Adoption; Illegitimacy; Paternity Actions.

3 Audio Cassettes
ISBN: 0-15-900283-4 $39.95

Federal Courts

Professor John C. Jeffries
University of Virginia School of Law

TOPICS COVERED: History Of The Federal Court System; "Court Or Controversy" And Justiciability; Congressional Power Over Federal Court Jurisdiction; Supreme Court Jurisdiction; District Court Subject Matter Jurisdiction—Federal Question Jurisdiction, Diversity Jurisdiction And Admiralty Jurisdiction; Pendent And Ancillary Jurisdiction; Removal Jurisdiction; Venue; Forum Non Conveniens; Law Applied In The Federal Courts; Federal Law In The State Courts; Collateral Relations Between Federal And State Courts; The Eleventh Amendment And State Sovereign Immunity.

3 Audio Cassettes
ISBN: 0-15-900296-6 $39.95

Federal Income Tax

By Professor Cheryl D. Block
George Washington University Law School

TOPICS COVERED: Administrative Reviews; Tax Formula; Gross Income; Exclusions For Gifts; Inheritances; Personal Injuries; Tax Basis Rules; Divorce Tax Rules; Assignment Of Income; Business Deductions; Investment Deductions; Passive Loss And Interest Limitation Rules; Capital Gains & Losses; Section 1031, 1034, and 121 Deferred/Non Taxable Transactions.

4 Audio Cassettes
ISBN: 0-15-900284-2 $45.95

Future Interests

By Dean Catherine L. Carpenter
Southwestern University Law School

TOPICS COVERED: Rule Against Perpetuities; Class Gifts; Estates In Land; Rule In Shelley's Case; Future Interests In Transferor and Transferee; Life Estates; Defeasible Fees; Doctrine Of Worthier Title; Doctrine Of Merger; Fee Simple Estates; Restraints On Alienation; Power Of Appointment; Rules Of Construction.

2 Audio Cassettes
ISBN: 0-15-900285-0 $24.95

Law School ABC's

By Professor Jennifer S. Kamita
Loyola Marymount Law School, and
Professor Rodney O. Fong
Golden Gate University School of Law

TOPICS COVERED: Introduction; Casebooks; Hornbooks; Selecting Commercial Materials; Briefing; Review; ABC's Of A Lecture; Taking Notes; Lectures & Notes Examples; Study Groups; ABC's Of Outlining; Rules; Outlining Hypothetical; Outlining Assignment And Review; Introduction To Essay Writing; "IRAC"; Call Of The Question Exercise; Issue Spotting Exercise; IRAC Defining & Writing Exercise; Form Tips; ABC's Of Exam Writing; Exam Writing Hypothetical; Practice Exam And Review; Preparation Hints; Exam Diagnostics & Writing Problems.

4 Audio Cassettes
ISBN: 0-15-900286-9 $45.95

Law School Exam Writing

By Professor Charles H. Whitebread
USC School of Law

TOPICS COVERED: With "Law School Exam Writing," you'll learn the secrets of law school test taking . In this fascinating lecture, Professor Whitebread leads you step-by-step through his innovative system, so that you know exactly how to tackle your essay exams without making point draining mistakes. You'll learn how to read questions so you don't miss important issues; how to organize your answer; how to use limited exam time to your maximum advantage; and even how to study for exams.

1 Audio Cassette
ISBN: 0-15-900287-7 $19.95

Professional Responsibility

By Professor Erwin Chemerinsky
USC School of Law

TOPICS COVERED: Regulation of Attorneys; Bar Admission; Unauthorized Practice; Competency; Discipline; Judgment; Lawyer-Client Relationship; Representation; Withdrawal; Conflicts; Disqualification; Clients; Client Interests; Successive And Effective Representation; Integrity; Candor; Confidences; Secrets; Past And Future Crimes; Perjury; Communications; Witnesses; Jurors; The Court; The Press; Trial Tactics; Prosecutors; Market; Solicitation; Advertising; Law Firms; Fees; Client Property; Conduct; Political Activity.

3 Audio Cassettes
ISBN: 0-15-900371-7 $39.95

Real Property

By Professor Paula A. Franzese
Seton Hall Law School

TOPICS COVERED: Estates—Fee Simple; Fee Tail; Life Estate; Co-Tenancy—Joint Tenancy; Tenancy In Common; Tenancy By The Entirety; Landlord-Tenant Relationship; Liability For Condition Of Premises; Assignment & Sublease; Easements; Restrictive Covenants; Adverse Possession; Recording Acts; Conveyancing; Personal Property—Finders; Bailments; Gifts; Future Interests.

4 Audio Cassettes
ISBN: 0-15-900289-3 $45.95

Remedies

By Professor William A. Fletcher
University of California at Berkeley, Boalt Hall School of Law

TOPICS COVERED: Damages; Restitution; Equitable Remedies (including Constructive Trust, Equitable Lien, Injunction, and Specific Performance); Tracing; Rescission and Reformation; Specific topics include Injury and Destruction of Personal Property; Conversion; Injury to Real Property; Trespass; Ouster; Nuisance; Defamation; Trade Libel; Inducing Breach of Contract; Contracts to Purchase Personal Property; Contracts to Purchase Real Property (including Equitable Conversion); Construction Contracts; and Personal Service Contracts.

3 Audio Cassettes
ISBN: 0-15-900353-9 $45.95

Sales & Lease of Goods

By Professor Michael I. Spak
Chicago Kent College of Law

TOPICS COVERED: Goods; Contract Formation; Firm Offers; Statute Of Frauds; Modification; Parol Evidence; Code Methodology; Tender; Payment; Identification; Risk Of Loss; Warranties; Merchantability; Fitness; Disclaimers; Consumer Protection; Remedies; Anticipatory Repudiation; Third Party Rights.

3 Audio Cassettes
ISBN: 0-15-900291-5 $39.95

Secured Transactions

By Professor Michael I. Spak
Chicago Kent College of Law

TOPICS COVERED: Collateral; Inventory; Intangibles; Proceeds; Security Agreements; Attachment; After-Acquired Property; Perfection; Filing; Priorities; Purchase Money Security Interests; Fixtures; Rights Upon Default; Self-Help; Sale; Constitutional Issues.

3 Audio Cassettes
ISBN: 0-15-900292-3 $39.95

Torts

By Professor Richard J. Conviser
Chicago Kent College of Law

TOPICS COVERED: Essay Exam Techniques; Intentional Torts—Assault; Battery; False Imprisonment; Intentional Infliction Of Emotional Distress; Trespass To Land; Trespass To Chattels; Conversion; Defenses; Defamation—Libel; Slander; Defenses; First Amendment Concerns; Invasion Of Right Of Privacy; Misrepresentation; Negligence—Duty; Breach; Actual And Proximate Causation; Damages; Defenses; Strict Liability; Products Liability; Nuisance; General Tort Considerations.

4 Audio Cassettes
ISBN: 0-15-900185-4 $45.95

Wills & Trusts

By Professor Stanley M. Johanson
University of Texas School of Law

TOPICS COVERED: Attested Wills; Holographic Wills; Negligence; Revocation; Changes On Face Of Will; Lapsed Gifts; Negative Bequest Rule; Nonprobate Assets; Intestate Succession; Advancements; Elective Share; Will Contests; Capacity; Undue Influence; Creditors' Rights; Creation Of Trust; Revocable Trusts; Pourover Gifts; Charitable Trusts; Resulting Trusts; Constructive Trusts; Spendthrift Trusts; Self-Dealing; Prudent Investments; Trust Accounting; Termination; Powers Of Appointment.

4 Audio Cassettes
ISBN: 0-15-900294-X $45.95

Employment Guides

A collection of best selling titles that help you identify and reach your career goals.

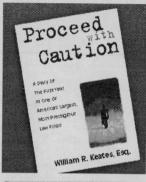

The National Directory Of Legal Employers
National Association for Law Placement

The National Directory of Legal Employers brings you a universe of vital information about 1,000 of the nation's top legal employers— *in one convenient volume!*

It includes:

- Over 22,000 job openings.
- The names, addresses and phone numbers of hiring partners.
- Listings of firms by state, size, kind and practice area.
- What starting salaries are for full time, part time, and summer associates, plus a detailed description of firm benefits.
- The number of employees by gender and race, as well as the number of employees with disabilities.
- A detailed narrative of each firm, plus much more!

The National Directory Of Legal Employers has been the best kept secret of top legal career search professionals for over a decade. Now, for the first time, it is available in a format specifically designed for law students and new graduates. *Pick up your copy of the Directory today!*
ISBN: 0-15-900248-6   **$39.95**

Proceed With Caution: A Diary Of The First Year At One Of America's Largest, Most Prestigious Law Firms
William R. Keates

Prestige. Famous clients. High-profile cases. Not to mention a starting salary approaching six figures.

In *Proceed With Caution*, the author takes you behind the scenes, to show you what it's really like to be a junior associate at a huge law firm. After graduating from an Ivy League law school, he took a job as an associate with one of New York's blue-chip law firms.

He also did something not many people do. He kept a diary, where he spilled out his day-to-day life at the firm in graphic detail.

Proceed With Caution excerpts the diary, from his first day at the firm to the day he quit. From the splashy benefits, to the nitty-gritty on the work junior associates do, to the grind of long and unpredictable hours, to the stress that eventually made him leave the firm — he tells story after story that will make you feel as though you're living the life of a new associate.

Whether you're considering a career with a large firm, or you're just curious about what life at the top firms is all about — *Proceed With Caution* is a must read!
ISBN: 0-15-900181-1   **$17.95**

Guerrilla Tactics for Getting the Legal Job of Your Dreams
Kimm Alayne Walton, J.D.

Whether you're looking for a summer clerkship or your first permanent job after school, this revolutionary book is the key to getting the job of your dreams!

Guerrilla Tactics for Getting the Legal Job of Your Dreams leads you step-by-step through everything you need to do to nail down that perfect job! You'll learn hundreds of simple-to-use strategies that will get you exactly where you want to go. You'll Learn:

- The seven magic opening words in cover letters that ensure you'll get a response.
- The secret to successful interviews every time.
- Killer answers to the toughest interview questions they'll ever ask you.
- Plus Much More!

Guerrilla Tactics features the best strategies from the country's most innovative law school career advisors. The strategies in *Guerrilla Tactics* are so powerful that it even comes with a guarantee: Follow the advice in the book, and within one year of graduation you'll have the job of your dreams… or your money back!

Pick up a copy of *Guerrilla Tactics* today…and you'll be on your way to the job of your dreams!
ISBN: 0-15-900317-2   **$24.95**

Beyond L.A. Law: Inspiring Stories of People Who've Done Fascinating Things With A Law Degree
National Association for Law Placement

Anyone who watches television knows that being a lawyer means working your way up through a law firm — right?

Wrong!

Beyond L.A. Law gives you a fascinating glimpse into the lives of people who've broken the "lawyer" mold. They come from a variety of backgrounds — some had prior careers, others went straight through college and law school, and yet others have overcome poverty and physical handicaps. They got their degrees from all different kinds of law schools, all over the country. But they have one thing in common: they've all pursued their own, unique vision.

As you read their stories, you'll see how they beat the odds to succeed. You'll learn career tips and strategies that work, from people who've put them to the test. And you'll find fascinating insights that you can apply to your own dream — whether it's a career in law, or anything else!

From Representing Baseball In Australia. To International Finance. To Children's Advocacy. To Directing a Nonprofit Organization. To Entrepreneur.

If You Think Getting A Law Degree Means Joining A Traditional Law Firm — Think Again!.
ISBN: 0-15-900182-X   **$17.95**

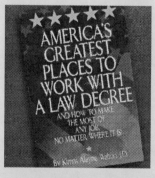

America's Greatest Places To Work With A Law Degree
Kimm Alayne Walton, J.D.

"Where do your happiest graduates work?"

That's the question that author Kimm Alayne Walton asked of law school administrators around the country. Their responses revealed the hundreds of wonderful employers profiled in *America's Greatest Places To Work With A Law Degree.*

In this remarkable book, you'll get to know an incredible variety of great places to work, including:

- Glamorous sports and entertainment employers – the jobs that sound as though they would be great, and they are!
- The 250 best law firms to work for between 20 and 600 attorneys.
- Companies where law school graduates love to work and not just as in-house counsel.
- Wonderful public interest employers – the "white knight" jobs that are so incredibly satisfying.
- Court-related positions, where lawyers entertain fascinating issues, tremendous variety, and an enjoyable lifestyle.
- Outstanding government jobs, at the federal, state, and local level.

Beyond learning about incredible employers, you'll discover:

- The ten traits that define a wonderful place to work…the sometimes surprising qualities that outstanding employers share.
- How to handle law school debt, when your dream job pays less than you think you need to make.
- How to find – and get! – great jobs at firms with fewer than 20 attorneys.

And no matter where you work, you'll learn expert tips for making the most of your job. You'll learn the specific strategies that distinguish people headed for the top…how to position yourself for the most interesting, high-profile work…how to handle difficult personalities… how to negotiate for more money…and what to do now to help you get your next great job!

ISBN: 0-15-900180-3   **$24.95**

Presented by The National Law Journal

The Job Goddess column is a weekly feature of the *National Law Journal's Law Journal Extra,* and is written by Kimm Alayne Walton, author of the national best seller *Guerrilla Tactics For Getting The Legal Job Of Your Dreams.* View recent columns or e-mail the Job Goddess with your job search questions on the Internet at www.gilbertlaw.com